PRAISE FOR *THE DRIVE*

"How far would you go to make sense of a tumultuous childhood, better understand an imperfect parent, or bring some peace to the most heartbreaking tragedy a family can experience? In her expertly crafted memoir *The Drive*, Teresa Bruce travels to the ends of the earth. With refreshing honesty, an attentive eye, and her husband Gary and dog in tow, Bruce takes us on an emotional and thoroughly rewarding ride, artfully weaving an inspiring life story that veers between memory and dreams and the space in between."

—Franz Wisner, bestselling author of *Honeymoon with My Brother* and *How the World Makes Love*

"Teresa Bruce takes us along on an enthralling mid-life road trip through the landscapes of Latin America and those of her own heart. In a story by turns harrowing and heartfelt, she shows how to dive into the past and emerge renewed."

—Elisabeth Eaves, author of *Wanderlust* and *Bare*

PRAISE FOR TERESA BRUCE'S
THE OTHER MOTHER: A REMEMOIR
AND DOCUMENTARY
GOD'S GONNA TROUBLE THE WATER

"Filled with the wisdom of a creative genius."

—*Foreword* Magazine

"Poignant and eloquent, this is a graceful exploration . . . "

—*Booklist*

"Invigorating . . . "

—*Kirkus*

" . . . Loving, contemplative and nuanced."

—John Leonard, *New York Magazine*

THE DRIVE

THE
DRIVE

Searching for Lost Memories on the
Pan-American Highway

Teresa Bruce

SEAL PRESS

ISBN: 978-1-58005-651-9
ISBN: 978-1-58005-652-6 (e-book)

Library of Congress Cataloging-in-Publication Data for this book is available.

Published by SEAL PRESS, an imprint of Perseus Books, LLC, a subsidiary of Hachette Book Group, Inc.
1700 Fourth Street, Berkeley, California 94710
sealpress.com

Cover Design: Laura Klynstra
Interior Design: Jack Lenzo

Printed in the United States of America
Distributed by Hachette Book Group

LSC-C
10 9 8 7 6 5 4 3 2 1

For Gary and John John, with me and beside me.

CONTENTS

CONTENTS

THE ROAD

We are marooned in the center of a country in the center of a continent. It would be better to be lost, comforted by the possibility of search and rescue. But my husband and I have driven here on purpose, searching for the remains of my childhood home. Somewhere between the mountainous Bolivian outposts of Mizque and Aiquile, the dirt track we are following narrows to the width of a hospital gurney and then doubles back on itself in a hairpin turn. Manageable, actually, if it weren't for the fact that it does so directly under a waterfall. This particularly contorted switchback is pinched under a flood-swollen river gushing to a gorge below.

Gary stops our one-ton truck and vintage camper just shy of a pummeling cascade. Another ten feet forward and neither one of us will be able to get out of the vehicle. On the driver's side—the inside corner of the hairpin left turn—a sheer cliff plunges three hundred feet. There is no guardrail or shoulder; the road is perfectly aligned to the terrifying drop-off. On my side is a low overhang, water-carved out of a mountain face and so claustrophobically close that opening the truck's door will impale it into solid rock.

The roof of the camper might squeeze under the overhanging ledge, but if the back wheels slip we will be swept over the edge in an instant. The road is too narrow and unstable to turn around, so if we chicken out we will have to negotiate hours of mud ditches and washboard road in reverse.

We are days off course already, on a dubious detour forced by washed-out bridges along the Pan-American Highway. There is no guidebook or app we can consult to tell us what to do, and the road is dissolving before our eyes. I visualize a wave of mud with our beautifully restored 1968 Avion camper riding its crest like a surfboard. Not even two years into our married life together, Gary and I would be swallowed whole, our quest to find the camper I grew up in submerged in grief and second-guessing.

It is told-you-so infuriating, the kind of unfair that gushes out in hot tears when it would feel much better to punch something. We quit amazing jobs and sold a house on Capitol Hill in Washington, DC, to take this trip, leaving a trail of friends and family questioning our sanity. Men fired guns over our heads in Mexico and Nicaragua. We depleted most of our budget to ship the camper around the kidnapping narco-traffickers of Colombia. My intestines are pickled in Cipro, and Gary carries dengue fever in his blood. There are ashes from an aborted llama fetus scattered on the camper bed.

All for nothing. The road is impassable. After seven months of driving we will have to console ourselves with platitudes. You can never go home again anyway. It's the effort that counts. Better to have tried and failed than never dared a leap of faith.

Gary squeezes my hand. We are standing behind our dented, road-bruised camper in helpless silence when the sky splits. It pours with enough force to obliterate the road on either side of the hairpin waterfall. The weight of our decision lifts; we both realize that turning back now would be as dangerous as going forward. We run back to the truck, lock the hubs into four-wheel drive, and climb in.

Steam obscures the windshield so we inch forward in first gear, driving almost blind. I am too scared to talk but we can't hear each other anyway. The sound of the downpour becomes deafening when the waterfall hits—first the truck's hood and then the camper's aluminum roof. I have the absurd sensation of driving through a car wash on a roller-coaster.

"Can I come any closer on your side?" Gary shouts as he begins to take the inside curve. I roll down my window, which is under the protection of the rock ledge overhang, and yank the side-view mirror toward me to give us another few inches of clearance. We can't afford to get wedged in so we will have to bump our way through by feel. My heart tastes cold and metallic lodged in the back of my throat.

The back end starts to fishtail to the left, like someone is tugging at the corner of a carpet underneath us. Gary steers the front wheels into the deepest ruts for traction. My side of the camper begins to scrape the cliff wall. Solid rock is gouging into its thin aluminum skin, peeling back reflector lights and rivet strips like tortured fingernails.

"Are the back tires holding?" I yell.

"I can't tell. Open your door in case we have to jump."

It takes a second to sink in. If the road gives way, our only hope of survival is both of us clambering out the passenger side before the camper plummets into the ravine.

I brace my left arm against the dashboard and crack open the truck door. It is so heavy I can barely hold it off the latch while I peer under my armpit at the road below. Gary drives and I watch for signs that the tires are slipping. Mud spins up and into my eyes. I let go of the dashboard to wipe my face, and when my weight shifts the momentum of the swinging-open door starts to take me with it.

Chapter Two

JOHN JOHN

The greatest adventure of my life began with the greatest tragedy of my parents'. I was only six years old, so my memories of that devastating catalyst are less of the actual events and more of smells and sounds. I was on my first sleepover in our hometown of Banks, Oregon—thirty miles west of Portland—when my father knocked on my friend's front door and told me I had to leave. Right now.

My father never cried, but that particular day tears were streaming down his bearded face. He was shaking and he smelled sour, like sweat and throw-up swirled together. He didn't stop shaking and never said a word on the long drive home. We drove through the four-way stop sign without stopping, over the bumpy railroad tracks without looking left and right, past my babysitter's farm without blowing kisses, and past our two horses in the meadow with no noise from my father but shuddering gasps and wet snorts. He sounded like he was choking. He didn't honk the horn at Simba, our dog, who chased us

5

all the way up the rutted, muddy driveway through the woods. He just held my hand so tight I thought it would break.

He took me to our single-wide trailer. It was as still as a coffin. My maternal grandmother, Nellie Mae, was there, my Aunt Ronell and Uncle Tim, the neighbors, and my baby sister, Jenny—but not my little brother, John John. I didn't notice his absence at first; I thought something had happened to my mother. She was lying facedown on her bed, one arm hanging off the side like the dislocated shoulder of a broken Barbie doll. I was told not to bother her. It was hot and the trailer smelled of salmon casserole and venison nobody was eating. Somebody had lined up pictures of my brother on the counter where we normally colored and cut out paper dolls.

John John had a head-bobbling belly laugh triggered by the words "say cheese." In the photographs I sit next to him, trying to smile pretty, but my little brother looks like he sees something silly behind the camera—pants falling down, a pie flying through the air, Tweety about to trick Sylvester.

Except at Christmas. As a baby on Santa's knee he appears about to vomit. In the next Christmas picture he is lurching for my mother. In the third one his chin is quivering and the veins on Santa's hands are bulging with the strain of holding him. He looks a lot braver in the other pictures lined up on our coloring counter. Like the one where he's helping Daddy cut down a Christmas tree in the woods while my mother and I wait in the front seat of the car in case we have to beep the horn to warn them somebody is coming. Or the one where he's sitting quietly, right beside his daddy, waiting for a deer to tiptoe into a sunny spot. By the time he is three he is almost as tall as his daddy's hunting rifle.

I was about to ask why pictures of me weren't lined up on the counter too when my father finally told me John John was "gone."

"It's okay, Daddy, he probably ran away. He's copying me. Again," I said, tugging on my father's jeans. He lurched toward the toilet and I had to run to keep up. I sat Indian-legged on the yellow linoleum floor bunching up tissue paper for my father to wipe his mouth. He heaved and I prattled through it, as only a six-year-old girl who doesn't want to say how scared she is can prattle.

"Maybe he went to see South Africa Granny and Grandpa. They live really far away, remember?"

South Africa was where we mailed finger-painted hearts and I-love-you notes in envelopes that took lots of licking to stick on all the stamps. My mother told us it was hot there, so grannies and grandpas have really big refrigerators and lots of magnets.

"Let's go find John John now, Daddy; he might want some hot chocolate already."

Hot chocolate had worked when I ran away a few months earlier. I was mad because my little brother wasn't doing what I told him. He sat in his lions-and-tigers high chair letting oatmeal dribble down his chin like it didn't matter that he didn't wear a bib anymore. He wasn't getting in trouble; my mother was taking his picture like it was cute. Not listening to me at all. So I stood on my chair, leaned over, and bit him as hard as I could, right through his ear.

"That's it, Little Miss, you're getting your mouth washed out with soap," my mother said. She yanked me from my chair and marched me to the sink horizontally—like a battering ram. I wouldn't say sorry even after two twirls of the Palmolive bar between my teeth. That's when I decided to run away, all the way up to the fence that kept our horses from eating the neighbor's grass. Which is where I changed my mind. There had been hot chocolate waiting for me when I got back that night. Little marshmallows on top when I said I was sorry—even though I wasn't really.

Now my father was heaving, and my mother's arm was dangling off her bed, and somehow it was all my little brother's fault. I kept saying, "John John will say he's sorry too." But nobody was listening to me. He probably wouldn't get his mouth washed out; everybody would think it was cute.

Just like everybody thought it was cute when he played his favorite game: truck driver. It went like this: John John would wait at the end of our driveway for Daddy to come home from a long day driving the town dump truck. He would climb into Daddy's lap and steer all the way home. His feet would pedal through the space around Daddy's shins like this was what made the engine go. Anything he could reach to tug became a make-believe air horn: Daddy's beard, the rearview mirror, the gear stick.

Only this time he hadn't waited for Daddy at the end of the driveway. My mother was home alone, watching my baby sister inside the trailer, and I was at my very first sleepover. My father's pickup truck was parked in our yard. John John must have climbed in, pretending to steer it like all the times he sat on Daddy's lap. Somehow his little swinging feet kicked and released the emergency brake. The truck started to roll backward down our steeply sloping driveway. He managed to open the driver's-side door, but the force of it flung his tiny body under the left front tire.

My mother found him, too late.

Chapter Three

THE PARENTS

M y parents are trading the United States for Latin America,
right before my wedding. Which they don't know about yet,
so I'm trying not to take it personally. After all, it's not the first time
they've packed up their passports and headed south. My father is a big
believer in burn-down do-overs, and my mother never questions him.
That's always been my job. And I've forgotten to give him notice.

At most I had thought introducing my fiancé might be awkward.
We are already living together in Washington, DC—a continent
away from my father's reality. Until now Gary has just been a figure in
photos I occasionally mail home, someone who has suddenly turned
"my" plans into "ours." To make things easier, we have decided to
divulge our wedding plans on my father's turf: a ramshackle house in
Oregon surrounded by a smattering of nonoperative vehicles up on
blocks.

I've never noticed how fragile the whole compound looks, like a heart I'm about to break. My father will be happy for me, I tell myself. True, his oldest daughter is marrying a man he hasn't even met. But I'll distract him with enthusiasm, make him laugh before he cries. "So Dad, whatcha thinking dowry-wise, to make up for your favorite daughter? I do come with a lot of useful skills after all these years of surviving on my own."

I'm waiting for the comeback, the "What skills? Mastery of the microwave?"

But Gary isn't even through the first cup of my mom's watery coffee, microwaved from the crusty pot of Folgers she brewed that morning, when my father trumps our big announcement.

"Well I hope you're planning on eloping, because your mother and I will be long gone," he says, pouring his own cup of coffee down the kitchen sink drain. The sound trickles away and leaves a heavy silence. "The rain's stopped. Come on, I'll show you."

I check my mother's face for a reaction but she's watching my father, following his lead. There are no misty eyes, hugs, or even congratulations. Neither of my parents asks a single question. Where or when we'll tie the knot doesn't matter since they won't be there anyway. It feels as if I've announced I'm making meatloaf for dinner and my father has a few things left to put away in the garage before he's ready to eat.

Gary and I follow him outside, mouthing the words "what the hell?" to each other at the exact same time. Shocked? Hell, my father isn't even curious. I squeeze Gary's hand as we pick our way through an obstacle course of engine parts and sawhorses draped with extension cords. The unfamiliar frame of a motor home stretches along the length of the muddy driveway, a dinosaur's carcass in the process of de-extinction. Dad's latest escape vehicle, I surmise.

"We're selling this shit hole," my father declares. My cringing eye roll doesn't faze him. "Never should have come back to the States from South Africa in the first place. As soon as I finish the new rig, the Bruces are moving to Nicaragua."

I've told Gary about the first time my father built a camper. It was in 1973, when I had just turned seven. It reminded me of Frankenstein's creation. My father welded tractor-trailer-size side-view mirrors onto the camper that looked like giant, rectangular ears. The Jeep's square engine was the jutting chin. My parents' bed cabin thrust out over the cab like a high, bulging forehead. Together, the truck and camper were transformed into a 14,400-pound monster I called home.

"It was my first try. It was so damn heavy I had to swap out the Jeep's axle with one from something bigger," my father tries to explain to Gary. "Then the wheel bolt patterns didn't match, so I welded a plate to fit over the old studs."

His plan had been more linear than logical. In the consuming grief of the months after John's death, my father picked up a pencil and plotted the farthest spot away from Oregon possible to drive: the end of the Pan-American Highway. We only made it as far as Bolivia, but now, apparently, he is planning to charge the same windmill again. And not even my wedding will stop him.

But if I'm sulking, just a little, Gary seems intrigued. He inspects the dashboard console speakers, sticks his head inside freshly finished cabinets that smell like sawdust. His own father built two family homes in Wisconsin, and I can tell that Gary is impressed with my father's ingenuity.

"So you built the original one from scratch," Gary says, more acknowledgment than question. My father nods, as if building the rolling home of my childhood was no big deal. "I wonder if it's still out there somewhere?"

"In the Bolivian outback? Not bloody likely," my father snorts. "Sold it to a rancher who probably chopped it up for firewood eons ago."

My mother tags along, seizing each pause in my father's rants with strings of linked-together words too rushed to interrupt.

"We-finally-found-an-island-off-the-coast-of-Nicaragua-where-the-land-is-cheap-enough-and-we're-going-to-call-it-Corn-Island-Dive-Resort-and-we'll-build-a-hut-maybe-called-Sea-Hunt-like-the-old-TV-show-for-when-you-and-Jenny-visit-and-you-can-get-all-your-rich-advertising-clients-from-DC-to-come-spend-their-money."

She runs out of breath by the time she remembers why we're standing there. "Of course you can come too, Gary. Since it looks like you're going to be part of the family."

That Gary doesn't whip out his cell phone and call a cab back to the Portland airport right this second seems pinch-myself lucky. But not as lucky as later, after he and my father have had a few beers out in the garage. Gary stands behind me at the kitchen sink, pulls my hands out of sudsy dishwater, dries them off with a towel, and places a loose diamond in my open palm.

"You've got your dad all wrong," he tells me. "He doesn't show it, but he's really happy about the wedding. Otherwise he'd never let this go for such a bargain."

I turn the stone over in my hand: one carat, maybe more. It seems heavy and vaguely familiar, like I've seen it in another setting. Literally.

"A bargain? Wait a minute. Are you telling me this wasn't a gift?" I ask.

"Practically the same thing," Gary replies, holding the diamond up to the light. "He's got a generous streak, your old man. I could never have afforded anything nearly this perfect. Straight from the heart of Africa."

Which is when I remember where I've seen it before. On my mother's right ring finger when she smuggled it out of South Africa. It was the only way we could get our money out of the country, Dad had explained at the time. Foreigners couldn't leave with cash.

"Okay, so he's ingenious, too," Gary says. "That's one hell of a chance he took."

"Not as much of a chance as the diamond seller took when he gave them to my father with only 10 percent down," I say. The diamond my father has so graciously discounted for his future son-in-law was never paid off in the first place.

My father offers to let us sleep in the unfinished motor home, but he hasn't installed a propane heater yet so we opt for the bedroom where I spent the last two years of high school. I warn Gary about its Pepto-Bismol-pink walls and gymnastics ribbons still thumbtacked in a rainbow arch over the bed. He plunks our suitcases down, and I smile at the bowl of fresh-picked blackberries my mother leaves on my white dressing table. It's not the only welcome-home gesture. My father has meticulously taped a clean layer of plastic sheeting over the window that's been cracked since I was fourteen. But what Gary is staring at is a fax machine, still in its cardboard box.

"What's this?" I ask my mother.

"I guess it's your wedding present now," she says. "Daddy and I were going to give this to you for Christmas—you know, so you can fax us all the dates and credit card numbers when scuba divers want to make reservations for Corn Island Dive Resort."

It is at this moment that I realize my mother has no idea what her daughter's life is like. I am a vice president in the creative division of a global public relations firm, a woman who eats more meals on airplanes than at home. My fifteen-year-old dog, Wipeout, spends so much time at the Maryland farm where she goes when I'm away that the two women who run the farm have their own set of keys to my house on Capitol Hill. I have a full-time production manager who coordinates my schedule and makes travel reservations and an administrative assistant who files my expense reports. I haven't touched a fax machine in years.

The first time my parents ran away from Oregon, I was a child with no choice but to tag along and little responsibility along the way.

Now I hear my mother's intonation rising at the end of every sentence. She's trying to talk and smile simultaneously, and I realize that she wants me to be the grown-up.

"It's a wonderful fax machine, top of the line," she says. "It'll make it so much easier for you to take care of our bills and bank stuff. Instead of relying on the mail."

Sure, no problem, I feel like saying. Why don't I file your taxes, too? I've got so much free time on my hands.

"Bev, really, you shouldn't have," Gary says, making like the gift is much too thoughtful or generous, but my mother is tone deaf to the joke.

I'm still stunned. I've just introduced my mother to the man I'm marrying. I don't expect her to flutter around me making guest lists, but a fax machine for a wedding present?

"Mom, isn't it supposed to be something borrowed or something blue?"

She looks away, chirping and hopping around the fact that there will be no wedding shower, no motherly words of advice. She is flying south, following my father again. I have always been her accomplice, the one who can talk my father down from the ledges of his leaps into the unknown. The fax machine is my mother's way of saying *please be there if I need you. Always be my lifeline.*

Gary is still shaking his head in disbelief at the clunky machine in front of us.

"So, right about now you're probably wondering what kind of craziness you're getting yourself into," I say, hoping he'll laugh.

He does. "As long as it's only hereditary and not contagious."

Gary and I met on my first agency shoot in DC. He's a cinematographer, watching scenes unfold through a tiny viewfinder while I conduct the interviews and direct the content. He is discovering I have no such power over my parents. They have the capacity to careen off balance and spin assumptions into unfamiliar planes. Their eagerness can be rough, their intensity overwhelming. The words they choose are not diplomatic; their thoughts tumble out uncensored.

I understand this because I know what happened to my parents and why their default setting is to yank the cord from the wall. But I haven't told Gary. So I decide to drive him out to a graveyard a half hour away, without my parents. We stand in the Oregon drizzle looking down at a slab of rose-colored marble.

Our Son
John McDonald Bruce
1968–1972
His love and laughter live forever

It's a lie, that headstone. My younger sister and I are still afraid to say our dead brother's name out loud. Jenny doesn't ask our father for parenting advice or brag to him about her two boisterous sons. Maybe it's because her youngest boy has John John's eyes, but my father takes no joy in playing with his grandsons. He chooses to keep them at least a continent's length away. He was robbed of a son, and being a grandfather is a consolation prize he resolutely, selfishly rejects.

My mother's scars are not so visible, so close to the surface. If anyone asks, she says she lost a son, not that he died. She greets her grown daughters with baby-love words: "How's my number-one Princess?" and "Does my Sunshine need a hug today?" as though this will resurrect the world we shared before my brother died.

John is an unspoken absence in all our lives, and standing over his grave with Gary at my side I don't know whose childhood is really buried here.

"He was there one day and then just gone. I never got to say good-bye."

I nudge the toe of my shoe against a weed that's attached itself to John John's neglected headstone.

"We don't have to accept the fax machine, you know," Gary says as he draws me near. "You don't have to be the parent."

I love this man but he can't fathom the extent to which the past paralyzes the family he is about to marry into.

"Nobody just says no to my father."

There's another way, he tells me. We sit on damp Oregon soil, backs against the gravestone of my father's son. One hundred miles south of here, Gary's son, Alex, is studying philosophy at the University of Oregon. He is so happily immersed in college life that he barely remembers to call home.

"I needed to make sure Alex was settled," Gary says. "And he is. He's not a kid anymore."

I have no idea where this is leading.

"Your parents were younger than we are when they took off for South America, right?"

I nod. For two nights now we have sat in the dark, in a wood-paneled living room with orange shag carpeting, listening to the purr and click of a slide carousel projector. Gary's head is full of faded color images to match the tall tales my father tells of our journey down the Pan-American Highway in that ridiculously heavy homemade camper. There are no mentions of my missing brother; the slide-show version of the trip drowns grief in glory and erases agony with adventure. There we are, sleeping in the shadow of pyramids in Mexico. Skinny-dipping in volcanic craters in Guatemala. Breaking down and being rescued by a Sandinista newspaper publisher in Nicaragua. Getting thrown in jail in Panama. Surrounded, at gunpoint, in Colombia. Scaling the heights of Machu Picchu. Selling the camper to buy airplane tickets to South Africa, where my father's parents would dust us off and squeeze Jenny and me tight enough to make up for the grandson they would never meet.

"What if we take a trip like that of our own?" he asks. "Your dad has all the old maps and your mom kept a journal. We could try to find the original camper in Bolivia. You could finally say good-bye."

He's telling me that nothing about my crazy family will scare him off. It is both a sweet thought and a ridiculous proposition. We both have careers, successful ones. We are just beginning our lives together. We don't need to escape or run away from anything.

Chapter Four

THE WEDDING

It annoys me that my father thinks I've taken his advice. We are indeed eloping, on a beautiful beach near the Tulum ruins along Mexico's Mayan Riviera. But it's not because I still do everything my father says. It's just that a big wedding isn't rational when none of our family can come. Alex can't take time off midsemester. Gary's parents are too old to fly. Mine are on a container ship headed to Nicaragua.

"Doesn't matter anyway," Gary says. "We can always drop in on them when we drive down the Pan-American Highway."

There it is again, that graveside proposition to retrace a journey thirty years in my past. Driving thousands of miles to search for a homemade camper abandoned in the wilds of Bolivia isn't logical. I'm not the type to quit a six-figure job that sends me to shoots all over the world on business-class flights. And there isn't time to consider the idea anyway. Not with the wedding a week away.

Mexico only officially recognizes civil marriage ceremonies, so between shoots I've scouted out a Mayan judge willing to conduct one on a stretch of beach beside the thatch-roofed bungalow I found online. I've arranged for blood tests and scheduled everything around Mexico's required waiting period. But when we drive to Tulum's courthouse to pay the fees, we are told that for the ceremony to be legal we must have four witnesses: two for the bride and two for the groom.

"I never saw anything about that on the Internet," I sputter, all of my fastidious planning about to be derailed by an overlooked detail. "Or in any of the guidebooks."

"It's okay, Teresa, nobody's grading you," Gary comforts me. "We'll figure something out."

The solution presents itself over shots of tequila that night at the empty hotel bar. I'm translating my favorite Spanish toast to Gary: health, wealth, and love, and the time to enjoy them. It's a musical-sounding phrase that lights up smiles on the faces of bored beach bartenders. Gary buys a round for all four of them—Armando, Basilio, Enrique, and Juan Antonio—and then steps aside to let me do the talking.

"We're trying to get married tomorrow," I tell our new friends. "But we need four witnesses. Are you guys doing anything at, say, sunset?"

It turns out we are not the first couple to require emergency wedding witnessing, and each of the bartenders calmly reaches into his apron pocket and hands me a Mexican identity card.

"Just take these to the judge first thing tomorrow so he can put our names in the computer," Juan Antonio says. He laughs at the shocked look on my face. Four total strangers have just handed us their official identities. "It's cool, we know where you're staying."

Gary proposes his own toast, to me. "We would never have gotten this far if you weren't such a left-brained perfectionist."

"To the smart Señorita Teresa," Juan Antonio says, raising his shot glass.

"Would it spoil all this sucking up to tell you that the whole up-tight left-brain/free-spirit right-brain theory has been disproved?"

"No," Gary answers, downing his drink. "But how very left-brained of you."

Beachside elopements are utterly romantic but not terribly pre-dictable. A half hour before sunset the next day, Enrique runs up the steps to our bungalow.

"The judge is here," he says. "Can you guys do it right now in-stead of sunset? We're getting slammed at the bar."

Before I met Gary I don't know if I could have laughed and said, "Sure, no problem." Or if I could have handled the German nudists who decided to park their baby stroller, cooler, and beach blanket right in front of our almost-sunset ceremony. I'm not sure what is more surreal: the fact that they're both beginning to strip off their clothes or that they're arguing so loudly they drown out the soft voice of the Mayan judge in front of us.

I'm aware only of Gary's arm around my waist, turning me closer to him, and Juan Antonio adjusting his position to my left, just enough to shield my eyes from a hairy German ass striding defiantly into the ocean waves.

A PART OF ME WANTS TO LINGER IN THIS COUNTRY WHERE A WEDDING is reason enough to stand up for strangers. I remember traveling through Mexico as a child, and there is something nostalgic and comforting in its warm sand, nylon hammocks, and punched-tin lan-terns swinging from ropes between palm trees. But our honeymoon is cut short because I have to fly to Honduras to scout for an upcoming corporate-brand film.

I am still feeling sorry for myself when the plane touches down.

I have been to this country before, as a seven-year-old stowaway in my father's Frankenstein camper. When a power outage zaps the air-conditioning of the Intercontinental Hotel, it is just a sweaty slide back in time. I was too young, cocooned in my father's sturdy beast, to understand the turmoil stirring just under the surface of this and almost every Central American country in the 1970s. By the time my family reached Honduras, the sight of men with machine guns slouched under banana trees was as normal as the barefoot kids who brought us bread when we camped for the night.

So it feels natural, in a way, to have an armed driver deliver me from location to location in modern-day Honduras, dodging crater-sized potholes on the long drive up a mountain to Lago Yojoa. I will be bringing a crew here to film one of the country's first aquaculture operations: tilapia cordoned off from the rest of a freshwater lake nestled in a depression formed by volcanoes.

I am suddenly, acutely aware of my little brother's absence. John John loved playing with plastic boats in the bathtub of our trailer in the woods of Oregon. He should be the one paddling out on a ninety-five-foot-deep lake, not me. The atmosphere is exotic and ethereal and catapults my memories of Central America from the faded images of my father's slide show to a vivid immediacy.

My client ties up our canoe at an elaborate floating dock where I snap photographs of workers dumping sacks of pelleted fish food into the netted underwater enclosures. In a whirling instant the surface is transformed from placid to frothing with hungry fish, and I realize that the money shot will be underwater. But from the surface of Lago Yojoa it is impossible to tell whether Gary will be able to shoot without underwater lights.

There is only one thing left to try: taking a look for myself. Somewhere buried in my backpack is a disposable, waterproof camera—a low-tech backup just in case I need to take location pictures in a downpour. I'm wearing a bathing suit under my clothes and strip down to it while my client turns his back.

I'm about to take the plunge when one of the workers shouts out a warning. He points to the watch I've forgotten to take off my wrist. I gulp. It was the first present Gary ever gave me and I'm about to ruin it. I'm shoving it into the change pocket of my jeans, wadded up on the dock, when I realize it's probably just as stupid to jump in with my wedding ring on. It's the first time I've taken it off since Tulum, and I have never felt more naked as I do diving headfirst into thousands of slippery tilapia.

The bulging, glassy eyes of the fish seem to magnify underwater, especially when a woman with a disposable camera plunges into their midst. I am literally kicking my way through walls of tilapia, my bare skin bumping against fluttering fins, gaping fish lips, and solid flanks of glittering scales. I lift the camera toward the surface, shooting into streams of sunlight.

Back at the surface I'm still gasping as my client hands me an empty burlap feed bag and points to my soaking wet hair.

"Oh, that's okay," I tell him, too exhilarated even to shiver. "It'll just dry off on the boat ride back."

He bites his lip. "Um, actually it's not that. You just might want to clean off a bit. It'll be harder to get out when it dries."

I run my ringless hand through my hair and discover that it is smothered in tilapia poop, clumps and strings of it clinging to every strand of hair. The burlap sack simply grinds it deeper into my scalp. I reach for my shirt and wipe my face. Yup. Coated in a fine layer of fish excrement. Time to get back to a hot shower as quickly as possible.

I'm in such a hurry that I yank my jeans up over still-wet, sticky thighs. I don't even hear the splash. In my peripheral vision I spot a swarm of tilapia following my shiny silver watch as it sinks to the depths of Lago Yojoa. I would bawl, but then the fish shit would stream into my mouth. My heart stops as I remember the second piece of jewelry I shoved into my jeans for safekeeping: my wedding ring.

I'm scared to poke my fingers where the watch once was. I feel the metal rivet of the change pocket first, too studded and small. This can't be happening. I dig around, my fingers clumsy and numb from the cold water. But finally I feel it, the thinnest ridge of everything-is-going-to-be-okay poking into my hip. I hold it there, pressed against my flesh, until my breathing returns to normal. I slide it onto the ring finger of my shaking left hand and clasp my fist against ever losing it again.

Someday a chef is going to slice a Honduran tilapia into filletts and discover an undigested Kenneth Cole watch. It may still tick, counting down the seconds and minutes of an overscheduled, stressed-out woman's life. I haven't seen Wipeout in three weeks. I don't really have time for epiphanies but one seems to have caught up with me.

I am rushing through what should be the best year of my life, cramming the hours of every day with ambition and obligation. But it is my watch at the bottom of Lake Yojoa and not my wedding ring. If that isn't a sign to slow down and reboot my priorities, then I don't know what is.

I call Gary the minute I get back to the Intercontinental Hotel in San Pedro Sula, hair still crusty with fish poop but too desperate to hear his voice to shower first.

"You'll never guess what happened," he says, before I get a word in. "My dad found a 1968 Avion truck camper in the Milwaukee classifieds. He says it's in pretty good shape and the guy only wants $1,200 for it."

Without hesitation I tell him to send Joe a check and start looking for a truck big enough to handle it. We'll need something dependable on the Pan-American Highway. As soon as this film is over we are going to find the camper of my childhood.

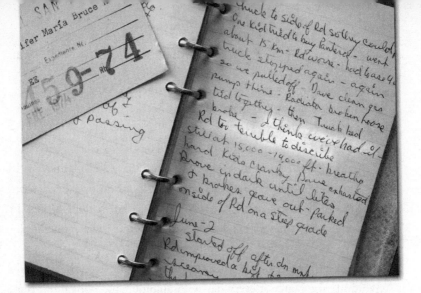

Chapter Five

THE JOURNAL

've given notice at the agency, and it feels like I am balancing on a precipice. Or maybe the trip is an approaching avalanche. I will be unemployed for the first time since I was sixteen. My stomach muscles cramp with doubt, and in my dreams I am utterly incapable of controlling anything. Clearly, ditching a career plan requires a plan of its own.

I unwrap five packs of colored sticky notes and peel everything off the walls of Gary's three-room office. We've been living here ever since selling my row house on Capitol Hill to an incoming congressional staffer.

Wipeout nervously paces around the boxes marked for storage, her nails clicking on unfamiliar hardwood floors. Her silky white fur is falling out in clumps, and her watery brown eyes stare up at me for answers. Gary and I have taken to whispering, late at night, as though she can overhear us debating the merits of every friend and relative who has offered to keep her until we come back.

But Wipeout's arthritis is so bad she can't jump into the backseat of the new four-wheel-drive, diesel-engine Ford F-350 we bought after Gary's dad found the camper. She is almost sixteen years old, filled with cancerous lumps and bumps and steadily losing weight, but at seventy pounds still too cumbersome to lift. It takes both of us to coax her up a sturdy plastic ramp that slides between the seats; she has reached a state of anxiety that is soothed only by the comfort of having us both in sight at all times.

Everything but our nearness is about to change, and I am as nervous as Wipeout. I can't imagine how life without our working partnership will work. I produce, Gary shoots: our interlocking parts fit so snugly you can hear the seal lock. Without that purpose, will we still be airtight? This trip isn't a leave of absence; when we come back, nothing will be waiting. I've already hired the senior producer who will take over my job at the agency. Gary sold his camera to buy the new truck. When the trip is over we will have to reinvent ourselves, start over in a new city, make a new home, build new careers. We aren't twenty-something backpackers; we have everything to lose if this goes wrong.

So many things could. We are newlyweds who will be forced to spend every day in the same vehicle, with no personal space to retreat into if it gets too stressful. What if Gary discovers I'm a better producer than I am an unemployed wife? What if I can't handle a year without deadlines, assignments, and a steady paycheck? Everyone we tell about the trip professes to be wildly jealous. It sounds so spontaneous and artistic. Who hasn't dreamed of throwing caution and logic to the wind and embarking on the ultimate road trip?

In all honesty, me. The slides in my father's carousel have seared unsettling images into my memory. A huge, clunky camper created in the aftermath of a tragedy. The man who built it crouched beside the busted wheels of an old truck on the new Pan-American Highway. A skinny seven-year-old with choppy bangs and buck teeth standing beside a cherubic little sister. A mother with vacant, tired eyes.

"There isn't a script to follow, Teresa," Gary says when he finds his office transformed into a strategy room. "We don't have to come up with a time line. We'll take as long as we need to take, or at least until we run out of money. That's the beauty of this."

The thought of a life without alarm clocks and schedules thrills him, and he's trying to make me think of this trip as a journey, not something to cross off a list of accomplishments. He loves to drive and can't wait to leave behind congested city streets. For him this is a chance to exchange rush hours for the rush of hours and hours on the open road. But he's wrong about me having no script to follow. I do have one. It belonged to my mother.

JANUARY 1, 1974—MEXICO
Took Dave's wallet and all our money—told police.
Went home. Some day

MARCH 29, 1974—COLOMBIA
Drove on bad road until we hit valley and got truck
fixed. Camped by river

MAY 16, 1974—PERU
I was sick—back door trots. Got shot for cough, napped
all day

My mother gave me her journal when she left for Nicaragua. It is a faded, pink, three-ring binder the size of a Harlequin romance. Every night for nearly a year, she documented what we ate, where we stopped, and who was sick. She also recorded sixty-one separate truck breakdowns along the Pan-American Highway. It is more like a ship's log than a keepsake, and in it I find evidence of everything that could go wrong.

"Does she ever find a positive thing to say?" Gary asks when he thumbs through the delicate pages. "We should chuck this thing. It's got to have bad karma."

"Are you kidding? It's perfect," I answer. "I can cross-check all my lists against actual risks and proven mistakes."

Under each mental picture of the journey that began when I was seven, I create a sticky-note storyboard of all the ways this trip will be different, better, safer. From the journal entry about my father's stolen wallet I bullet-point our strategy: less reliance on cash (times have changed and there are ATMs everywhere), separate sets of credit cards in case either one of us is mugged, codes and passwords backed up on laptops and hard copies stashed with Gary's parents, and a phone tree of embassy contact numbers taped to the case of a portable satellite phone—the kind favored by war correspondents.

"Should I start a column of sticky notes under 'back door trots'?" Gary asks, still teasing me. But diarrhea was the least of it. My mother's journal documents almost daily vomiting (mostly mine), chronic dental problems, broken bones, unexplained rashes, concussions from high-altitude blackouts, and worse.

FEBRUARY 5-11, 1974
Met local news publisher and enjoyed house
facilities while there. 1st Teri sick, then I. Doctor
said malaria?

I fill almost an entire sticky pad listing what will become our traveling pharmacy: prophylactic antibiotics, bandages, splints, gauze, syrup of ipecac, rubbing alcohol, laxatives, antidiarrheals, muscle relaxants, a year's supply of birth control, antiseptic creams, snakebite kits, emergency iodine tablets, and expensive water bottles with microbial filters. Then I start on a list of medical tests and checkups to schedule before my company health insurance plan runs out.

"You do realize that most Latin American countries have doctors," Gary reminds me. "They won't turn you away. Nobody wants a gringo to die in their country."

I keep writing notes to myself. Compare costs of emergency traveler's insurance plans. Investigate helicopter evacuation policy. Gary raises a bushy eyebrow.

"What? I know a producer who had to get airlifted out of a country. It happens."

In truth I am thinking of my mother and how lonely and scared she looks in all my father's photographs. For her, the Pan-American Highway might as well have been a road to the moon. There was precious little any ordinary American knew of it back then; Latin America only made news when natural disasters struck or bloody coups erupted. This was the period when Moscow and Peking had more publicly acknowledged interest in Latin America than Washington did.

Word that Guatemala's government was executing leftist challengers at children's birthday parties did not make it to Banks, Oregon. Neither did the fact that El Salvador was in the beginning of two decades of bloody civil war, or that thousands of people died in the overthrow of Chilean president Salvador Allende.

My mother prepared the best way she could, focusing on the needs she could imagine. I remember her filling Tupperware containers with oatmeal and peanut butter. She bought first-through third-grade books to homeschool Jenny and me along the way and took first aid classes, just in case. She sat in on some Spanish classes at the community college but dropped out when my father ridiculed her awkward pronunciation.

"I never did have his natural ear," she says.

I scribble a new note, this one on the green pad denoting Gary's to-dos: sign up for Berlitz course. Gary scratches it out and writes his own. Buy Spanish CDs and listen as we go.

Where I am obsessing over the dangers my parents faced on the original trip, Gary finds the journal's descriptions of food more harrowing than stolen wallets and malaria. By the time we reached Ecuador, my mother was documenting what we ate for breakfast, lunch, and dinner, and it was dismal.

> **MAY 4TH** Oatmeal (L) banana sandwiches (D) toasted cheese sandwiches

> **MAY 5TH** Oatmeal and bread (L) bread and bananas (D) spaghetti

> **MAY 8TH** Pineapple, bread (L) bananas, leftover rice (D) spaghetti, bread, pop

"Is this considered camping food?" Gary asks. "Because you should know, my idea of camping is a bad Holiday Inn."

"More like a combination of being broke and Mom not knowing what to do with anything from local produce markets."

He picks up a stack of pink sticky notes. "Let's call this color fuchsia. For food."

He's beginning to see the logic in my color-coded defense against feeling overwhelmed. Under the fuchsia food column he sticks reminders to pack cookbooks, a crème brûlée torch for blackening the skins of fresh peppers from markets, and a dish-drying rack that could double as a grilling surface for outdoor campfires.

"I thought you said you never camped?"

"I'm thinking of it as a mobile, backyard barbecue."

The phone rings and we take a break while Alex interrogates his father about the new truck. I listen to one side of the conversation.

"Teresa's dad had a piece-of-shit used truck that couldn't handle the weight of the camper, and it broke down almost every day. I'm not planning on spending a year on the side of a road."

There is a pause and Gary laughs. "We'll see." Alex wants the truck when we get back. Despite the banter, I know Gary aches with missing Alex, and this journey will lengthen the miles between them.

"Can't Alex take a year off and come with us?" I say, only half-kidding. "There's a kid bed in the camper. He'd fit if we just chop his legs off at the knees."

Gary laughs but I know he's wished it too. "If he was seven, like you were, that'd be one thing. But this is his moment. I could never give that back to him." It is settled.

De. OCTUBRE. del.. DOS MIL TRES

HAROLD RIVAS REYES
CONSUL GENERAL

Chapter Six

THE DOG

Alex's legs are safe, but there is still the issue of Wipeout. She was born in Mexico and I sneaked her into the United States illegally when she was a year old. She's too big to sneak back. She has outlasted every job, every apartment, and every boyfriend in my life, but my standing in *her* world diminished when Gary joined our little pack. She lavishes on him a degree of adoration that would make a less balanced woman jealous.

Every so often I remind them both of the risks I've taken for her. There was the time in Mexico, when I was in my twenties, that I had to find a way to take her with me on a long-distance bus back to the border. I tried poking air holes in a duffle bag and singing the song that always soothes her—"How Much Is That Doggie in the Window?"—while I zippered her inside. Even when she stopped kicking and thrashing it was impossible to walk upright with sixty pounds biting into one shoulder. So I bought a bright-red leash for her and a white cane for me and pretended to be blind. Wipeout thought the cane was a stick I'd toss for her and bolted up the bus steps yanking me behind her. Even now, she can jerk my shoulder out of its socket if she sees a squirrel. It's just that now her legs give out first. To take even a healthy dog on a yearlong road trip through Latin America is far from logical.

"Wipeout is too weak," our friends say. "We'll keep her until you get back." This whole idea is crazy, they really mean.

"So this is what my parents went through," I tell Gary. "Only they took even more flak. Instead of a sick old dog they were taking two little girls."

I can't bear to contemplate the absence of Wipeout. There is little likelihood she will hang on until the end of the Pan-American Highway, but I had to leave one family dog behind thirty years ago. Selfish though it may be, I cannot do it twice.

"Unwrap another stack of stick-its," Gary says. "White, of course. For Wipeout." She's coming with us, he really means.

I am giddy with relief, and our celebration begins with tequila we saved from the honeymoon. The bed is already in storage so we tumble onto a futon on the ground, clothes fluttering down atop cardboard packing boxes. I don't hear Wipeout clicking into the bedroom, but I feel her wet nose as she sniffs the edge of the futon.

"Get out of here, girl, we're getting busy," I say, nudging her with a knee.

She must think that we have lost our minds, wrestling on what to her looks like a dog bed. She plops herself down right behind Gary's bare body, and we become three layers of a crescent moon howling with laughter.

"You better get used to it," I tell him. "In a camper things are even cozier."

Our final week in Washington, DC, passes in a blur of vet and consulate visits seeking visas for Wipeout to enter Mexico, Guatemala, Honduras, El Salvador, Nicaragua, Costa Rica, Panama,

Ecuador, Peru, Bolivia, Argentina, and Chile. That's right: canine visas. I never knew there was such a thing, but not only do we have to pay a fee, in advance, for Wipeout to enter each country legally; we're also supposed to know the exact dates of entry and exit.

"We're driving, not booking a flight," I sputter to the consulate official. "Can't we leave the transit time blank?"

Even with my father's meticulous maps I have no idea how long it will take to drive through each country.

"The whole point is not to have a schedule!" I can hear the tone of my own voice: pissy bordering on pleading. For the first time in my life I am trying not to commit to every detail in advance. I want to slow down and absorb what flew past me as a child.

But I have no idea how long Wipeout will live. I don't dare let on that the canine in question needs pills to control her bladder, chews herself bloody if she's left alone too long, and only makes it upstairs if Gary carries her. We may need all twelve visas or she might not make it through Mexico. So I pore through the dates in my mother's journal, subtracting days lost because of truck breakdowns and sick kids and, under protest, fill in arrivals and departures for every country.

Back in Gary's office, I let down my defenses. "They're going to take her away from me and it's all my fault." I may have satisfied bureaucrats behind counters, but even a control-freak producer can't predict the timing of a road trip as complicated as this one.

"That's not going to happen," Gary comforts me. "I have a plan." He hands me an iron and the first of twelve canine visas. "Okay, babe, ease the steam under the edge of this foil stamp and it'll come right off the original."

My hands shake, but the steam button sends puffs of moisture into the gluey substrate between foil and document. The seal of official permission lifts right off.

I stand, sticky foil stars and disks attached to my thumbs while Gary scans the unsealed visas of a dozen countries into Photoshop. In a matter of minutes, he erases the dates I was forced to commit to and then prints out exact duplicates with everything filled in but the lines for entry and exit. With trembling hands, I reaffix each foil seal to its doctored original document.

"There!" Gary says when the last one is finished. "Just before we get to each country's border we'll fill in whatever date we want, and no one will be the wiser."

Wipeout will begin her final road trip with a portfolio of forged documents, a scheme I assume will impress my father. Instead, over a crackling long-distance telephone connection, he tells me, "Some illiterate border *aduanero* is going to want a hell of a bribe to let that mutt through."

My father's tone gives him away; this isn't about Wipeout. My parents are living forty miles off the coast of Nicaragua now, their plan to build the island dive resort mired in permissions waiting for appropriate payoffs. My father doesn't know who will talk to lawyers in Spanish for him, who will wire him money when he runs out, who will forward his mail and shred his bills when I am gone. I have chosen Gary over him, to follow our dreams instead of his.

"I'm telling you, you'd be better off not taking her."

"I can't believe I'm hearing this, Dad. You drove two little girls into a dozen revolutions and you think *we're* getting in over our heads?"

Chapter Seven

MEXICO

Wipeout's wet nose rests on my left shoulder as the Ford F-350 creeps toward a checkpoint dividing the United States from the country where she was born. We've removed the useless, tiny backseat and replaced it with a carpeted bench so she has room to stretch out and sleep along the way. Underneath this platform is a locked wooden box storing spare parts and valuables we don't want every border agent to see: computers, camera gear, satellite phone, cash. Wipeout is a willing decoy and guard—she paces with excitement and sticks her head out the driver's-side window when Gary rolls it down to show our passports.

I am both nervous and exhilarated, clutching Wipeout's documents in sweaty hands in case they're demanded. But the border agent just waves us through to a fee station, warily backing away from the drooling seventy-pound dog displaying every tooth she still possesses. Over a period of forty-five minutes between Nogales, Arizona, and Nogales, Mexico, we pay seven different clerks a total of $275 to stick holograms on our windshield and fastidiously enter copies of our driver's licenses, the title to the truck, insurance receipts, and passport photos into some presumed database of foreigners passing through.

"What was our daily budget again?" Gary asks as he starts handing out our credit card instead of our rapidly thinning stash of cash.

I do the math. "One fifth of how much we just got fleeced."

"You don't know that," Gary says. "We weren't singled out as far as I can tell." It's irritating how easily he can roll with punches the producer in me can't. Luckily I built some wiggle room into the script I'm not supposed to be following. I pull out my mother's journal to see if the crossing knocked the breath out of her as well.

> **DECEMBER 16, 1973**
>
> $2 fee at customs. Trucked stopped side of road in desert.

Maybe not. Even in 1973, two dollars couldn't have seemed unreasonable. The diesel engine purrs as we pull out onto our first Mexican highway, and despite the shock to my projected budget I feel invincible. This is going to work. Wipeout and Gary are with me, and I am ready for everything ahead, open to the pure adventure of it. I've prepared well enough to relax, confident that this new truck and this new journey will somehow lead me to the camper of my childhood. Cocooned in air-conditioned comfort, the first day of my new life flashes past the windshield. It is a suffering desert landscape—scorched sand, withered trees, and shriveled towns—but I am as excited as I was at seven.

We haven't passed a supermarket since leaving Nogales, Arizona, but flyaway plastic bags snag on every brittle stump of a bush. These shredded North American garbage kites are the only splashes of color, relief from grey monochrome monotony. This stretch of northern desert, the fastest overland route to Mexico's coast, will never grace the cover of a guidebook or tourism website. I turn away from the occasional dead dog, smacked by semitrucks and left to bake along the road. I wave at children gathering scraps of discarded tin cans, their bare feet hardened against the sizzling asphalt by thick layers of blackened calluses. They wave back with gap-toothed smiles, transfixed by the sight of a beautiful silver castle on wheels.

THE AVION IS A GIFT FROM ANOTHER ERA. ONE WHEN CAMPING WAS glamorous and pickup campers were more stylish than most people's homes. She is constructed entirely of aluminum panels, like an airplane, and weighs only twenty-two hundred pounds—a fraction of my father's Frankenstein beast. Even so, balanced on teetering stacks of bricks in the driveway, the Avion looks like an elephant on toothpicks. Gary's parents have restored her to a lustrous silver shine after years of neglect. Joe winterized all the pipes. Angie reupholstered the worn, orange seat cushions with a velvety African safari print of zebras and rhinos. The Avion is airtight, riveted against whatever tests we will put her through.

The camper's original owner saved the sales brochures and instruction manuals that came with her. They are full of glossy photographs of a buxom woman in satin capri pants admiring the all-in-one toilet and shower compartment and the full-sized oven with three burners. "This compact castle lets you live like kings and queens wherever you go—even way back in wild bush country!"

NO CLAIM SEEMS TOO EXAGGERATED WHEN WE PULL THE TRIUMPHANT Avion into an empty RV campground in San Carlos, Mexico, on our first night. Even with hips stiff from three hundred miles of desert driving I feel regal mixing two gin-and-tonics over our compact sink. It's so hot inside the camper that we slip into swimsuits and carry our celebratory cocktails across a two-lane highway to the beach.

I fling off my flip-flops and dig my toes into searing hot sand. I am standing in the first footprint of my childhood odyssey. The beach is flecked with thumb-sized pebbles of deep jade. I roll them in my palm, and when the glistening seawater evaporates they fade to the olive green of a long-ago memory. Wipeout chases Gary into the waves, and they both howl like shipwrecked castaways too long in the sun. I hang back, spinning and skipping in the beige sea foam.

When the vomiting starts, hours later, it is the same color and consistency: a frothy mix of bile and tonic. I abandon the Avion, too claustrophobic to puke inside our compact, all-in-one toilet. I stagger to the campground's restroom in pitch-black night with Wipeout underfoot.

"Gross," I moan, begging Gary to take her back to the camper. She has pushed her way into my stall and is licking my chin, eyeing the puke-covered toilet bowl rim.

On our second day in Mexico, the air-conditioning inside the truck struggles to keep up with the desert temperatures, and a visible suspension of particulates streams through the vents with the thick, sweet scent of Freon.

The soothing blue sea disappears from sight, and the shoulderless asphalt hovers and seethes on a baked, colorless horizon. I roll down my window, and the desert smells like the inside of a Laundromat dryer. Each time Gary pulls over so I can vomit again, the heat presses down on my lungs and I can hardly draw the breath to heave.

There is a beach town ahead promisingly called Las Glorias, but the Avion's plastic water tank cracks when we hit an unpainted speed bump, and all thirty gallons of our chlorinated water supply seep into the carpeted camper floor. By the time we reach Las Glorias, three hours later, the thermometer inside the Avion reads 114 degrees. Every air-conditioned hotel is full, so we park on the beach.

"Can you feel that?" Gary asks, turning my flaccid body to meet a breeze coming off the ocean. "Try not to panic. This wind will keep the bugs away so we can open all the windows and let the camper cool down. You'll be able to sleep it off."

I have to hold onto the truck's back tire to keep from falling into pools of my own vomit. My throat feels like it has been scored with a rake. Sand is plastered to my knees and my lips are caked. Gary ties Wipeout to the truck next to a cooler of water, and we walk to the outdoor pool of the nearest hotel. It is dark and no one sees us opening a chaise lounge to the completely horizontal position. I lower myself stomach first with my face between two sagging rubber slats. When I throw up in my sleep at least I won't choke to death.

The next morning I roll into the pool and let the cool, over-chlorinated water wash away the stink and stickiness. We make our way back to the camper, but not even Wipeout's joyous, sand-flinging morning greeting revives me.

"Your parents might have let you puke your way through Mexico," Gary says. "But I'm taking you to a hospital. Mazatlán looks like the next big city; there's got to be one there."

DEC 20TH, 1973

Drove our big rig through narrow streets and parked
by a square to watch kids breaking piñatas in a church-
yard. I bought a dress for 90 pesos.
Camped by the beach—pretty. Teri sick.

Gary thinks it is pent-up stress that is coursing through my bowels, but I know the truth. I am being punished for a decision I made a little over a week ago.

Chapter Eight

THE GUN

I called my father for advice before the drive began, and even after a week on the road the disbelief in his voice still rings in my ears.

"Come again?" he had sputtered, from a neighbor's phone in Nicaragua. "This line must be crappier than normal because I know you didn't just ask me what kind of gun to get."

Ever since I was a teenager I have harangued my parents about the evils of guns. The fact that they only used them to hunt deer, which stocked our freezer all winter, did not temper my haughty judgment. I became a sulky, vegetarian know-it-all who listened to the Smiths' "Meat Is Murder" over and over on her Sony Walkman. That's when my father gave me my nickname.

"Hey Miss Information, are you forgetting how I almost shot myself?"

I was seven at the time, and I still remember how his face got sweaty and grey—like canned tuna when you press the lid down really hard and squish out all the juices. It happened in Bolivia, during a shakedown for a bribe. A border guard demanded to inspect the camper, and my father had forgotten to put his revolver back in its hiding place after cleaning it. He spotted the gun lying on the bed and shoved his way past me to conceal the illegal weapon—by sitting on it. He squirmed and scooted all the way to the left of the bed like he was dying to go to the bathroom.

"The inspector searched all around the camper," my father always says when he gets to this part of the slide-show version of our life on the road, "but not under my ass."

He can laugh about it thirty years later, but I can't push back the walls of fear closing in as Gary's parents finish restoring the Avion in Milwaukee. I print out random, unverified stories from the Web about kidnapped tourists, gang shoot-outs, American women mistaken for foreign baby-snatchers, violent guerrilla insurgencies, and military clashes with indigenous peoples.

"I'd feel safer with a gun," I tell Gary, when Alex is out of earshot. I can literally see my husband's patience with my paranoid overpreparation departing his more rational brain like quivering waves of heat.

"Listen, babe, we're still technically residents of Washington, DC," he says. "We don't have the right to vote and we sure as hell can't buy a gun."

Fear can be so powerful it creates its own logic, and nothing Gary says stops me from fixating on the worst possible outcomes. Our beautiful camper is so conspicuous we get truckjacked and stranded. Wipeout gets hit by a car and there's no vet to put her out of her agony. We naively stumble into a coup or a civil war like my parents did. One of us is held hostage by narco-traffickers.

Gary keeps trying to reason me down from my mental cliff. We make a pact. If at any time either one of us gets a bad feeling about a place or situation, we will tell the other and immediately turn around. No second-guessing each other's instincts. It is a pledge that comforts me on many levels but not enough to give up on the gun.

My scenarios are convincing enough that Gary's eighty-one-year-old father caves in and buys a pistol for me. In roughly one week, we will be crossing the Mexican border with a gun registered in Wisconsin under the name of Joseph Geboy. Whatever he thinks of his new daughter-in-law Joe keeps to himself.

"I've been thinking of a place you can hide the gun," he says instead.

I can't let on that I haven't thought this far ahead. I watched my father build a secret hiding place thirty years ago and now I watch Gary's father do the same.

"See right here, where you put your feet when you sit down to eat at the table?" Joe has been working on the camper for weeks and knows it far more intimately than we do. "Well, that's just a platform, a false floor. There's a storage space underneath. If we lay carpet over this whole thing and piece it in where the floor lifts up, I don't think anyone will see the seam."

It's perfect, so of course I have to make it more complicated. "Let's store our books under the floor too." I am thinking of my father's ass in Bolivia, his bare gun out in the open. "No border guard is going to dig through all these paperbacks to find a buried gun."

While Gary and Joe piece together carpet segments, I get down on my belly and shove the gun as far back under the false floor as I can reach. Then I stuff in forty-two books.

"What about this box of bullets?" Gary asks when I am finished. Out come the paperbacks, one by one, and I realize that if we ever need to use this weapon it will take me fifteen minutes to get at it.

"Let's hope the bad guys give you lots of warning," Joe mutters as he tacks down the last carpet nail.

JOE WOULD NEVER TELL ANYONE ABOUT THE GUN OR ITS HIDING PLACE, but my guilty conscience makes me blurt out the secret as soon as we reach Prescott, Arizona. I choose my audience well for this confession: Gary's older brother, Michael, his wife, Carol, and their seventy-two-year-old friend, Nancy, have just opened a bottle of wine to celebrate our arrival. We are spending one last weekend with family before entering Mexico. Staring at three disbelieving faces, I feel a little of the guilt-laced defiance that flows through my father's veins. I can't back down now; better to make light of it.

"No border inspector will suspect we have a pistol, not with this fearsome guard dog for protection," I say. Wipeout lazily licks her privates and then falls asleep.

Carol gets on the Internet to research the legal ramifications of getting caught with a gun south of the border. The first site she finds is not comforting.

"Bullet point one (no pun intended)," she begins to read out loud. "You will go to jail and your vehicle will be seized. Bullet point two: you will be separated from family. Bullet point three: you may get up to a thirty-year sentence in a Mexican prison. Ignorance of this law will not get you leniency from the police."

Michael brings up Napoleonic Law. "Basically it's the opposite of the way it works here. In Mexico, you are presumed guilty and must prove your innocence. Good luck with that."

The silence of a stupid idea hangs in the air. I am proving I am as bullheaded as my father, only these people don't know him and therefore cut me no genetic slack.

"Well, obviously you're going to do what you're going to do," Nancy says at last. "I just have one question. Do either of you know anything about guns?"

This is how I find myself firing a gun for the first time in my life, the day before we enter Mexico. Nancy, as it turns out, owns several guns and has driven through Mexico in her own RV—with her firearms locked safely in a cabinet back in Arizona. She offers to show us the basics, and we sheepishly follow her to a firing range in the hills above Prescott. Wipeout stays with our camper, guarding a pile of forty-two paperbacks.

My palms itch and the gun's first report reverberates in my cramping stomach. I squeeze my eyes shut to keep from crying.

"Teresa, look at me," Nancy says. "You have to be ready to actually kill someone if you pull the trigger in Latin America. Then you'll have to drive the hell out of there without looking back."

Gary maintains his composure. It turns out years of holding cameras steady translates into decent aim, and Nancy is temporarily distracted by the fun of showing him how to shoot.

"Squeeze, don't pull, the trigger," she coaches. "Brace for the kick and keep breathing."

Later, in a garage filled with deer-antler carvings and bullet-riddled target-practice posters, this five-foot-tall woman with sensible silver hair shows us how to clean the gun.

"Don't forget, border dogs can detect cleaning fluid as well as gunpowder." I don't ask her how she knows this. She hands me a box of ziplock bags. "Wear gloves, keep everything separate, and use these to throw away the evidence." She means evidence of cleaning, I tell myself, not that she thinks we'll ever have to fire the gun. We write down Nancy's e-mail address and promise to keep her posted along the way.

"I still think it's a bad idea," she says as she drops us off at Michael and Carol's house.

I know she's right. I will enter Mexico a suspicious, armed intruder—not the open, appreciative traveler I want to be. This gun is me hanging on to every wrong turn and fateful twist in my mother's journal, coloring my future with fears I need to outgrow. I have disrupted my inner equilibrium between rational and irrational, trust and distrust, and I struggle to push down the bile beginning to fester in my guilt-twisted intestines.

Chapter Nine

BREAKDOWNS

Driving a camper through Mazatlán quickly becomes a hangover without the fun of getting drunk. Overweight, underdressed tourists spill off the sidewalks. The streets slowly squeeze together until all the city's faded glamour empties out into a dingy port and ferry terminal. Gary periodically pulls over to avoid me puking inside the cab, and I must look like the oldest spring-breaker who ever hurled humiliation into a gutter. But we pass no hospitals so we settle for a shabby hotel that allows dogs.

By the time Gary locks up the camper I am blacking out on the hotel's toilet, coming to with strings of vomit connected to the flush handle like a spider's web. My arm drops off the toilet seat and the back of my hand makes a loud smack on the cool tile floor. I'm convinced someone has slapped my face, and I have no idea that I am talking to myself. *I want to go home.*

I start to cry. In reality, the only home I now lay claim to is a 110-degree tin can parked on four wheels outside, but I am imagining our solid row house on Capitol Hill and its soft, handwoven Afghan rugs. The sloppy coating of Lysol on the hotel's bathroom floor isn't quite thick enough to blanket the smell of diarrhea. It sounds over-dramatic, even to the voice in my own head, but to actually return to the United States means facing the desert again. And if I have to go back out into that heat, I will not survive.

Please don't let me die in a Mazatlán motel.

I picture turning back after less than a week in Mexico. Gary and I walked away from the peak of two careers to retrace this journey. We are supposed to be on an exotic sabbatical, so confident in our world-traveling skills that we leap without a landing pad. The explo-ration, the journey itself, is more important than the outcome, goes this plucky narrative. But who would hire us again if we have nothing to show for it, no adventures to document?

It is an even darker fear, though, that has reduced me to a woman who speaks in a submissive, little-girl voice every time she asks Gary to pull over. My inner dialogue is just as pathetic.

If I can't tough this out will he still love me?

It is utterly unfair to doubt the commitment of a man willing to drive to another hemisphere to find the camper I grew up in. But our marriage is untested. There are not enough shared moments and fond memories to compensate him if I bail out on this joint adventure. I will end up like my mother, using baby love words to try to hold the past together.

My body ricochets between panicked hot flashes and cold-sweat chills, but there is no one to call on my fancy satellite phone, and all the traveler's health insurance in the world can't compensate for my hemorrhaging hopes and dreams. *Stop it,* I tell myself. My par-ents went through much worse, and my mother managed to reduce the misery to incomplete sentences in a little pink journal. She never turned back and neither will I.

Just stop retching and stand. When I flush the toilet, something glistens as the globs of phlegm swirl out of sight. I am so dehydrated that my wedding ring has fallen off my finger.

Every fiber of buck-up unravels, and my sobs morph into gasps for air that Gary hears even over the white noise of CNN in the bedroom.

"I'm going to get help. Stay here and try to pull it together," Gary tells me. He doesn't know why I keep pointing into the dingy toilet bowl. "If you keep crying you'll hyperventilate and scare Wipeout."

His words force me to at least fake being calm. Somehow, even though I'm the one who speaks Spanish and asks all the questions, Gary finds a pharmacy clinic and returns to fetch me.

After a cursory exam, a Mazatlán doctor says I have gastroenteritis and need a drip to restore my fluids. The nurse lifts my feeble arm and straps my veins to a hanging pump of electrolytes, Cipro, and Valium. Six hours and $380 later, I am human again. Not well enough to face the heat inside the Avion, but well enough to stagger back to the hotel. When she sees me, Wipeout's paws slide out from under her as she runs into my outstretched arms, and I don't care what toilet bowls she's licked.

I lie in bed watching CNN news anchors babble on about the war in Iraq, something that until a week ago I diligently followed, and my entire childhood journey through Latin America suddenly makes more sense. Only hours earlier I thought I was teetering at the edge of death, but my parents actually fell over it and landed on a ledge just wide enough to crawl along by feel. A grief-blinded mother and father drove off into an unknown continent without investigation or research not because they were inherently irresponsible but because they couldn't imagine anything worse than what they had already endured.

ON OUR SIXTH DAY SOUTH OF THE BORDER, GARY AND I LEAVE MAZATLÁN and set off down Toll Highway 15 headed for the fishing town of San Blas. This is the town that became my father's "See, we weren't crazy" moment in the family slide show. He parked our giant camper right on the beach, and there are pictures of my little sister and me licking huge ice creams, wearing ponchos, and smiling. A stranger would never have suspected I was secretly glad the ice-cream man didn't have orange-and-vanilla sherbet, because that was John John's favorite flavor. It was still raw, his gone-ness, but in San Blas somehow the ocean didn't seem to sting as much.

Thirty years later I roll down the truck windows and let the wind lift and flow through my fingers. This is the Mexico of my childhood: colors as rich and waxy as my darkest crayons, smells sticky-sweet and steamy. Some of the drugs are wearing off; others are kicking in. I don't hear the blood racing through my temples anymore. I don't feel like my intestines will disintegrate with every exhale. I am both embarrassed at how close to death I believed myself to be and prostrate before the power of fear. I am at that stage of timid relief when instead of talking about what happened I'm happy just to wiggle my toes.

The thought occurs to me that perhaps by this point on the first trip, the younger version of me had recovered as well. So I dig in the glove compartment for a letter my aunt saved for me. It is the first letter from the road that my mother airmailed home, and instead of mentioning me it chronicles six major truck breakdowns.

> Well it seems our dream trip has turned into a nightmare. The rim on the back wheel seared off and we limped into town and replaced it with a used one . . . we are getting broker by the minute.

In comforting increments Gary and I pass a Ford dealership, a Goodyear tire shop, and a Hyatt. My body and courage may fail me again, but if our truck breaks down I will never have to write a letter like this one. I turn the letter's tissue-thin pages with a flutter of something akin to survivor's guilt.

Used wheel seared completely, found a place to fix the wheel. Trying to get brakes fixed too. They fixed for $20 and a jack in trade. Got truck going but wire to starter came off. Dave adjusted carburetor while I did laundry. Waiting for wheel now.

I put away the letter to let the scenery lift my spirits. The dry-biscuit desert gives way to mustard-and-olive-colored fields and then to emerald tropics in the state of Nayarit. Along this daylong stretch of highway, Mexico transforms from *Treasure of the Sierra Madre* to *Night of the Iguana*.

None of this beauty finds its way into my mother's journal. From San Blas forward, it reads like instructions for the damned:

1. Break down near dusk.
2. Spend night on side of road.
3. Limp or tow into nearest town.
4. Fix (barter for parts if possible).
5. Drive a little.
6. Repeat.

While my father stayed behind in garages, my mother, sister, and I wandered off to find markets, Laundromats, and playgrounds. From these uncertain explorations grew the grand sense of adventure I would forever link to Mexico.

I remember sucking on my first stalk of raw sugarcane, extracting what felt like a delicious secret. I have wanted a pair of black leather pants with silver buttons chained down the seams ever since I saw them on the legs of mariachi singers in Guadalajara cafés. We had stopped to share a bottle of orange soda, and the singers serenaded our table with such vein-bulging passion that it made my mother blush.

But with every unplanned repair stop my father was forced to consider the possibility that the truck would bankrupt us long before we reached the end of the Pan-American Highway. We would never reach Brazil or Tierra del Fuego; we might not even get to Guatemala. So he added a PS to my mother's letter asking her to wire $1,000 to us, care of the US Embassy in Panama City.

> We have had more problems than we anticipated. Some could possibly have been avoided in advance by more careful analysis of the truck's capabilities but the remainder, such as the cost of gasoline and repair bills, were unforeseeable.

My father never admits he is wrong; if he is one hundred miles off course he will claim he picked the scenic route on purpose. He is only half joking when he says, "With a little humility, I'd be perfect." So I am startled by the tortured content of this letter to my aunt. Between the lines is a chagrined acknowledgment that a camper and truck topping fourteen thousand pounds had crippling consequences, and that my belligerently independent father was even more afraid of quitting, of failing, than I am.

But my parents' misery was escalating at the point where I have turned the corner on my own. Where my mother was starting to panic, I am starting to relax. In the highlands of central Mexico it is finally cool enough to camp inside the Avion instead of renting expensive hotel rooms. We are no longer dashing across deserts and cranking the air-conditioning, so our daily diesel bills become more manageable.

For the first time it sinks in that we have no deadlines to meet, planes to catch, crew to direct, edits to review, or clients to impress. Gary stops checking his watch; I don't have to tell him we're a scene behind schedule, losing the light. I stop consulting the map every five miles; our journey is not a storyboard I have to direct.

The hills lining the toll roads are covered in fields of blue-grey agave: the exact shade of the color I've loved most since I was a kid and never known why. It is a hue familiar and mysterious at the same time, as if created to fill its own spectrum of light. The agaves layer the countryside in bursts of milky luminescence between tilled rows of rich, brown earth. The jagged edges of each frond are softened only in the shadows they cast, and driving past them is hypnotic and transporting. When we come upon a man in a horse-drawn cart we find ourselves pulling off the highway to follow him. He leads us to the town of Jala, the name of which I know only because of a hand-painted sign announcing our arrival.

"Welcome to life without maps or GPS," Gary says.

As the road changes from asphalt to cobblestone, I thumb through the journal to see if my mother wrote of this town. I search my guidebooks for more information but find nothing there either. For the first time since we crossed the border I have no reference point upon which to base an expectation. I possess no convenient cataloging of Jala's contents; there is no compass for my internal reaction.

It is only when I stop searching that I realize Jala has discovered us, not the other way around. Its streets are obviously designed for horses and there are few cars. With our huge camper and loud diesel motor, we feel intrusive and conspicuous so we park on the widest street and spend the rest of the afternoon exploring on foot.

Jala is as clean and beautiful as a movie set, and yet there is nothing staged about it. People go about their business repainting signs, sweeping sidewalks, and rocking in chairs behind bougainvillea-draped wrought-iron gates. Cats yawn and arch in front of architecture that borrows from their feline grace. Inner courtyards shelter rocking babies and gurgling fountains. Doors and windows are flung open to receive the slanting light, offering wafts of musky masa flour and pungent cilantro to the wind. Vendors at the corner of the town square sell slices of watermelon from ice-filled coolers and hot boiled corn from propane stoves.

Schoolgirls in pleated skirts and embroidered blouses ask if they can pet Wipeout. They whisper admiration into her supple ears: "Que linda" and "Te amo." She closes her eyes and pulls her faded black lips into a contented smile, basking in the echoes of her pampered puppyhood.

One girl asks me if I have any daughters. I point to Wipeout. "Solo ella."

Her schoolmates laugh. No really, señora, another of them asks, how many children do you have? She holds up ten fingers, in case I don't understand. I shake my head. She tucks one thumb away and I tell her no, not nine children, none. The dog asleep on my feet is like my baby. I got her from a man selling puppies on a street corner not so far from here. So tiny she fit in the palm of my hand. Sixteen years later, she takes up my entire heart.

It's a game now. The girl counts down from nine fingers until there are none left, only open, questioning palms. No children at all? How do I explain that where I come from, when girls grow up and get married, motherhood isn't a given? I've never yearned for children or felt quite together enough to handle the responsibility. I could barely squeeze a patient, low-maintenance dog into the crazy schedule that my life once was. I point to Wipeout again and smile.

Then the first girl asks how many puppies does Wipeout have? We go through the giggling ten-finger countdown again, and in the end the girls scamper off, disappointed. No babies. No puppies. The strange American lady and her old Mexican dog are lucky they found a nice man. Otherwise they would have only each other.

In the distance, horseshoes click and a motorcycle sputters to life. From a far-off radio, an accordion squeezes a lurching ballad. Parents and grandparents look up at us with measured curiosity when we pass—as if we must be lost.

I have never felt more found. I rest my head in Gary's lap on a cool, tiled bench and do absolutely nothing but listen to Wipeout pant. I could linger in Jala for days, but there are no hotels, campgrounds, or even empty parking lots. We are not meant to stay here or change anything we've seen, and the fact that we can drive away is both a gift and a reminder of how disconnected this transient life will be.

We have decided to untether ourselves from the technology of the life we left behind, both to minimize distractions and to experience the journey as it unfolds without instantly defining and disseminating it. Our camper's roof is aerodynamically dish-free. The aftermarket GPS I bought back in DC has proven uselessly out-of-date, so we bury it in the locked box under Wipeout's platform. We are not filming ourselves or posting adventure-cam footage on the Internet. We are sharing no photos or updates. My laptop has no wireless access to anything; it is simply an updated version of my mother's pink journal. We will ration even our reading; after the forty-two paperbacks multitasking as gun camouflage run out, we have no way of downloading more books or newspapers on e-readers. Family members have the number to our satellite phone, but barring emergencies our only contact will be made during twice-a-month stops at Internet cafés. The first is in Guadalajara.

We're huddled over a desktop computer the size of a small oven when we open a coded e-mail from Nancy, our firearms instructor back in Arizona.

"How is the package?" she asks. "Remember to thoroughly clean everything inside the package once you open it." I laugh, to mask the guilt of making an old lady worry. And to make light of the nagging sense that my insistence on the gun has introduced a bulky, unspoken tension into our marriage.

"I'd shoot myself if I had to drive every day, all day, with my husband," reads the second e-mail we open from a friend back home, ignorant of her pun. "Aren't you worried you'll get sick of each other?"

A part of me is worried, but I know that if anything drives us apart it won't be uninterrupted together-time. The chance to tear months out of a calendar is too rare to waste with bickering. Working together around the clock isn't new to us. Filling entire days without assignments or appointments is a window flung wide open to the sun.

"So, about all this free-time, ditching-the-alarm-clock thing," I mention to Gary as he grills fresh eggplant and chicken over an outdoor fire pit. We are the only people camped in a deserted RV park in the hills near Guadalajara. "How long do you think it'll take for two Pavlovian-conditioned humans to wake up without that panicked feeling of oversleeping?"

Producers backtime each element of a broadcast—subtracting the running time of each video and commercial to track, precisely, when every segment should start and end. On the road I'm finding that mileposts are harder to predict: we know how far the truck can go on a tank of diesel but not necessarily which towns along the route might have a gas station. The time it takes to find ice, propane, or water is equally unpredictable, and we are learning to look for campsites while there are still hours left of daylight. Each morning there is no pressing need to get up by any particular time, and this feels unnaturally delinquent.

"I'd give it another week," Gary says. "But if you're feeling like a slacker you're welcome to sleep outside and let the songbirds be your wake-up call."

Compared to the complexity of shooting videos in foreign countries, simply traveling through them is refreshing. Gary isn't responsible for hundreds of thousands of dollars of camera equipment. I am telling my own story instead of a client's, and it is sugarcane-sucking, mariachi-pants thrilling.

Chapter Ten

MEZCAL

When a man on the side of a deserted road to Chiapas waves you down with a machete, it takes a big gulp of positive thinking to pull over. But we have slurped at the fountain of Mexican tranquillity for two straight weeks, and this man is wearing a sombrero so worn thin it barely casts a shadow over his work-sloped shoulders. If he is part of any plot to murder passing drivers, then his only accomplice is a donkey too exhausted to lift its head. It plods in a yoked ring around what looks like a smoking brick fire pit, and when our diesel engine clatters to a stop we see a structure in the distance that in a Norman Rockwell painting might pass for a lemonade stand. The man slides his machete behind a twist of rope that serves as a belt holding up his baggy pants and trots toward the Avion.

"He either needs a ride or he's trying to sell something," Gary guesses. "Do you have any pesos handy?"

I can't think of anything I need to buy from a machete-waving campesino until I see what's burning in the fire pit: the charred hearts of giant agave plants. We have been flagged down to sample Mexican moonshine: mezcal. It is a one-man, one-donkey operation, and we are Martin Garcia's only customers in days. He's more surprised than we are that two gringos who stepped out of a rolling fortress are now approaching the counter of his lean-to and agreeing to taste his wares.

A few days earlier we camped in the agave fields of an American expat cashing in on mezcal's rising notoriety, so I think I know what to expect. But when I lift the husk of a coconut-shell shot glass to my lips, I get a whiff of the difference right away. If I ever needed nose-hair clipping before, I will never again. I hesitate, not wanting to offend Martin but certain his mezcal is meant for stronger guts than mine.

Gary has no such reservations. He tosses his sample back and lets the vapors collect for a second before reopening his mouth to exhale.

"That's the smoothest fire I've ever swallowed," he says. "Tell him the only thing I taste is the plant. It's magnificent."

It turns out that Martin's Spanish is much better than mine, even though it's his second language too. He's a native Zapotec whose family goes back hundreds of years in the Oaxaca Valley, and when Gary tries to stop him from pouring another shot he smiles out of one side of his mouth and tells him to relax and let the woman drive for a while.

We agree to buy some mezcal to go, but that's when the transaction hits a snag. Martin doesn't have any inventory on the shelf. His customers are mostly Mixtec and Zapotec Indians who bring old jugs from home to fill. The closest thing I can scavenge from the camper is an almost-empty glass jar of pickles. I feed the shriveled cucumbers to the donkey while Martin rinses out our container with a few drops of mezcal right from the spigot of his copper still. It kills the pickle smell instantly, and he dips the now-disinfected jar into a fresh vat to fill it. We drive away with a gallon of 100-proof mezcal for the equivalent of three dollars.

THERE IS A POINT IN SOUTHERN MEXICO WHERE BOTH COASTS ARE pinched so close together that the Atlantic and Pacific winds collide onshore. The gusts of the Isthmus of Tehauntepec are so famously violent that truckers are permitted to drive across it only in the morning, before the day's building heat exacerbates the crosswinds. The fact that no trucks are in sight when we begin the crossing should be a warning, but there is mezcal in the back and a campground to reach before we lose the light.

Compared to the graceful Oaxaca Valley, studded with its outcroppings of ancient holy sites and fortresses, the isthmus is as difficult to admire as it is to pronounce. Even in the high, top-heavy Avion we can see nothing but drab scrub jungle, tilted almost horizontal by the constant wind. The air is so thick with humidity that the horizon is a blurry smudge, and neither one of us notices the two massive oxen camouflaged in the underbrush.

They lumber out onto the road, shoulders hunkered down against the wind. Gary has less than thirty feet to maneuver and not nearly enough time to brake. He guns it, heading for the opposite lane and hoping the oxen don't spook and run for the other side. It may be the howling wind, but I could swear I hear the sound of horns scraping along the length of the Avion as we hurtle past.

I HAVE FORGOTTEN ABOUT THE GUN HIDDEN UNDER THE FLOORBOARD OF our camper until we are flagged to the side of the road again, five hours from Chiapas. In a single moment it is as if the generous spirit of Mexico spits me out, my I-think-I-am-above-the-law taste too bitter to tolerate.

I can't tell if the checkpoint is military or routine law enforcement, but there is no mistaking the intensity of the serious men in dark blue uniforms. Cars are stopped in both directions. Drivers raise and keep their hands in the air; trunks and hoods of cars are flung open like gaping mouths. The air smells of submission, and German shepherds sniff and strain against their leashes, thrilling in it. Guards with rifles pace the aisles of passenger buses while others, with nightsticks, bang on the gas tanks underneath. Women stand in ditches, hushing babies, while their young sons drag suitcases off rooftops for inspection.

The driver in the car stopped behind us walks up to Gary's window. "Hey guys, my name is Gaston, from Mexico City," he says, in perfect English. "I lived in the States for a while so I recognized your plates. Looks like this is going to take a while."

Gaston explains that it's a weapons search, so routine he takes advantage of the delay to socialize. He removes his Ray-Bans and dangles them over the side-view mirror while he chats with Gary. I squirm with dread, but Gaston and Gary trade philosophy and theory. Gaston views these searches as evidence that those in power are afraid those without power will take up arms.

"The poverty here is a ticking time bomb," he says. "The only thing that has prevented a major rebellion, a revolution really, is that we haven't had a Martin Luther King. We haven't had a Che. When the poor people find their messiah, they will take back the power."

The Avion is far too conspicuous. I can't look at Gary, knowing that if these cops or soldiers find the gun I insisted on bringing, he will be the one to go to jail. I want him to yell at me, blame me, anything but calmly chat with Gaston and trust that I can talk my way out of this.

Silently I debate the merits of "I don't know how that weapon got there" against "May we please make a contribution to a worthy cause you recommend?" I can think of nothing remotely worthy of testing aloud on Gary.

"¿Qué estás buscando?" I ask when a soldier finally slaps his open palm on the hood of our truck. I have forgotten to insert the respectful *usted* in my blurted demand to know what he is looking for. There is neither amusement nor annoyance in the unblinking eyes of my inquisitor, and the presence of a growling, seventy-pound dog on the backseat does not faze him.

"He's going to search the back," I translate for Gary. With clipped courtesy the man with an assault rifle slung over his shoulder is explaining that all guns and ammunition will be confiscated. He's apologizing for the inconvenience, but the word "please" before "disembark from the vehicle" does nothing to soothe my nerves.

My hands tremble and I drop the keys in the dust twice before I manage to unlock the dead bolts on the camper's door.

"Es un camper," I prattle. "How do you say 'camper' in Spanish? ¿Una casa rodante?" I trace the outline of a square house on rolling wheels in the air between our faces as if this is a game of charades. I am hoping to distract the soldier with obsequiousness, to make up for my earlier grammatical insult. I don't know which is racing faster, my heart or my mouth.

"Se llama Avion," I tell him, trying to explain that the brand name of the camper is the same as the Spanish word for airplane. *Please laugh at me now, or at least smile.*

My panicked strategy is to get in first and sit at the kitchen table with my feet firmly planted on the section of carpet that covers our gun's cubbyhole. Planting his ass over an illegal gun worked for my father in Bolivia; I can think of no better plan myself. But the soldier leaps inside before I can pull out the step stool to hoist myself up. I am eye-level with the camper's floor, and Joe's slice in the carpet looks amateur and obvious. I look up at the soldier's face to keep from staring at the hiding place, and for a second his disgusted grimace doesn't make sense.

The smell hits me at the precise moment I see the shattered pickle bottle on the floor. Somewhere between the isthmus winds and hitting speed bumps the size of felled logs, our pantry door flew open, and Martin's mezcal did not survive the fall. Hours of hundred-degree temperatures inside the camper accelerated the disintegration process of mezcal- and dog-piss-covered carpet fibers. The stench could peel the aluminum off the camper's frame.

The gagging soldier doesn't open a single cabinet or look under any cushions. He spins around so fast that the heel of his boot leaves a soggy indentation in the carpet just millimeters from the gun's hiding place. In less than thirty seconds the search is over.

"Me disculpo por la interrupción. Vaya! Por favor," he says, imploring us to drive this stinking vehicle away. He fumbles with his clipboard and diverts his eyes from mine. I have no idea what is going through his mind except avoiding the embarrassment of retching in front of a woman. As I lock the camper door's two dead bolts behind him, I give silent thanks to Wipeout's aging bladder. Not even the most suspicious, hostile, anti-American inspector would pick up a putrid urine- and mezcal-fermented carpet to discover a false floor and hidden .38 Special.

Chapter Eleven

SHOOT-OUTS

I am giddy with relief, but by the time we find a campground for the night the relief is replaced by retching. Lab results might define what is happening to me as a recurrence of gastroenteritis, but we both know by now that it is my body's way of punishing me for the gun. We go for a walk through a mango grove, and even though it is my favorite fruit I know better than to fill my bowels with ammunition.

We watch as Wipeout ambles up to a grazing goat about her size. I barely get my camera out in time to document the meeting of the species when the goat lowers its horns and rams into Wipeout.

A better mother would have leaped to her dog's defense but I am laughing too hard. Wipeout takes two steps backward and shakes herself, like she just got soaked with water instead of head-butted. She looks over at us, making sure we're watching.

Gary realizes what is about to happen. "No, she's not that dumb, is she?"

Wipeout has always been more beautiful than brilliant, and she does not let an insult pass. She backs up two more steps and charges directly at the offending goat. Their equally thick skulls meet with a loud smack and this time it is the goat who retreats.

If we had any of Martin's mezcal left to toast our hardheaded mutt, we would have poured her some too. But instead Wipeout falls into an even deeper sleep than normal, on the ground next to the cot I've set up inside a mosquito tent so that I don't have to climb out of the camper in the dark to puke. I lie on my back, stroking the head of a dog as dim-witted as I am. I will spend another night punished for owning something I have known is a bad idea since I was seven years old. All I have to do is reread my mother's journal to remember why.

> JANUARY 13TH, 1974
> Finally made beach, not without battery trouble . . .
> Met some Canadians . . .
> played guitar, and drank. Good time

My father didn't give a second thought to the gun hidden next to his bed when we arrived in southern Mexico. That is, until one night on a beach near Puerto Angel, when we woke to a series of lights flashing out over the ocean. I remember the darkness criss-crossed by flashlight beams, like a laser version of cat's cradle. I was poking my fingers through the streams of light, trying to catch one for Jenny. Then, from just to our south, came different lights—longer and brighter.

"Must have been boats approaching, but I couldn't figure out what the hell was going on," my father describes it now.

Gunfire broke out all around us. We didn't know it then, but police were using our camper as a shield in a shoot-out with drug smugglers. I could feel bodies bracing against the aluminum panel that stood between our homemade red sleeping bags and the outside; each new thump rocked the sticky mosquito strips hanging above my head.

"I don't suspect they had any idea there were two little girls inside that camper," my mother remembers with an almost forgiving tone.

I am far less magnanimous. I could feel hot pee soaking through my sister's nightgown, but I drew her closer anyway. Her hair smelled like salt and bug spray, and her heart was beating like a trembling bird. I watched my father slide open the secret door beside the bed and grab the gun we were never supposed to touch. He tiptoed to the door and crouched, in firing position, ready to defend his family to the death.

He was doing the only thing he knew how, but it didn't make me feel safe, not then and certainly not now. If he had fired, our camper would have been riddled through with bullets. The South African grandparents who had never met John John would never have met my sister or me either. But my father tosses it off like a funny scene in a Keystone Cops movie. Maybe because she always takes her cues from him, my mother also managed to make a joke out of the night her daughters could have been shot.

JAN 14TH, 1974
Had visitors in the night—Mexicans with guns.

That's it. Eight words. A haiku requires more syllables than my mother managed. I have no idea whether she was always like this or if the ability to erase reality was a survival skill she developed, triggered by my brother's death. But tonight I am sleeping on a coffin-size cot not a day's drive from what might have been my childhood grave, so all I can do is laugh about it too.

THERE IS NO HINT OF DANGER WHEN GARY AND I ARRIVE IN THE MOUNTAINS of Chiapas, only the feeling that we've somehow missed a border and arrived in another country. In a sense, we have. The indigenous population, led by a mysterious, rarely seen rebel leader known as

Subcomandante Marcos, is demanding autonomy from Mexico and setting up separate schools, hospitals, and governing councils.

The air thins and new colors draw together, dense and loud. Gone are the pearly tones of sand and hazy grey humidity of the Isthmus of Tehuantepec. In one day's drive they have changed to loamy reds and piney greens. The winding flatness heaves and struggles into peaks and ravines, closer with every twist and turn to a piercing blue sky.

We plan on using a wooded campground on the outskirts of San Cristobal de las Casas as a base for exploring the ruins of Palenque—a half day's drive away through the Lacandon Jungle. But the severity of Mexico's daily summer thunderstorms and the stress of constant traveling are taking a toll on Wipeout. She chews on her paws, legs, and tail whenever we leave her to buy groceries or ask for directions. On the afternoon of our arrival in Las Casas, even the benign activities of setting up camp unnerve her, and she paces between and underneath my feet. While we are taking showers I hear the first crack of thunder. I run back to the camper but Wipeout is gone.

Gary and I circle the campground, wrapped in towels and calling her name. We check under the truck and inside the guardhouse, in case she is curled up behind the watchman's television. I imagine her on a desperate limp back to Washington, DC, in the driving rain, but as we pass an orange VW bus, a young Dutch couple slides open the side door.

"Are you looking for a dog, big and used to be white?"

Wipeout has jumped through their door, panicked, dripping wet, and bleeding from the feet. These travelers, homesick for their own dog, are sharing tuna sandwiches and bottled water with her. They give her back to us with sympathy and reluctance; she has stolen much more than their supper.

I have spent almost half my life comforted by having Wipeout one step behind me. Now is the season when I must comfort her, and the anxiety in her watery brown eyes is heartbreaking. Listening to Wipeout's labored breathing, in a camper just big enough for the three of us, I worry how much longer I can protect her. She is scared and suffering.

"I think the heat will be too much for her in Palenque," Gary says. "Let's leave her with the camper here in San Cristobal, where it's cool, and take one of those group tours." The Dutch couple says we can leave Wipeout with them for the day; she will be safe.

We wake before dawn to a violet campground shrouded in cool fog and pile into a twelve-passenger van. We are joined by an Israeli couple on their honeymoon, an older French couple, two graduate students from the UK, and a Mexican grandmother with her pregnant daughter and sullen son-in-law.

The first two and a half hours are uneventful. Tall spruce and pine trees poke their evergreen heads through the mist blanketing the valleys. I write my name in the condensation of my breath on the window, and my ears begin to pop when the van spirals down a one-lane road.

"I wish I were driving," Gary mutters.

Until this moment, we have felt like travelers, not tourists, and I am suddenly homesick for the Avion. I know how to act, what to do inside a camper. When I was seven I colored pictures and practiced my Spanish. Now I ask directions, read maps, and negotiate with strangers. Gary mans the wheel of the machine that has replaced his camera. He checks the tires, the gauges, the propane and water levels. On the road he decides how fast, how close, how risky. I talk, sob, vomit, and recover, and he somehow manages to ignore these distractions and keep us alive.

If we were in our own camper now I could nod off, confident in his meticulous checklists and nondistractible judgment. Instead, our lives are in someone else's hands, and the churning in my intestines is not purely motion sickness. Each switchback seems more violent than necessary, every curve too blind to pass. There is nothing between us and the ravines below. I have an uneasy sense that this whole excursion is a mistake, but it doesn't rise to the level of invoking our mutual, instinct-trusting pledge, so I keep my worries to myself. Without our own wheels we couldn't turn around anyway.

"Is it me, or is it getting really hot in here?" I ask Gary, nervous sweat beginning to collect above my lip.

He pushes open my window and I can smell that something's changed. The approaching jungle reminds me of damp, tangled sheets just pulled out of a washing machine. The air is heavy and crackling with heat; it wants to expand but there's no place to go. It must be 100 degrees with 100 percent humidity by the time we descend into the jungle crossroads of Ocosingo.

Suddenly, crowds of men fill the road, blocking the way to Palenque. My first, panicky thought is Zapatistas, but instead of the black rebel ski masks made famous by Subcomandante Marcos, these men are dressed in straw hats, dusty-looking jeans, and flannel shirts—like loggers at a lynching. Huge bulldozer tires, filled with boulders, form a blockade, and we are instantly surrounded.

For some inexplicable reason the French woman opens the sliding side door of our van and the crowd surges toward us. There are machetes and guns. I can make out questions like "¿Turistas?" and "¿Por Palenque?" The presence of the Mexican family and pregnant woman probably helps our situation, considering that the next question I hear shouted over the sea of heads is "¿Hay gringos?"

The French woman, in heavily accented, indignant English, replies, "We are Europeans, not fucking Americans."

Gary and I try not to meet anyone's gaze. We don't dare speak to each other for fear of our accents giving us away. He puts his arm around my shoulders and pulls me closer. He wants to protect me, but he can't. This is the province where, not quite ten years ago, Zapatista freedom fighters rioted against the North American Free Trade Agreement and paramilitary groups massacred villagers as payback. A man with a pistol in his belt slowly pulls it out—I am staring at the muzzle through the thinnest pane of window glass. I look up and see anger and resentment in the man's eyes. Against the outside world he is powerless, and I can't blame him if he thinks of a gun as some measure of control. But I also see fear, and in this he is no different from my father.

Nothing I have done to prepare for this moment will save me. All my worrying, researching, insurance purchasing, and gun smuggling leave me as unprotected as my parents were on a beach thirty years ago. Fists are shaking and machetes waving, and the driver quickly pulls a U-turn and guns the accelerator. I'm so afraid he'll run somebody over that I can't look forward. I can't look behind me either; I would rather be shot in the back than see it coming. I can't even look at Gary; if there is fear in *his* eyes I know it will dissolve me.

The most I can worm out of the driver is something to the effect that the Zapatistas are ghosts, ancient history, and the protest is just over Ocosingo natives wanting private tour drivers to go on strike. They routinely block the road to Palenque in protest even though it is the only way goods or services get into or out of the Lacandon Jungle. I deduce that our driver is considered a scab and a sellout to foreigners.

The crowd surges, and men hold their guns up in the air, safe from shoving elbows and lunging shoulders. I clamp my hands over my ears, pre-recoiling. Colors start to blur and angry faces fall out of focus. Our driver does not even roll down his window to negotiate. Nothing he can say will ever convince the protestors to let us through. Anything might be the flash point. Hands rock the van and sticks smack the windows as we retreat. The gunshots I have been expecting fire into the air. I feel as trapped as I was in my red sleeping bag soaked through with the terror of my little sister.

When they realize we will never reach Palenque, the French and Israeli couples begin demanding that the driver issue a refund. They have every right to be furious with a man who drives tourists into known conflict zones, but it is easy to see why indigenous people prefer living off the land to placating tourists. It's harder to fathom anger so deep, disillusionment so raw, that they routinely cut off their own lifeline in protest.

Chapter Twelve

SAINTS AND LITTLE DEVILS

I f we needed a nudge to leave Mexico it comes during our final fuel stop. It is approaching ninety-five degrees, and there is a cattle truck in front of us, the rural type in which slaughterhouse-destined animals are penned behind hand-painted wooden slats. But dozens of men with guns stand in the back of this truck, black eyes peering out from holes in heavy, knit ski masks.

"Right now I am hating our DC license plates," Gary says. "Those guys are Zapatistas."

The masked men jump down and reassemble around the truck bed in a wary pattern, choreographed for vigilance. It is at once exotic, mundane, and revelatory. The roadblock we encountered at the entrance to Chiapas was never about finding tourists with .38 Specials hidden in their vintage campers. It was about intimidating these men and their supporters. The indigenous revolution is still real and armed, but even freedom fighters have to stop for Doritos and diesel.

Part of me wishes I had the nerve to walk up to them and ask a million questions, but the smarter part just wants to get the hell out of this place where Americans have no business interfering.

As Gary fills our tank with our last drops of Mexican fuel, I replay the slide-show version of the country we are about to enter in my head as a distraction from the masked men. To a seven-year-old girl, Guatemala was Willy Wonka wondrous. All it takes is tracing the smudge of my father's fingers along the highways of his folded maps and the names of towns jump out in double-Dutch rhymes: Chichicastenango, Huehuetenango, Sololá.

I picture black-haired girls with long braids down their backs and instantly leap into the rhythm of twirling jump ropes: cha-cha and tango, way-way-to-go and so-long-ago. Even my mother's journal sings along.

JAN 17. 1974

No hassle. Beautiful country. Clean.

JAN 18-22

Food cheap—fish dinner for four $1.7

It was a new year, and for my family Guatemala was a fresh start. Nine days we wandered through this country the size of Tennessee and only one night passed in the misery of a repair shop. Even my father's refusal to pay a bribe to cross the border resulted in only one night camped, in protest, in front of the immigration office.

"How did he get out of that one?" Gary asks.

It is one of my father's favorite stories. Apparently I wandered into the aduanero's office the next morning, introduced myself in Spanish, and somehow charmed the guards into letting the camper through with only a cursory inspection and no payoff. Considering that Guatemala was two decades into a thirty-six-year civil war that left two hundred thousand people dead, I do not expect my husband to completely swallow my father's seven-year-old-saves-the-day recounting of history.

"Let's try a safer border crossing" is Gary's way of telling me he doesn't.

We bypass the main Guatemala border crossing, still renowned for relentless searches and shakedowns, in favor of what guidebooks describe as the "easier" frontier in the mountains. When we arrive there is no "Welcome to Guatemala" sign, just a mechanical gate salute in the straight-up position. It looks more like a flea market in a chaotic delivery alley than an international border. Women waddle between semitrucks selling fresh fruit and bottled water. Grandfathers pedal bicycle carts, saving energy by grabbing onto the side mirrors of slowly passing cars. Young men wave wads of quetzals in the air to exchange for Mexican currency, but nobody wearing anything remotely like an official uniform pays attention to us.

While Gary stands guard next to the Avion, I drag Wipeout and her dossier of permission slips into an unmarked wooden shack filled with crates of live chickens. Wipeout strains against her leash while a guard leafs through page after page of her documents, every one of them upside down. After fingering the impressive stamps and embossed foils, he asks for a dollar and pencils a check mark in an otherwise blank ledger. That's it—all of my reputed charms are utterly unnecessary.

Since we are already in the mountains, we decide to deviate even farther from the course my parents followed and drive to the village of Todos Santos. It is not along the Pan-American Highway; we seem to be driving down the slope of a gravel pit. Exuberantly painted hand-me-down US school buses called "chicken buses" hunt and peck their way around fallen boulders, creating blinding clouds of dust in their wake. Landslides have wiped away entire chunks of hillside, and we slip and skid between foot-deep wheel ruts.

Still, I can't shake the giddy sense of adventure. We're finally abandoning the familiarity of my father's maps and my mother's journal and simply exploring. But I'm not the one behind the wheel, straining to keep the camper upright. Gary is focusing so intently on the cratered road ahead that he hasn't said a word in forty-five minutes.

"So there must be a reason they named this town Todos Santos," I toss into the tense silence.

Gary is a long-lapsed Catholic, and the only time I've seen him blush was before we were married, when his mother bragged about his short-lived stint as an altar boy back in Wisconsin.

"Don't you remember any saints we could start praying to, just to get us there in one piece?" I figure it's worth a try, anything to ease the tension in his jaw and grinding teeth.

"I think it's time to try out the four-wheel drive instead," Gary says as he gets out and kneels in mud beside the front wheels to lock the hubs in place. The truck grips the earth and chews up ruts and boulders like a jaguar ripping through the flesh of its first catch. Wipeout slides from one side of her platform to the other, and water bottles and sunglasses fly through the air. It is strangely exhilarating until I remember the thirty-five-year-old Avion swaying from side to side overhead.

I reach over to rub a charm hanging from the rearview mirror. The mirror itself is useless because the camper blocks the back window. We are using it as a hook from which to hang a growing chain of good luck charms: my grandmother's Navajo ring with its huge chunk of traveler-protecting turquoise, a Mayan calendar amulet for wisdom of the elders, and a fang-shaped piece of jade and silver to ward off the evil eye. The truck skids to the left, and suddenly the entire necklace of charms flies off the rearview mirror.

"So much for all the saints," Gary finally laughs. "It looks like we're on our own."

Hours later, we descend into the village of Todos Santos: a two-kilometer strip of houses, restaurants, and markets wedged in a ravine between mountains. The peaks soar four thousand meters on either side, and we are trapped in a different century.

"If we go any farther we won't be able to get back out," Gary says. The truck will soon be pinned into a one-lane, dead-end road, at which point turning around will require squashing small children or livestock. There are no gas stations here, no parking lots or rest areas, and certainly no campgrounds. We will have to ask landowners for overnight camping privileges.

It can't be all that different from negotiating location fees for films, I tell myself. When we pass a farmer tilling a plot of land, I lean out the passenger window and offer him the equivalent of five dollars to let us park. It may be because I'm a woman, but he doesn't ask questions or even look me in the eye when I hand him the quetzals.

"That was almost too easy," Gary says as he searches for the driest patch of grass.

"Don't be so paranoid," I tease him. I am feeling smugly self-confident. Every system has a set of rules, and I take the farmer's co-operation as a sign that I am already mastering Guatemala's.

Nine little ruddy-cheeked boys approach as a group while Gary sets up the camper's awning. It's eerily silent. These kids, unlike any we've encountered on the trip so far, make no attempt to tell us their names or ask where we're from. They just stare, without even blinking. If they possess any curiosity at all it must be satisfied through some sort of painless mental answer extraction. Just when it's starting to creep me out, Wipeout climbs down her ramp and the boys erupt with shrieks and squeals. All we needed was an ambassador, even one with wobbly legs.

"She's too beat to walk all the way into town with us. What about hiring these kids to watch her for the afternoon?" Gary asks me. "They look like they could use something to do."

We are eager angels, their cherubic faces say to me. They plop down in the soggy grass and let Wipeout make her own approach. Her slobbery tongue knocks off sweaty straw hats, and she nuzzles under pink-and-purple woven vests to identify their little boy scents. They collapse in giggles when her feather-duster tail tickles their chapped chins and bright red lips. I reach into my pockets and divvy up coins among the nine boys.

"Muchachos, protegen por favor mi perra." I ask them to guard her.

Gary takes a group portrait of Wipeout's new guardians, and the kids immediately strike a pose. I could swear some of them are flashing gang signs. "Where the hell did they learn that?"

"I guess we haven't driven far enough away from the US," Gary says. "That, or one of these little guys must have a satellite dish at home."

We leave Wipeout under a huddle of boys stroking her silky white fur and fighting over the right to lift the water bowl to her lips.

It is two o'clock when we make it to the Todos Santos Saturday market, but vendors are already packing up their wares. There are only a few blankets with peppers and flowers still spread on the ground in front of the white stucco Catholic church.

The street is jammed with chicken buses, revving their diesel engines to signal impending departure. The air is choked with exhaust and dust; feathers and chaff swirl around our ankles. It is part farm, part carnival, and the atmosphere is alien and familiar all at once. I walked through countless markets just like this one, clinging to my mother's hand, and I feel just as out of place now, as if my uninvited body is taking up too much physical space.

Gary and I climb uphill to watch the mayhem from a perch in the town square, which overlooks the road. It is like stepping into one of my father's slides. There is no evidence of any other foreigners, not even a scraggly backpacker in sight. Women wearing long skirts the blue of spun night sky huddle in the shadows, babies strapped to their backs by sarongs woven through with emerald greens and fiery magentas. I catch them sneaking glances at us, but the minute I smile, eyes drop to the ground and whispers stop.

The two of us, in dusty cargo pants and wicking fleece, are the most unisex-looking, conspicuously underdressed people in the square. The traditional *traje,* or indigenous costume, worn by the men of Todos Santos is black leather riding chaps over red-and-white candy-cane-striped trousers.

"See what I meant about Guatemala?" I whisper. "Willy Wonka Land."

The men's jackets have padded collars and cuffs, embroidered in iridescent blues and purples. Even their straw hats are jubilant, decorated with padded woven bands under studded strips of leather.

By four o'clock the sun is falling behind the high peaks of the surrounding mountains. We hurry back to the camper, and there is barely light enough to see that Wipeout's entourage has turned into a mob. There are at least fifteen kids squatting under the awning, and another ten descend as we approach. They poke at our pockets, demanding money, and Wipeout howls in relief when she sees us.

"Tu, tu, tu, and tu," I point to every grubby face I recognize. "Ya les di dinero." They have already been paid, but I am arguing with them in Spanish. Every single boy holds out his hand as though we'd never met before. They have transformed from sweet little animal lovers to hustlers in the space of three hours.

"I don't think they understand me," I shout to Gary. "They probably speak Mam or some other Indian language."

"If we give in now and start handing out money, it'll never end," Gary shouts back, over their heads.

A few boys start swinging on the awning bars, which strain perilously against the aluminum skin of the aging Avion. One boy cops a quick feel of my left breast, probably just checking to see if there is actually a woman under my androgynous, monochromic American clothing. Another pelts Wipeout with tiny pebbles, and his friends throw clumps of mud at the camper. Gary and I chase them in circles and eventually they scatter.

At Todos Santos elevation it takes fifteen minutes for a breathless American woman to bring a teakettle of water to a boil, but instead of a whistle I hear a commotion outside the camper.

"What do they want now?" I groan. The little rascals are back. Even Wipeout whimpers.

"Think like a kid," Gary says. "A Guatemalan kid. You made a promise."

It takes a second for the scope of my stupidity to sink in. The money changers at the border didn't bother with exchanging coins into Guatemalan equivalents. All the pesos and dimes I so magnanimously showered on the kids for babysitting Wipeout won't even buy them chewing gum in Todos Santos. No wonder the little saints turned into devils.

I fling open the door to jump out and make amends but my right leg flails through three feet of empty space. My hamstring takes the brunt of a brutal landing—the step stool we leave outside the back door is tucked under the arm of a boy who can run much faster than a limping cheapskate.

"Think of the karmic balance," Gary says as he boosts me back into the camper. "Next week some other dumb travelers won't believe their luck. They'll find a brand new step stool for sale at the Todos Santos Saturday market."

Chapter Thirteen

THE
FUNDAMENTALS

I am finally sipping a cup of tea, throbbing right thigh wrapped and elevated, when an otherworldly shrieking begins. Even through the protective hull of the camper, it sounds as though a man and a woman are being stuck through with pitchforks. They take turns, building on each other's frenzy, and the sound is so tinny and shrill I can't tell when one round of shrieking ends and its echo continues.

We lean out for a look and the wailing seems to be emanating from an unassuming, one-story outbuilding with a homemade wooden cross hung above its door.

"That little church, all the way across this valley?" I ask, incredulous. The church is nothing like the grandiose Catholic cathedrals I associate with Latin America.

Gary points to loudspeakers and megaphones strung all along a telephone wire from the building to the road. It appears a Pentecostal church service is under way. The racket ricochets between mountain peaks. We sinners are a captive audience.

"Crank down the air vents and close all the windows." Gary barks instructions like the captain of a sinking ship. "I'll sandbag the door with towels."

In a matter of minutes the camper has gone from halcyon to hellish. The din is claustrophobic, and even though I know that the message is intended for everyone within earshot, it seems personal. We are unwelcome intruders.

"What the hell are they saying?" Gary asks.

I have no idea. There seems to be no distinction between words; syllables bleed together in incomprehensible babble. We might as well be aliens who crash-landed on another planet. A headache is working its way to my frontal lobe, and I'm actually grateful I don't speak the language of our torturers. If I could, the hellfire being spewed through this isolated town would surely translate into something like, "Skirtless, barren woman: repent and return to the United States or burn in a lake of fire forever!"

I've read of the rise of Pentecostalism in Latin America—how some scholars credit its fundamentalist, zero-tolerance attitude toward alcoholism for a reduction in domestic violence in remote villages.

"At least women and men seem to share the pulpit," Gary offers, but I am certain that whatever brimstone being broadcast is far from tolerant or egalitarian. Why else would it be force-fed via loudspeaker the minute the sun goes down?

We try taking a walk, but cupping hands over our ears blocks even less of the noise than the camper did.

"Isn't this how the CIA tortures political prisoners?" Gary shouts.

Maybe it's some sort of revival, or a religious holiday that Lonely Planet and all the other guidebooks missed. It would be absurd if it weren't so disorienting. Everywhere we walk, the sermon follows. It's as though the loudspeakers have eyes and we're under shrieking surveillance. Shadows lurk in stinky ditches paralleling the gravel road, and the stars throb and pulse instead of twinkle. We take it for the Morse code of fallen angels warning us to return to the safety of the Avion.

Back in the camper, we sit on either side of the collapsible shelf that serves as our dining table, wadding toilet paper into our ears. It is impossible to have a conversation, but we try, just for the distraction.

"Could it still be the same two people?" Gary asks, and I know he's thinking it's impossible for vocal cords to survive this long. But there is no mistaking the timbre of the male preacher's voice and the scratchy rasp of the female's. We switch to passing notes, like this is an awful junior-high lecture on civic responsibility or personal hygiene.

"Worse than . . . the fingernails of fifty witches on a chalkboard," I begin.

Gary snorts. Not that I can hear it. "Bagpipes. Wait. Make that deaf kids, learning to play bagpipes."

I'd laugh, but any extra noise resonating in my eardrums might burst them. "Deranged woman screaming. In labor. Strapped to tracks. Freight train bearing down."

Gary flips the paper over. "Willy Nelson concert. Inside a bomber. During an air raid over Vietnam."

This I can trump. "Wouldn't know. Before my time." We switch to gin rummy, but even playing cards requires a degree of concentration impossible to maintain under continuous auditory assault. After the first hour we empty the aspirin bottle. After the second hour, I wrap every scarf I own around my ears like a mummy. The torturous din continues nonstop for three hours, reverberating within the camper walls like a scream in a tiny tin can.

I'm hallucinating. The camper windows appear to be vibrating. The door bulges and contracts, like the fabric covering a speaker. When the woman wails, the pilot light in the propane heater falters and droops, and when the man takes over, the flame shoots out in licks of fiery red. Then I realize it's actually Wipeout's tongue licking, and the fiery red is blood oozing from her groin and paws and dripping into her matted white fur. She is biting herself in anxiety, the canine equivalent of a panic attack. This is worse than any one thunderstorm or fireworks display has caused so far.

"Remember when we started out," Gary shouts, "how we decided if any place along the way gives either one of us the creeps, we're out of there, no arguing or second-guessing each other?"

"Is there enough light to leave right now?" I interrupt him. But I know the answer. The gravel road to Todos Santos is internal-organ bruising even in the daylight. I unwrap the scarves from my head and tie them around Wipeout's paws, and together we lift her into the bed so that our weary bodies and aching hearts shield her from some of the suffering.

We escape at the crack of dawn, pelted by a fresh round of preach-shrieking from the roadside loudspeakers. For three days we drive through highlands of alpine forest and mud huts, grateful for silence. Wipeout doesn't even lift her head to sniff the mountain air. Her appetite is gone, and we have to coax her to pee. We pass sparse, open-air markets in towns so small that maps ignore them. Women almost drop the bundles they carry on their heads as they pivot to watch our silver camper rumble past.

This is how my parents must have felt for our whole journey. They drove down the newly opened Pan-American Highway and into worlds without phones, electricity, or running water, let alone trucks with houses strapped on top.

Gary stops to photograph the stark landscape. It looks stone-aged, a muted palette punctuated by wildflowers in blood-red, cone-shaped flares. Through his lens my nomadic childhood comes rushing back. I am shadowing my parents but the context has evolved.

Miles from any village, we encounter twenty men walking down the middle of the road. When we slow down to drive around the

Chapter Fourteen

WIPEOUT

My father got stoned for the first time on the shores of Lake Atitlán, and I approach Guatemala's most famous tourist destination with skepticism bordering on premeditated disillusionment. My only reason for stopping is to find a vet for Wipeout and a jeweler to replace the wedding ring that dropped off my dehydrated finger into a Mazatlán toilet.

I imagine Lake Atitlán surrounded by expat colonies of aging American hippies and annoyingly crunchy, yogic Mother Earth–speakers. The guidebooks call Panajachel, the town that mushroomed at the base of this volcanic caldera, "Gringotenango." It isn't altogether fair—the town has just as many Europeans as Americans, and almost immediately I find a German jeweler who promises a new, handmade silver ring in a few days. Billboards advertising high-rise condos with free Wi-Fi and indoor gyms almost block the view of the lake. If tourism has ruined any point along the Pan-American Highway it is surely here; even the water has been contaminated by invasive bass brought in to stock the lake for American vacation dollars.

Still, the slide-show version of Lake Atitlán dances like a happy devil on my shoulder, whispering memories I've treasured since I was a little girl. Mountains ringing the lake like the points on a queen's crown. Water so clear I was embarrassed to watch my parents skinny-dipping. An earthy mix of strange smells: incense and frying fish. And everywhere the sound of campers laughing and singing, even my mother.

JAN 18–22, 1974

Stayed on public beach . . . bought clothes for all . . .
met lots of people—Jack and Carol there. Swam

My parents met up with the same group of travelers who had camped with us the night of the shoot-out in Mexico, and we stayed in one place for the longest time since the trip had begun: five whole nights under stars too many to count. Lake Atitlán was Shangri-la for wanderers and dropouts, too idyllic to have lasted, says the devil on my other shoulder.

The public beach where we camped still exists, but to reach it now requires dodging vendors selling Polaroid photo ops with dejected-looking ponies. Telephone poles are plastered with posters advertising an Astral Travel Camp and Vegan Meditation Center in the nearby village of San Marcos. Panajachel itself is a souvenir gauntlet of shell windmills and stuffed frogs, Mexican sombreros and American base-ball hats. A paunchy American in a faded Hawaiian shirt asks Gary if he's interested in some "really sweet weed," and I wonder if he's the same guy who convinced my father to light up, live a little.

It all seems like a tackier version of colonialism, culture shock after a week in the highlands. The only Guatemalans in sight are running souvenir stalls or giving tourists lifts to the lake in rickshaw taxis. A few tents dot the shoreline, where a drizzle of a river empties

into Lake Atitlán, but there is no way to drive our heavy truck out that
far. Luckily Gary and I have made other arrangements in Panajachel.

The twenty-three-year-old son of a friend from Arizona is vol-
unteering for the year in a medicinal herb garden, a community
health-care project. Shawn, and his girlfriend, Susie, arrange for us
to park our camper and stay in a private bungalow among fragrant
herb terraces. We warn them that we are traveling with an inconti-
nent, cancer-stricken old dog suffering from panic attacks, but they
welcome us anyway. After a week without a real shower, we shamelessly abandon the Avion and embrace the comforts of what they call
the "casita," the little house. After all my gringo-bashing it feels like
cheating, relaxing on teak deck chairs provided by the woman in San
Francisco who owns the place.

This absentee landowner, undoubtedly vegan and chakra-
mindful, formed a weaving cooperative for women widowed by the
Guatemalan civil war. The widows still live in distant villages, without electricity, but at least now there is a market for their skills and
they earn a living wage. Susie volunteers at the co-op, helping the
women choose colors more likely to entice American interior decora-
tors and high-end home magazines.

"Native women roll their eyes at all our earth tones and natural
dyes," she says. "To them, bright neon colors signify life and freedom. They'll pick turquoise or Day-Glo magenta any day over taupe
or black."

It is the kind of casual revelation that only happens far from
home, a contradiction that proves assumptions foolish. What I judge
gaudy is joyful to women who have survived much worse than I can
imagine.

Wipeout licks my ankles like a good-night kiss before she falls
asleep, and she is once again the snoring puppy who adopted me in
Mexico. For sixteen years she has planted herself at my feet when it is
time to rest, grounding me. Susie puts a pillow under her head, hands
me another Gallo beer, and asks if my parents were hippies.

"No more than we are. They just kind of stumbled into the stereotype."

When my parents met other Americans, the child not with them was never introduced. It would have been natural for fellow travelers to assume my charismatic father and timid mother were tuning in or dropping out. All the young Canadians, Europeans, and Australians that Gary and I meet assume that we are free-spirited wanderers too. The real motivation for this drive would be a chat bomb dropped into discussions about camp spots and roadblocks. It isn't practical, my quest to find my rolling childhood home and say a thirty-years-too-late good-bye to a three-year-old-boy. How could I explain that it's not that I still grieve my brother but that his unspoken history is so powerfully present.

I had a chance, the first time I camped at Lake Atitlán, to look into the future and find out whether I would ever be able to forget John John. But I was seven years old, and it had been thirty-seven days since I said good-bye to all my friends in second grade at Banks Elementary School. I was more concerned they would forget me. Even a walk along the shores of the lake wasn't enough to stop home-sick, sorry-for-myself tears from gushing out when I met the woman I've called "the gypsy lady" ever since.

She was camping at the far end of the beach, and I thought she looked like the star of *I Dream of Jeannie* with her long hair and lay-ers of colorful skirts. Her wrists tinkled with the sound of copper bracelets, and she told me she had a crystal ball inside her tent that could predict my future. That this crystal ball turned out to be invis-ible seemed perfectly logical at the time, and I didn't say a word as she moved her hands through the air in the shape of an orb. I finally blurted out a question.

"Does it show if I will ever have another friend?"

"Oh, yes," she said, smiling. "Many friends. In fact, each time you move to a new country or start a new school, you will find more friends, even closer friends than the ones you used to have. You're a very lucky girl to get so many chances."

Where once I had been an unwilling passenger in my parents' escape, the gypsy lady made me feel like a daring stowaway, discovering new worlds. I left her tent jackpot happy, and now, drinking Gallo beer with new friends not far from that very spot, I am filled with the same hopefulness.

In the spirit of the gypsy lady, the next day we take Shawn up on an offer to visit the pinnacle of Lake Atitlán's New Age subculture: Las Pirámides of San Marcos La Laguna. The ferry chugs away from the clamor of Panajachel, and within minutes it's as if we are traveling back in time. Other than a few tourists the boat is filled with locals taking goods to markets along the lakeshore route. Men wearing traditional woven *traje* sit on one side, napping, while women sort through sacks of beans, limes, and chili peppers. The lake is glassy and smooth, and little kids who've never held computer games in their hands jostle for position to lie on their stomachs and drag their fingers through the water.

We disembark at a rickety wooden dock with a hand-painted sign declaring the destination. Underneath the San Marcos sign is the same poster we saw in Panajachel; it promises better health through the one-month moon course at Las Pirámides Spiritual Retreat and Yoga Center.

"At least we'll have a good lunch," Shawn says. "Can't go wrong with a vegan buffet."

The pyramid part of Las Pirámides is more suggestion than literal—a scattering of tent-size rustic wooden structures with pointed tops peek out from clearings in the scrubby brush. They're too low to the ground to be anything other than sleeping quarters, but the whole complex seems abandoned. No one greets us or asks what we're doing on private property; we must look like foreigners authentically seeking authenticity. I'm feeling a bit like a spy, here to judge rather than join in, so I buy some dried purple basil and wormwood powder from an old Mayan man shuffling a few steps behind us.

He points to two larger structures—pyramid-shaped meditation centers—and taps his watch. Apparently in five minutes something important happens. I'm trying to be open-minded but this place feels anything but sacred, and I picture the meditation center filled with the drooping breasts and faded tattoos of potheads past their prime.

Instead, the pyramid disgorges dozens of the most beautiful young foreigners I have ever seen in one place. They all seem to be under thirty and they're laughing and chatting in half a dozen different European languages. The energy is radiant and palpable, enough to disarm even the most determined skeptic. Whatever it is they're studying here, these are eager, appreciative students. The women in particular are luminous, like they've just swallowed the sun.

"Forget astral travel, they should put these women on the poster," I whisper to Gary. "The place would be booked solid."

We follow the followers into a dining structure and, at only slightly inflated prices, dive into a crunchy meal of quinoa, root vegetables, and dehydrated fruit snacks. I've dabbled in vegetarianism for close to twenty years and haven't created or consumed anything as tasty. I can practically feel the toxins draining from my body.

"Don't go overboard," Gary warns me. "It's a long ferry ride back. Without bathrooms."

Only two people join our table and I'm surprised when they don't return my attempt at conversation. Instead, their faces drape into benign smiles, and they lean toward each other and touch foreheads before picking up their silverware.

"What's that all about?" I whisper to Shawn. The two diners appear to be pantomiming with gentle hand gestures and facial expressions.

"I'm not sure but I've heard that the last week of the moon course is supposed to be silent," Shawn says. "Part of getting to another level."

An entire week without talking seems more like torture to me, and I leave San Marcos mystified by its spiritual pilgrims. I'm bursting with questions, and on the ferry ride back I find someone to ask—a thirty-nine-year-old Guatemalan man traveling with his four-year-old son. He offers only his first name, Saluo, and explains in halting Spanish that it means blessed with fortune.

I do the mental math and realize that Saluo probably fought in the civil war that was raging across Guatemala when my family unknowingly traipsed through the country. He's surprisingly eager to talk about it. He loved guns, he says, and reenlisted many times after his mandatory service was over. Even though he saw many atrocities, he tells me he was still drawn to guns and violence after the war and ended up as a security guard in Guatemala City. The man gently stroking the top of his son's head seems like he is describing another person in another lifetime, and when he builds up to a long pause I realize he is setting the stage for a plot twist.

"And then I found God," it comes. "I left violence behind me. Alcohol behind me. The only thing that matters to me now is God, my wife, and that my son never know the life I led."

He speeds up with the energy of the evangelical. He leans so close I can feel the hot breath of conviction. In Saluo's earnest fervor I hear the passion of the loudspeaker preacher in Todos Santos. I try to smile, channeling the calm acceptance of my silent lunch companions. He is putting his past into perspective, offering thanks for an option other than violence. It doesn't matter how I define the continuum of logic to lunacy; the truth is that I am just as much a seeker as this man. Or as the beautiful vegans meditating under stunted pyramids. Or as my father, smoking really sweet weed so that he could float, for a while, away from the memory of my little brother.

Lake Atitlán is a gift that I am beginning to appreciate, a respite from the world of knowns and certainties. It is gently preparing me to accept that there are things I can't even understand, let alone control.

Meanwhile, Wipeout is weakening by the day. Summer thunderstorms are increasing both in strength and frequency. Children are afraid to touch her: she twitches, howls, and bleeds from everywhere her teeth can reach. Even guard dogs give her wide berth. We've stayed longer than we planned, unwilling to uproot her again. I can't bear the thought of putting her to sleep, but it is even worse to think that she might die along some nameless stretch of the Pan-American Highway, her last days unsettled and transient and with no place to bury her.

After dinner on our fourth night in the casita, Gary and I walk her down to the shore for a dip in Lake Atitlán. Just a mile away from the hustle of Panajachel, there is serenity and privacy. A thousand soothing shades of blue sky float above the clear water on invisible terraces of wind. The volcanoes rise so steeply from Lake Atitlán's shores that the sun can't set at the same time here. The evenings are a staggered affair; each cove and jutting point burns to its "good night" alone.

If only the golden light would linger on Wipeout a little longer. In better days, she bounded into lakes and oceans, swimming after rubber ducks and tennis balls. Now she checks to see if I am coming in with her. She hobbles out slowly, until the buoyancy of the cool water lifts her off her aching legs and the rhythm of the lake floats her gently back and forth. Gary takes a photo of her when she turns to see that we are still with her. She closes her eyes and sways in the water.

Her hips are so weak that Gary and I have to carry her up the hill to the casita, like a seventy-pound sack of potatoes. Shawn has made us a comfort-food dinner, macaroni and cheese, but there is no comforting Wipeout. Even a gentle rainstorm unnerves her to the point of biting a chair and breaking a tooth. I try everything I've learned from a lifetime of loving her, from the "How Much Is That Doggie in the Window" song to folding her soft ears in my fists and nuzzling her lumpy forehead. Nothing stops the quivering seizures of panic.

Susie offers me her cell phone. The number of a veterinarian who makes house calls is already on the screen, and I make the call I have been dreading. The groundskeepers, Tito and Chema, stop by, hats in hand.

"They say, if you want, they will prepare the earth," Susie translates.

I can't help feeling it is no accident that my journey with Wipeout is ending in Lake Atitlán. Her work with me is done. There is harmony and resilience in these waters—a strength that comforted me once is offering to do so again.

We are wealthy foreigners, and the groundskeepers barely know us. They have watched their country be torn apart by decades of war and poverty. They have every right to think I am overreacting, that my grief is somehow insensitive, given where it is playing out. Yet no one in this commercialized, contemplative, contradictory place ever tells me, "It's only a dog," ever offers anything but compassion and understanding. Even the German jeweler, who drops by the casita and finds me in tears, finds a way to comfort me.

"It's a symbol of eternity—no beginning or end," he says, placing my replacement wedding ring in the palm of my hand. "Loss is part of love, and life."

We agree on a time, the next day at sunset, and I wonder if Wipeout will make it that long. She pants all through the night, but each time I wake her she refuses to drink. She is wobbly on her feet, disoriented and unable to remember where the door is located to go outside. I have to rest my hand on her back as we walk to the garden in the soft moonlight.

The next day feels like there isn't air enough to inflate my collapsing lungs. We try taking Wipeout for a walk, but Gary, who can normally cover five or six miles without breaking a sweat, turns around after a few hundred yards. His muscles are aching; there is a ringing in his ears and a pounding behind his eyes.

Back at the casita he falls into a fitful slumber. By midday he has a fever of 103 degrees, and I have to lift both his head and Wipeout's to give each of them food and water. When the vet comes to the casita, he gives Wipeout a quick examination.

"I know how hard this is for you," he says, holding my hand. "But her passing will be peaceful and painless."

Gary's fever has drained the normal color from his skin and replaced it with sweaty blotches. He can barely walk; it's as if his body is staggering with sorrow.

"I think somehow I've managed to bust all the bones in my ankles, knees, and elbows," he groans.

"It's probably dengue," Shawn says. "The locals call it breakbone fever."

Susie and Shawn walk ahead of us to the spot the groundskeepers have prepared on the steep hillside. A tall, sheltering tree will be Wipeout's headstone. There are freshly cut flowers from the garden and scented candles flickering at the base of the tree. We are all crying, even the vet, but Wipeout is calm and ready. She is resting now where the thunder can't torment her and the deep waters of Lake Atitlán are always at her feet.

Chapter Fifteen

THE SHAKEDOWN

My mother's journal makes sense to me now. It is mechanical because she was. Taking out a pen and opening the little pink binder to a new page each night was a routine to follow. She wrote so that she could put each day without John John behind her. Pretty flowers, quaint cobblestone, *he's never coming back.*

Neither is Wipeout. I know that losing a sixteen-year-old dog in no way equates to the tragic death of a three-year-old son, but her absence is so fresh and disorienting that I keep turning around, convinced I've heard the huffing sound she makes when she flops to the ground at my feet. Her smell lingers in the seat cushions, the carpet, and my clothes—still covered in strands of her long white hair. My grief is instinctual; every speed bump sends my left arm flinging over the back of the seat to stop her from flying forward. At night I still wake every three hours in case she needs to go outside.

When I can't go back to sleep I turn on my laptop and write down every single thing I can remember, as if regurgitating details will keep her from disappearing. Whereas my mother minimized her words, I record pages and pages. But there is no structure or narrative; my thoughts are clumped into blunt bullet points.

- Found the church where dad's steps were stolen thirty years ago. It's the only church with a parking lot we could have camped in. The church looks the same but I don't remember all these stalls selling candy. Dixie cups filled with meringue. I'm sure those weren't there before. I would have eaten them until I puked.

I reread each entry before moving on to the next and find no comfort in the relentless, meticulous documentation. I want to wake up Gary so he can reassure me that this pettiness I see on the monitor, this ungrateful and ungraceful prose, wasn't in me all along. Surely he wouldn't have married me if it were.

- We're always getting lost. You can't trust Guatemalan directions. They all wave and say "todo derecho" but nothing is straight ahead. I want to scream with frustration.

The truth is that I am directionless without Wipeout. Without her I have lost not one discrete sense, like a person suddenly blinded; I have lost a degree of each of them. The gears in my heart and brain and muscles can't find their proper grooves and move me forward anymore. She was a soft, patient reminder to slow down and appreciate the balance and the beauty. I will have to relearn the best parts of myself.

Shawn and Susie try to help. They will travel with us as far as Antigua, guiding us through villages along the winding route with spirited discourses on the differences in *traje* (costumes) and indigenous languages. It is like trying to distract two zombies. They sit cross-legged on the back bench seat, but they cannot fill the space where Wipeout would have been.

We drive in such a daze that Gary doesn't see the traffic cop standing at an intersection of near-empty roads. He is holding a traffic sign painted green as if directing us through nonexistent road construction. As we approach, he flips the sign to the other side, fire-engine red. He fumbles for his whistle, almost dropping the sign in excitement.

"I think he wants something," I tell Gary. "Better pull over."

What he wants is to tell us that we have disobeyed him, have ignored the laws of Guatemala's roads, and could possibly go to jail.

"And where, exactly, would we find a jail around here?" Gary wants me to ask. We have passed no building more official looking than a *tiendita* selling *chicle* chewing gum.

"Adelante, muy cerca," the cop responds. "Somewhere ahead," I translate for Gary, a place as imaginary as our infraction. The cop begins embellishing his outrage, an extemporaneous monologue that I can decipher only in bits and pieces. It is not right to ignore a police officer. Our truck is very large and could have killed someone.

Gary's fingers are tapping the steering wheel as if he wishes it were the cop's chest. I don't know which seems less familiar: Gary's temper or the effort it is taking him to hold it back. I have never known the first or seen the second. I have no idea how to diffuse the situation or return to the normal pattern of our relationship.

"This is just machismo. We have to give him a way to save face," I suggest. "I'll try apologizing."

The sign was very far away. Of course we want to obey the law. He is right to be vigilant. In the future we will stop even if the sign says go.

"Doscientos," he insists. "Americano." The fine is conveniently in dollars, two hundred of them. Or we can try explaining to a judge why we almost ran over an officer of the law.

"Fine," Gary says. "Tell him to drive ahead of us and we'll follow him to see the judge. If he even has a police car."

But it is Friday afternoon, the cop counters. We will have to wait until Monday, behind bars. Unless we pay the fine to him, in person. He will make sure the judge gets it and our truck is not reported to Interpol.

Gary's forehead is dotted with sweat and his entire face is flushed. I have no idea if he's about to implode or if it is just residual dengue fever overheating the blood pounding through his temples. I reach for the wallet in the glove compartment, just to check. This is, after all, the country where my father was thrown in jail for refusing to pay a bribe, and I have no confidence I could rescue Gary from the same fate.

"What the hell are you doing?" Gary asks. "We'll just call his bluff. Put that away."

But before I can, three crisp twenty-dollar bills fall out on the bench seat, in plain view.

A deposit is a very good idea, the cop says. Maybe it will be too late today to report our violation after all. I lean over my sweaty, fuming husband and place the day's entire travel budget, plus breakfast and lunch tomorrow, in his fleshy hand.

"We are never, ever going to do that again," Gary says as he rolls up the window. We sit inches from each other but for the first time feel miles apart. "Unless you want to run out of money and hitchhike from here to Bolivia."

JANUARY 23, 1974
Antigua is a beautiful town. Teri's sandals fixed free.
Stayed under deserted gas station

Antigua is draped in fragrant bougainvillea, more inviting than any other town so far in Guatemala, but we drive right past its elegant cathedral and colonial *zócalo* and pull the camper up to a grungy gas station.

"I don't know," Gary says. "This looks pretty dodgy."

"Or providential," I counter. "We can start making up for that 'deposit.'"

Except for a modern, walled-off resort hotel across the street, it could be the same deserted spot my parents found. Shawn and Susie don't try to convince us to follow them to the youth hostel where they'll be spending the night; even sympathetic and understanding angels need a break from despair.

So they aren't with us the next morning to translate when someone raps on the door. If it were possible to pretend this elephant-sized camper is invisible, I'd curl up in the bed and hold my breath. The knocking is insistent; whoever this is has more endurance than we do.

I open the door and a rotund man with a handlebar mustache gallantly offers his hand to help me down, as if I were the visitor and not he. The audacity of it makes me giggle and I accept his chivalry. Gary jumps down right behind me, barely landing before the man grasps his hand in a vigorous, theatrical handshake. It's only then that I see a woman hanging back in the camper's shadows. It must be the fact that I'm half asleep and still mourning Wipeout, but she seems, well, furry.

"Me llamo Señor Jordan." The man's voice is resonant and deep, like he's announcing his arrival rather than merely introducing himself. At least he's speaking Spanish instead of K'iche' or Tz'utujil; there's a chance that even before I've ingested any caffeine I'll be able to figure out what he's selling. He hands me a red-and-white paper flyer with the headline "Jordan Bros. Circus—de Mexico." Ah, that's why he's patting his chest. He must be the owner, or maybe the ringmaster.

"I think he's inviting us to the greatest show on earth," I whisper to Gary. "Or at least in Antigua."

The freshly photocopied flyer shows illustrations of African lions, juggling clowns, and monkeys. Mr. Jordan points to a bullet-pointed list of attractions. The world's smallest pony is easy to translate, especially when standing next to a mustachioed man squatting in a Cossack position, pretending to hold reins and gallop. I have no idea what "*avestruces*" means, but Gary guesses "ostriches" when Mr. Jordan tucks his hands under his armpits and stretches his head into an imaginary pile of sand.

When the pantomiming ends, he motions for the woman in the shadows to join us. She stands two heads shorter than me and is covered in swirling, black body hair. She flashes a gleaming smile, and the gap where her two front teeth should be is so perfectly spaced I could swear they were intentionally removed.

"Mi esposa," he says with dramatic flair. "Bety la Fea." It's right there on the flyer: "Presenting . . . Betty the Ugly."

I'm debating whether it would be more insulting to act like the moniker isn't horribly demeaning or insist that his wife is merely hirsute when Mr. Jordan whips out a crocodile-skin wallet. It bulges with quetzal notes, pesos, and dollar bills and is securely attached to its owner's belt by a heavy silver chain.

"Tengo tanto dinero," Mr. Jordon proudly tells us. Then he points to the Avion. "¿Cuánto vale su casa rodante?"

We are barefoot, dogless, and dejected, and a complete stranger wants to buy the roof over our heads. My first instinct is to say yes. There's enough money in this ringmaster's wallet to buy two, one-way plane tickets to DC. Or to Gary's parents in Wisconsin since we don't actually have a house or jobs to return to.

This whole trip seems meaningless, more punishment than journey. I am searching for the camper that starred in the slide-show version of my childhood. All I am likely to find is a sad truth. I've already seen what happens when a camper echoes with absence. The blameless, beautiful Avion deserves more than the two empty people standing speechless next to it in a Guatemalan gas station.

"Don't just stand there," Gary says. "Tell him it's not for sale."

But instead, I ask Mr. Jordan and Betty the Ugly to come back again tomorrow morning. I have to think about it.

They drive off in a pickup overflowing with mattresses, plastic clown barrels, and empty cages, and the hair on Betty's arm flutters in the wind as she waves good-bye. For the first time, we lock up the camper to explore a city on foot without Wipeout. Her leash hangs from a hook inside the door, but I leave her water bowl by the back wheels anyway, just in case some other thirsty dog wanders by.

The entire day turns into a freak show, and we stumble aimlessly from one tent to another. First there is the parade that blocks the main street, with marimba music blaring from loudspeakers atop a flatbed truck. Following behind it could be the possessed residents of a nursing home. It's impossible to tell the ages of the dancers. Their faces are hidden under wrinkled rubber masks with stringy, silver hair and blacked-out teeth. Their synchronized steps seem to be some sort of deranged death march, the women staggering, unsteadily, as the men grope at overstuffed breasts and swaying hips. A boy in a Batman costume turns cartwheels and smokes a cigarette at the same time.

"The Jordan Bros. Circus has its work cut out to top this," Gary says, and I know that he too is still thinking of the offer to buy our camper. I picture a giant mural painted on its aluminum side, our compact castle converted into a traveling billboard. Step right up, it would declare. Forget the Pan-American Highway and a homemade camper rotting somewhere in Bolivia. The show must go on.

We're supposed to meet Shawn and Susie for lunch, and we wait for them in front of an Antiguan travel agency. The windows are plastered with colorful posters—carnival dancers in Rio and high-kicking Rockettes in New York City. It reminds me we're still in the same time zone as Gary's parents. If we sell the camper to the circus, Angie would have Wisconsin sweet corn, lake perch, and cherry tomatoes from her garden spread out on a gingham tablecloth, waiting for us.

Instead, we duck down a hallway between the travel agency and youth hostel and into what looks like a tapestry-lined harem tent. An indigenous woman sits in the center of dozens of steaming baskets. She lifts each container's woven cover for our inspection. Charcoal-grilled chicken parts in one. Stacks of soft corn tortillas in another. A cauldron of peppers and eggplants floating in fresh, cilantro-scented broth.

"Just point to what you want. You get four helpings for about a dollar," Shawn tells us. "Not even Lonely Planet knows about this place."

The only sound is the slurping of a half-dozen construction workers sitting on piles of wool rugs in almost complete darkness. The smells are intoxicating, the atmosphere as exotic as it is authentic. But the cramping in my stomach is so powerful that I'm afraid to sip even the soup.

Gary has convinced me to keep a food journal, like my mother did, to see if there's a pattern that might be repeating itself. Each night I log everything that has passed through my lips. I have been so afraid of eating anything fibrous, fermented, or unfamiliar that except for the delights of Central American bakeries, called *panaderías,* both lists could be straight out of a 1950s Midwestern garage-sale cookbook.

FIRST TRIP	NOW
Breakfast: pineapple bread	Breakfast: orange-chocolate bread
Lunch: bananas, leftover rice w/can soup	Lunch: olives, pickles, peanuts, beer
Dinner: spaghetti, bread, pop	Dinner: canned veggies, spaghetti

I swallow my last Imodium A-D capsule, and we head to a pharmacy for something stronger. I don't even attempt to read the fine print on the box of tablets I'm handed. A list of side effects will not tell me how to stop the hemorrhaging of my resolve. My body is as broken as my heart. The Jordan Bros. Circus offer could be a sign: get out before it gets worse.

There's time for one last stop before Shawn and Susie have to catch the bus back to Lake Atitlán, and they want to show us a flea market famous for antique Guatemalan weavings and carved figurines. I remember, out of the blue, that today is Gary's birthday. We pick out a delicate, intricately patterned head wrap that Susie says women used to wear for special occasions. It's long enough to encase a mummy—or a man recovering from dengue fever.

I'm tucking it into my bag when Gary and Shawn wave from an interior courtyard in the back of the building. They're standing behind some sort of brick alcove, shrouded in hazy smoke that makes it hard to see what has caught their attention. Susie raises a finger to her lips when we approach and whispers into my ear.

"It's a Maximón altar." Instead of the hard X sound like that in Maximilian or Mexico, the syllables in Maximón's name are held together by a soft, shushing sound. "The Catholic Church doesn't recognize him, but the locals think of him like a dark saint."

I've been reading about this mysterious Guatemalan highlands deity, always depicted as a carved figure wearing black with a cigar pinched between blood-red lips. Whatever it is that Maximón officially protects or bestows seems to vary from village to village. The only constant is that he expects booze and cigars in return. According to all the guidebooks, Maximón's physical location is supposed to be secret, his carved figurine paraded in public only by specially appointed believers one day a year.

My eyes sting and I swallow back a cough. Surely nothing good could come of interrupting the private, somber ceremony we have stumbled onto. A kneeling man and woman, their backs to us, squeeze each other's hands as two men wave bundles of burning herbs over their bowed heads.

I squint through clouds of copal incense. There's a waist-high carving of a man at the base of the brick altar. His face is black from soot and the tip of his stogie is a red-hot coal. A plastic bottle of Coca-Cola is tucked into the crook of his arm. In another context it might be comical, his outsize cigar a blatant phallic symbol. But here, even though the hot sun beats down into the courtyard, a cold chill makes me shiver.

This is no genial, macho offering of booze and cigars. We are eavesdropping on some sort of ancient fertility ritual. The men are hissing and spitting streams of alcohol through their teeth in Maximón's direction. The woman seems about to faint, and her husband closes his eyes and presses his hand into her stomach. I look down and find that I am doing the same thing to my own bloated gut. It is time to leave.

We walk Shawn and Susie to the bus stop, and I am actually grateful for the contractions in my lower intestines. If we hurry, I might make it back to the camper in time. The threat of imminent disaster excuses me from trying to thank Shawn and Susie enough. I couldn't fight back tears through a long good-bye or watch their smiling faces recede when all I'd want to do is run behind the bus taking them away. Two people we didn't know a week ago have carried us across a threshold, and seeing them wave through a dirty window would make it seem like they, and Wipeout, existed in another lifetime.

I am practiced by now in the art of hurrying as fast as I can without vibrating my digestive tract, and the camper has never looked more beautiful than when we arrive at the deserted gas station. But when Gary unlocks the door, the wave of trapped heat is enough to make me consider searching out some bushes behind the fuel pumps instead.

"I have a better idea," Gary says. "Just hang on."

He hops inside and fishes through our tiny closet for swimsuits and a change of clothes.

"Run a comb through your hair and put on these sunglasses. We're crashing the resort across the street."

It is a trick every traveler on a budget should learn. Walk into a five-star hotel like you own the place, and not a soul will say a thing when you stop at the lobby bathroom. Emerge wearing nothing but a huge smile and the bathing suit you've just changed into, and staff will point you in the direction of the swimming pool.

That locker-room shower you're supposed to take, the one to prevent hair gel and sweat-proof sunscreen from greasing up the water? A perfect place to shave off two days of stubble and to trim toenails caked with grime gathered from strolling through parades and bus stations in open sandals.

I stand under a pulsing showerhead, inhaling the perfumed aroma of tiny bottles of Bulgari shampoo and conditioner and thanking the gods of pampered tourists. It's bizarre how only three months ago I took such luxuries for granted. Whenever I had to travel I indulged in fully reclining airplane seats and noise-cancelling headphones. I ordered room service if I didn't feel like making reservations at a restaurant and never worried about running out of Imodium A-D. In most hotels the bathroom was bigger than the entire camper I now call home.

If we sell it to a traveling circus, that life is mine to lead again. I could get another job, buy another house, and compartmentalize these last few weeks as a bohemian sabbatical. But the woman in that parallel universe isn't quite in focus; her voice is a distant echo. She never had time to watch Batman smoke cigarettes while turning cartwheels or her dog butt heads with a goat in a mango grove.

Gary is already floating on his back in the cool, chlorinated infinity pool when I join him, and we swim until our freshly shaved skin begins to shrivel.

Chapter Sixteen

THE BROOMSTICK DEFENSE

We wake in the middle of the night to the sensation of the camper rocking side to side. My reflexes are slow; I am still tangled in sheets of grief and fear. It could be a powerful gust of wind, but I find myself yelling "¡No me moleste!" to the darkness—a phrase that roughly translates into "Don't bug me."

The rocking intensifies. A glass of water and Gary's reading glasses fly off the shelf at the base of our feet.

"Jesus Christ." Gary bangs his head sitting up. "Someone is trying to tip us over."

He climbs over me, jumps down from the bed, and yanks a broom from the plastic clamp holding it to the curved, wood-paneled wall. He unlocks the door, waits a second, and then kicks it open with his bare feet and leaps into the darkness. It is so quiet I can hear the sound of the broomstick slicing through the air. If there is an element of surprise he has seized it, but he is only one man against an unknown threat.

I drop to my knees, rip up the carpet, and start digging through the paperbacks burying the gun.

"Leave us alone!" I hear Gary shouting. "Get out of here. I know you're there."

I flatten to my stomach, extending my fingers to feel for the gun. It's back there somewhere. Every worst-case scenario rewinds through my mind. *You will be carjacked. You will be kidnapped.*

I claw the gun from its ziplock bag. It smells stale and metallic and feels cold and clammy in my quivering palm. I'm still staring at it when I realize that the rocking has stopped. The camper is dead still. I hear only the sound of Gary's footsteps, circling the Avion. He has stopped shouting at ghosts.

I am dangling the gun by its butt, like a little girl afraid to run with scissors, when Gary climbs back into the camper.

"What the hell are you doing?"

My hands shake as I drop the pistol back into its ziplock bag.

"It's just losing Wipeout," I say, as if this excuses me.

But I know it doesn't. I have failed a test I've been afraid of taking since the day we decided to drive from normal newlywed life into 24/7 togetherness and unpredictability. It's the test in which our relationship either strengthens or splinters over how we handle a crisis. Gary hands me the first of forty-two paperbacks, not saying another word. I crawl back into bed alone while he sits, staring out the window into the tar-black night.

THE NEXT MORNING, MR. JORDAN KNOCKS ON THE DOOR AGAIN, HOLDING up his wallet and asking if we'll sell our camper to his circus.

"¿Cuánto para la casa rodante?"

He is wearing a black tuxedo and dangling a fat cigar from the corner of his red lips like the reincarnation of Maximón himself. But

I have a question rather than an offer. Did he hear of any riots overnight, young people raging through the streets trying to tip over anything in their path?

"Pienso que no." He twists the ends of his handlebar moustache and
says he doesn't think so. It is Betty the Ugly who offers the follow-up
question.

"¿Antes o después del terremoto?"

"Wait, *terremoto,* I know that word," I sputter to Gary. "*Tierra*
means earth. . . . "

Gary starts to laugh. He doesn't need a translator. "Nobody was
attacking us. It was just an earthquake."

We are camped on the outskirts of a city surrounded by volcanoes, on ground so riddled with fault lines that the country's leaders long ago moved the capital to Guatemala City, yet the two of us
couldn't tell a temblor from teenage troublemakers.

I look over at Gary, still wearing the pajama bottoms that were
his only armor when he jumped out of the camper in the middle of
the night, and double over with laughter. I am married to a man who
battles earthquakes with broomsticks. He is married to a woman who
would sooner shoot them.

Mr. Jordan puts away his wallet, chews the end of his cigar, and
shrugs his shoulders; we are clearly too crazy to know a good deal
when we see it. The Jordan Bros. Circus will break camp and move
on, and so will we.

The Pan-American Highway has much more to teach us. Circumstances I am only beginning to understand forced my father to
abandon the camper he built, and no matter how much I want to
close that chapter of my childhood there is a chance that Gary and
I may never find it. This journey has no guarantees, and there are no
talismans or higher powers that can protect me against scares and
heartbreaks still to come. But I could never sell the Avion. I would
rather run away from one circus than rejoin the one I left behind.

Chapter Seventeen

EL SALVADOR

Guatemala is only a few hours behind us but worlds away. The men cutting grass along the shoulder of the Pan-American Highway in El Salvador use Black and Decker weed whackers, not machetes. They wear baseball caps, not straw hats tied with hand-woven ribbons. The camping section of the *Central America and Mexico Handbook* offers only this advice for the country we have entered: "Camping is not advised." It recommends registering with the US embassy if we plan on staying for more than a few days. "The legacy of many years of civil war is still visible."

The words seem to jump from the page to the road in front of us when we drive up on two men who stand between orange plastic cones blocking the highway. The butts of their semiautomatics, pressed into the asphalt, are like third legs in a pair of tripods. One cop gathers both weapons in his arms to free the other cop to lean over the threshold of Gary's window.

We are missing a sticker that should be under the visor, I translate for Gary. Something normally issued at the border.

"Ask him how he could see that we were missing a tiny sticker
before pulling us over."

For a second I consider relaying his exact words, just to be in
sync with my husband once again. Because while my intestines are
twisting in the knowledge of the actual illegal act we are committing,
transporting the gun, Gary seems to have driven right past fear and
into defiance.

The cop who spoke moves away from Gary's window to confer
with his partner. They haven't even named their price when Gary
sticks both of his arms out over the side-view mirror, crossed at the
wrist, fingers wriggling.

"Tell them they won't get a dime this time," he says. "I mean it. I
am never paying a bribe again."

I don't know if the cops or I am more stunned at Gary's panto-
mimed invitation for handcuffs. But the expectation is clear. All eyes
are on me. I am supposed to step up and somehow smooth this over.
Because I speak Spanish. Because I am a woman. Because I am the
one with lists and plans and practice in this sort of thing.

But instead I make the universal gesture for crazy, circling my
finger in the space next to my temple. I shrug, just a little, in Gary's
direction but in truth I am referring to myself as well. This is nuts,
loony, screwball—all the words I suddenly can't find in Spanish but
do not need. The cops have no fall-back move, no counter for insanity.
They wave us on, laughing, but I can't let it pass.

As Gary drives, I read aloud that El Salvador has the worst levels
of violent crime on the continent. The guidebook says kidnapping is a
constant threat, and the per capita rate of violent deaths is higher here
than in Colombia. But however justified, my lecture seems hollow
and shrill as we pass elementary schools letting out for lunch; cascades
of students in ties and white shirts wrestle under trees, chasing each
other around cows and then waving at our startling silver camper.

The camper that brought me to El Salvador the first time got more stares than waves. My family must have looked like dust-bowl evacuees from a Steinbeck novel, pulling into a gas station with one wheel wobbling under fourteen thousand pounds of misery.

> **JANUARY 27TH, 1974**
>
> Still wheel trouble. Stopped to fix at station. Jennifer
> fell out of camper and broke her tooth. Took her to
> hospital in N. San Salvador. Dr. saw her and gave med-
> icine. NO charge.

When my sister screamed that day, it wasn't a scream like when I took away a crayon she wanted. It was the kind that made everyone in the gas station run to the back of the camper and then turn their eyes away. A lot of blood comes gushing out of a two-year-old's mouth when her baby teeth smash against camper steps her tiny feet have missed.

My little sister was patient number 1,459-74 at Hospital San Rafael; a scrap of faded blue paper in the journal is the souvenir my mother kept of a wretched day. I wonder if she saved it because no one back home would ever believe her. This tiniest of Central American countries, just five years away from the tipping point of civil war, treated a two-year-old girl from a much wealthier country for absolutely no charge. And when Jenny was discharged from the hospital, the dental surgeon insisted that we camp at his farm on the coast while she recuperated.

Maybe I am trying to atone for pulling a gun on an innocent earthquake, or for becoming the kind of person who hides one under the carpet in the first place, but I try to put more faith in the El Salvador I remember than the one described in the Central American handbook.

In my mother's journal, in handwriting more delicate than hers, are the names of the dentist, Ernesto, along with his wife and three daughters and their address in San Salvador. Gary and I are only two hours from the capital, and it is as if Yolanda, Carolina, Fiorella, and Lorena are calling out from the pages of my past.

So much sadness filled the intervening years—750,000 died in the civil war, another 1,000,000 became refugees, and a 7.6 Richter scale earthquake struck in 2001—that there might not be a happy ending to this story. I decide to call my parents on the satellite phone to see if they know whether the dentist still lives in San Salvador.

"How old do you think he'd be now?" I ask. There's a long pause on the Nicaraguan end, memories too faded to help. "It's okay, Mom. How old do you think he was when you met him?"

The journal is in my hands, and without it my mother doesn't remember Ernesto at all. My father can't picture him either; there are no slides of this man to cue an entertaining story. El Salvador was an instrument of torture, trying to extract an admission of defeat one lug nut at a time. While my father spent hours underneath the jacked-up truck, my mother waited helplessly on beaches, grains of sand draining through her fingers like the money she knew would never be enough to last.

JAN 28TH 1974

Fix truck. Went to beach in La Libertad 2 nites. Good swimming.
Back to have wheel fixed again.

My parents must have blocked out memories of the man who was wonderful to our family at one of the lowest points in the trip—broke, a little girl with a smashed front tooth, and a truck whose wheels barely turned. I have a chance to thank him now. The only problem is that my father's map is thirty years out of date, and we get hopelessly lost trying to find the address in the journal. I spend an hour jumping in and out of the truck, directing Gary as he backs the Avion out of dead-end streets.

"Why don't we show the address to a taxi driver," he suggests at last. "You ride with him and I'll follow."

It is a brilliant solution to perpetually vague directions from strangers, and forty minutes later we park in front of a two-story brick home. There is a razor-wired patio on top of a garage and a bougainvillea-draped stairwell to the main entrance on the second floor. There is no name next to the doorbell, but the young woman who answers in a white tunic and apron confirms that we are at the right house.

"I should have worn a dress or something; I didn't really expect to find him," I whisper to Gary.

"Don't worry about it. Your mother still picked out your clothes the last time he saw you," Gary teases me. "If you got all dolled up he'd never believe it was you."

My hair is plastered to my forehead with sweat, and Gary untwists my collar as we walk up the stairs to the living room. Ernesto shuffles in. His eyes curve downward, too tired to register surprise. He smells faintly of aftershave, and the folds around his cheeks and chin are smooth and deep. He still dresses as though he has someplace to be: a starched striped shirt, polished silver belt buckle, and freshly pressed brown trousers. He extends his hand slowly to greet Gary, and I can see him wondering why we've come to see him: has he missed an appointment or forgotten an invitation?

I show him my mother's journal, opened to the page listing the address and names of his family. He brings it closer to his glasses and recognizes the handwriting on its faded pages.

"Yolanda," he mutters as we sit down beside him on a plastic-covered sofa. "Dios mío."

My parents never saw the home we are visiting now, so I flip through my mother's journal to the part where she describes the dentist's coastal farm.

FEBRUARY 2ND, 1974

Rich San Salvador dentist spoke English, wanted us to
stay with them. They own coffee plantation. Gave us
cream, beans and honey from the farm—good . . . Jen
face burned bad

I remember it like a bedtime story with Yolanda as the fairy god-
mother—there was fresh cream in our hot cocoa from the night's
milking, honey from her beehives, and beans from her vegetable
garden. Every morning Ernesto examined my sister's swollen mouth
and gave her more medicine and ice packs for the pain. He wanted to
practice his English, and my parents were a captive audience.

I remember little of the grown-up conversations; I was too busy
playing with the girls. Carolina and Fiorella were five and three years
older than me; their baby sister, Lorena, was the same age as Jenny.
They were the first children on our journey who could speak any English, and they reminded me of everything I was missing. I wanted
my own room again, not a sleeping bag next to my little sister in a
camper. We had races in their backyard pool—just like the ones I
used to win at the Hillsboro swim center. They rode horses—just like
the ones my parents had to sell to build the camper. They had a parrot
that perched on my shoulder and a dog who didn't have to get left
behind. Best of all, Carolina and Fiorella went to school. I wanted to
live with them forever; they knew how to French braid each other's
hair and how to balance books on their heads and walk at the same
time.

"We are practicing to be beauty queens," we told Yolanda as we
pranced around her patio in our bathing suits.

The farm felt regal to me; each night we folded linen napkins as
Yolanda set a table bigger than our entire camper. I flung myself into
the routines of a stable family: *Teresita, take another empanada; there*

are plenty more. Let me fix that sleeve for you; here's a dress that you can borrow. Time to put on hats, girls, you'll get sick from the sun.

I sobbed when it was time to leave, comforted only by Yolanda's hugs and Ernesto's promise: "If you are ever in San Salvador, you are always welcome to stay with us again."

Thirty years later, Ernesto picks up the story as if Gary and I are stand-ins for my father and mother.

"What a strange thing—life," he says, shaking his head and holding the journal in his delicate hands like a hymnal. "You never know what returns around again."

I feel like our presence takes him back someplace kinder and safer in his life, and his initial reserve melts into a gentle melancholy. His eyes well with tears as he describes his wife; he accepts a sip of water from my glass to loosen the words stuck in his throat. Yolanda was killed in a car accident two years earlier, and he speaks about her as if she will walk back into the room any minute.

"Her father is Italian and she can speak four languages, five if you count the way she talks with her hands."

His is present-tense love, and I can see her again, beckoning us inside for milk and cookies. Despite her privileged upbringing, Ernesto tells us, Yolanda loved the simple life of the farm on the coast. But ultimately she felt too vulnerable surrounded by the poverty of their neighbors and workers.

"We had to sell the farm not too long after you visited—during the first years of the civil war," he tells us. "Yolanda didn't like having to drive there with an armed guard in our car."

It is hard to reconcile this frail old man with the wavering voice as the "rich dentist" my mother described. He has silvered past the glamour of hired drivers and high society, and I cannot picture the world he is describing—until he brings out two oversized scrapbooks and spreads them on the glass coffee table before us. One is filled with family photos, postcards, and mementos, and the other with newspaper columns he has written since the 1950s. His jaw relaxes as we turn the pages, and he fiddles with a delicate gold cross around his neck.

My parents never discovered that the dentist who gave us shelter was also a correspondent and well-connected civic leader. There are photographs of Ernesto rubbing shoulders with politicians, shaking hands with academics, and presenting trophies on behalf of the San Salvador Lions Club. He skims over the photographs of himself and lingers on one of a young Yolanda taken on the occasion of her introduction to the Queen of England. His wife looks innocent and conscious of her beauty all at once, and nothing matters as much to Ernesto without her by his side.

Hours pass, and Gary and I never move from the sofa; we have front-row seats to a movie that hasn't been projected in decades. Ernesto's English is faltering now, so he asks me to translate for Gary and gently corrects me when I misunderstand.

"How did he manage to make it through the civil war, being so well-known and well published?" Gary asks.

"He says he avoided politics and made friends on all sides of the struggle."

Ernesto changes the subject and starts talking about his children, but while I listen I thumb through the articles he wrote. They are all political. He is telling us a truth that has developed, delicately, over time. This is *his* slide-show version of history. There are photos of him with Schafik Jorge Handal, leader of the left-wing guerrilla group FMLN.

"Handal es simplemente un amigo el míos de universidad," Ernesto explains, a college friend who just happens to be running for president at the moment.

"It's good to have friends in such high places," I try to joke, but Ernesto doesn't smile.

"Nada, y nadie, dura por siempre en El Salvador." He is saying that nothing and no one last forever in El Salvador. Ernesto was clearly connected but not too conspicuous. He was politically active but not threatening. He owned land in a country where most do not, yet he was kind to strangers in need.

He survived. Only to lose the one person who mattered most to him: Yolanda. Now Ernesto is biding his time, staying under the radar screen of public life and just passing the hours until he can be with his wife again. Gary and I have shown up on his doorstep and given him a reason to look back.

"Yolanda was so good to us," I tell him. "I can see why my mother asked her to put your address in her journal. She must have intended to keep in touch."

Ernesto struggles for words in English. "She was worried that something would happen to you and your sister. You were so thin, so fragile, and we didn't really think that your mother and father would make it."

The address Yolanda wrote in my mother's journal was never intended for correspondence, but for consolation—a way station on the long drive back if all else failed.

Ernesto wishes us luck on our journey, but he never asks about my parents. He is no longer concerned with the future. He lives in a world without the woman who gave it meaning, comforted that, for a few hours, someone listened to his stories and remembered his beautiful wife. I don't want to leave either one of them or face the San Salvador that now surrounds the dentist, where bougainvillea winds through razor wire on top of every cement wall. Men with semiautomatics guard the doors of children's gift shops. Escorts for delivery trucks lazily point rifles out of open windows.

It is growing dark, and as we stand to say our good-byes Ernesto brings out a small locked box filled with jewelry that belonged to Yolanda.

"Please, Teresita, you must pick a piece and wear it on your travels," he insists.

My eyes land on a beaded bracelet, and I roll my fingers over its tiny spheres of jade fastened by a sturdy barrel clasp.

"Shiny emerald green," Ernesto mumbles. "Just like her eyes when she cried."

I think of his daughters and for a moment I hesitate, wondering if Carolina or Fiorella would resent me for wearing a bracelet that belonged to their mother. But Ernesto just wants to keep some part of Yolanda alive and spread a little of her grace in this walled and gated country. And in his gesture is all the sweetness of El Salvador.

BORDERS

T he Spanish word *frontera* makes the line between one country
and another sound exotic, as though crossing it is adventurous
or at the very least pioneering. But the truth is closer to the English
word—*border*—at best boring and more often boorish and brutal. I
learned that lesson when my father drove through Honduras in a single day.

"Daddy, what does '*tránsito*' mean?"

The *entrada* visa stamped into my passport at the border allowed
us sixty days in country. But the part of Honduras dissected by the
Pan-American Highway is only a pinch along its Pacific coastline.

"Means we aren't stopping," he answered, sick of questions.

In just a few more hours we came to the border of Nicaragua, my
second passport stamp in one day.

"Daddy, what does '*prohibido efectuar trabajo*' mean?'"

"Means I'm getting you a dictionary next chance I get."

Central American border crossings along the highway. If we blaze
through the coastal section of Honduras as fast as my parents did, we
could be in Nicaragua by nightfall. But each line representing a tropical border on my father's map is actually two chances for a shakedown: one for the privilege of leaving the country on one side of the
line, another to advance into the next. Honduras is a fleshy slice of
grapefruit, released only by scraping both sides of the membranes
connecting a continent.

"So, Miss Information, what does '*tramitaro*' mean?" Gary asks.

We are in line on the El Salvadoran side of the Honduran border,
and six young men calling themselves *tramitaros* are huddled on the
running boards of the Ford. Clinging to its side-view mirrors, they
reach through the open window to hang onto the dashboard.

"Clearly something in the vein of traumatic."

I don't remember *tramitaros* competing for tips to shepherd my
father through borders. If these pushy entrepreneurs existed back
then, the sight of a Frankenstein camper on the verge of disintegration driven by a man with a Fidel Castro beard and fierce blue eyes
must have scared them off. Apparently they see Gary and me as much
easier targets.

They are all shouting that they speak perfect English, but only
one boy, who can't be older than sixteen, bothers to actually make the
claim in English instead of Spanish. So I hand him a few dollars as a
down payment and he shoos the rest of them off the bumper.

The truth is, I'll take any help I can get. Each frontera from El
Salvador south is more bruising than the last. There is nothing exotic or adventurous about the process. Money changers descend like
vultures, scratching and clawing each other for access to our wallets.
There are so many of them that I'm already feeling claustrophobic,
and my stomach lurches when I see drug-sniffing dogs. I think of the
gun under the carpet. These are countries unlikely to forgive Americans any trespass. In their eyes we've propped up dictators and trained

terrorists, instigating decades of the kind of instability that collapses economies.

I tumble through a wash-and-spin cycle of queues, stamps, and signatures like a sweaty rag doll. Everything is upside down and inside out, and I am too exhausted to fight. So instead of waiting for confrontations I quietly make offerings not yet demanded. I pay not to be robbed when Gary parks the truck under distant, shady trees, and then I pay inspectors so they do not inspect the camper. I pay for lunch breaks to be over on time and copy machines to not be out of paper. It is both proactive and paranoid, but to me it seems a small price to keep matches away from Gary's fuse. Until I open my mother's journal and find a solution more clever by half. In the land of five-dollar graft, nobody can make change.

FEB 4, 1974

Went through Honduras border. Started showing $500
travelers check. No problems.

By this point in the first journey, my parents had mastered the art of the con game. They sent me inside the customs offices with the check they knew could not be cashed, banking on my adorable, imperfect Spanish and big blue eyes, quick to fill with tears. My father refused to leave his vehicle; that $500 traveler's check had to last until Panama, where $1,000 from my aunt would be waiting if we made it that far.

Gary and I are not as desperate, and we declare a moratorium on self-righteous vows and rants. I tell Gary we are too lucky to begrudge these petty payoffs. He agrees to call them tips instead, tiptoeing around another no-bribe showdown. The *tramitaros* working so hard to convince me of their English skills might otherwise be beholden to vicious Honduran gangs. The girls selling overpriced bottled water are better off than those forced into prostitution or attempting to make it to the United States on their own. I am stunned by the cruelty of chance—we happened to be born on one side of an arbitrary line and these people were not.

Each crossing tops the previous in pure despair; women and children staggering under the weight of everything they're trying to carry to a new country, dogs fighting over rotting roadkill, downtrodden men hiding in pockets of shade from the blistering heat. It feels utterly indulgent, traveling in search of the abandoned camper that was my home, when in the opposite direction people are risking everything to leave theirs.

Gary doesn't even take out his camera; these are places of transition and people in the process of losing. It is too much to take anything, even a photograph.

FEBRUARY 5TH, 1974
Thru border again—Ugh—lots of time.

Those who drive through Honduras in a hurry are not seen as tourists but as instigators of trouble. Northern Nicaragua is a day trip from absolutely nowhere. To enter here requires explanation, and when I hand over our documents I feel as distrusted as a missionary, as suspect as a smuggler, and as unwanted as an immigrant. And that's before I try to pass off a color copy of our truck's title.

"Este título es una falsificación. Usted debe conducir un vehículo robado," declares the man behind the glass partition. He is waving the photocopy through an ultraviolet scanner and thinks the truck is stolen.

"No, es solamente una copia," I bluster, trying to explain that I thought the original might get stolen along the way. I dig it out of its hiding place under Wipeout's bench, but the damage is done. I may as well be dangling bribe bait.

"¡Su placa de la licencia es falsificación también!" Another Nicaraguan border guard decides our license plate is fake as well.

Washington, DC, "Taxation Without Representation" license-plate tags are preprinted and smooth to the touch; there are no raised letters or machine-stamped numbers. I can see how this would be suspicious even were they not manufactured in the city that orchestrated the Contra War. The entire office parades out to the camper to inspect the Ford F-350's license plate.

"¿Donde está el verdadero placa?" Another official demands to know where I've hidden the real plate.

I try to convince him I'm not lying this time—that all new license plates are made like ours. It doesn't work. Our license number and VIN are called in to Interpol. The border police chief declares the truck stolen until proven otherwise.

It is licensed to Gary and I am no longer an innocent, blue-eyed decoy. He is the one who must wait for five hours on a hard wooden bench in the merciless Nicaraguan sun. He is the one who would go to jail if they ever find the gun I insisted on. How I ever imagined that owning it would give me some sense of security or control seems mockingly ridiculous now.

I watch from under the camper's awning as men with machine guns pace back and forth, inches from Gary's intentionally expressionless face. They are imagining the accolades, picturing the reward if this gringo can be taken into custody. There is no wind to evaporate the sweat seeping through his clothes. I am not allowed to go inside the camper to get any water for him. I can see by the way he pinches the bridge of his nose that the eyeball-squeezing headache left over from his dengue fever has returned. I notice that he's lost weight; his long cargo shorts seem dangerously close to slipping from his hips.

He could easily reach into his pocket and pull out his wallet. Even twenty dollars each would probably be enough to bribe the men with guns. But I am watching what has become his new normal, and all I can hope is that he doesn't press his luck. If he goes too far we could lose the only means we have of driving away, the roof over our equally hard heads. Gary locks eyes with them instead and waits. He is calling their bluff, waving an invisible $500 traveler's check in the air. At last the phone rings and I can hear the police chief talking to someone, presumably Interpol. Gary is still staring down the guards when our passports are reluctantly stamped.

ON MY FATHER'S CRISPLY CREASED MAP, IT LOOKS LIKE A QUICK SIXTY miles from the Nicaraguan border to León, the birthplace of the country's most famous poet: Rubén Darío. But a mile away from the crossing the road turns to gravel. It is so dry and dusty that semitrucks and long-distance buses stir up a complete white-out in their wake. When the air clears, small cars are in ditches and dogs are dead.

It is a miserable four hours before we shudder to a stop at a six-dollar-a-night trucker's motel on the outskirts of León. It is far too hot to sleep inside the Avion, so we drag the sagging motel bed directly under the room's central ceiling fan and push the windows open through their metal bars. In a few hours it should be cool enough to sleep; there is plenty of time to explore the city first.

We've just started to walk when the skies open and it pours. Within minutes, streets flood and water slops over the transoms of living rooms. Rain pelts horizontally and we cannot see our feet or where the sidewalk ends underneath them. And then, just as suddenly, the deluge stops and the streets glow in a silvery light that forgives everything it took to get here.

> *Therefore to be sincere is to be strong.*
> *Bare as it is, what glimmer hath the star;*
> *The water tells the fountain's soul in song*
> *And voice of crystal flowing out afar*

—RUBÉN DARÍO

I am suddenly ravenous, and we sit down at a sidewalk café table overlooking rain-slicked stone lions guarding the León cathedral.

"Están mirando sobre el poeta Darío. Él duerme adentro."

A voice over my shoulder says the lions are watching over the famous poet laid to rest inside the cathedral. It belongs to a boy about as old as I was my first time here. He is barefoot, his zipper isn't quite closed, and he doesn't tell us his name. His hair is neatly combed and his face scrubbed clean. A full belly peeks out from under the one button fastened on his short-sleeved shirt.

"Tome mi fotografía, sólo diez cordobas," he bargains as he sits down on the empty chair at our table. It'll cost us ten cordobas, or about a dollar, to take his picture. I have never formed a mental image of what my little brother would have looked like if he had posed beside my sister and me in my father's slides of Central America. To me he is arrested in time, a tormented toddler forever on Santa's lap. But this boy's audacity is straight out of my father's playbook, and for the first time I have a sense of the savvy hustler my little brother might have become.

"Oh yeah, tough guy, how about one cordoba?" Gary counters, laughing as he holds up one finger.

"Okay," Tough Guy answers without hesitation, holding up ten fingers. "Pero, diez fotos." Either way, he's getting his dollar's worth.

We spend an hour watching vestiges of lightning and pressing our faces against the cool condensation of bottles of Victoria beer. I can't stop smiling at Tough Guy, but he prefers to assume serious poses for Gary's ten digital portraits, one elbow propped on the table and the other on his hip, eyes drilling directly into the lens.

He clearly isn't impressed by the results on Gary's viewfinder and motions for us to follow him to a small plaza behind the cathedral. Which is where an itinerant photographer named Jesús works. He uses a homemade camera that looks like a cardboard shoebox covered with leopard skin. For another ten cordobas we pose for him as Tough Guy supervises.

It's a primitive two-step process: a negative of a negative to make a positive, chemicals right there in a plastic bucket. The result resembles a daguerreotype—our gestures blurred and eyes glazed like travelers from another century. Gary snaps a digital photo of our oddly intimate portrait and offers to e-mail it to the photographer, but Jesús has never heard of the Internet.

Tough Guy spies another sucker sitting down for a beer and darts away before I can get close enough to pat his head, or, worse yet, hug him. I watch him leave, knowing something has changed. Time has relinquished a tiny piece of power over me. All the frustration and brutality of the border are behind us now, the dividing line a meaningless artifice. I have collected another entrada, but it is Nicaragua that has entered me.

Chapter Nineteen

THE PUBLISHER'S WIFE

Nicaragua did not agree with me as much the first time. We stopped in León only long enough for another wheel repair and then headed for the closest beach, Poneloya, this time not for my little sister to recuperate but for me.

> **FEBRUARY 5-11, 1974**
>
> Met local news publisher and enjoyed house facilities while there. 1st Teri sick, then I. Doctor said malaria?

My head begins to throb as I read those words. Why is there a question mark after the diagnosis? Was the doctor not certain or my mother not concerned? I flip through the pages, looking for another hospital admission card like the one she saved after my sister's fall in

El Salvador. Simple blood tests would have settled it; even in 1974 there were medicines we could have taken. All I find is one line she wrote a few days earlier, in Honduras.

Spent night on roadside. Got bug bites.

After twenty-one separate truck breakdowns and hemorrhaging savings, contracting malaria warranted only a shoulder-shrugging question mark from my mother. So much had already been taken from her: her three-year-old son, her home in the Oregon woods, and all contact with her own mother and sister. She had no power other than denial, and like the shoot-out in Mexico, malaria became just another visitor in the night. She never referred to it—or to the woman who nursed me back to health—again.

It is this woman's husband who has always played the starring role in the slide-show version of our time in Nicaragua. He's the one my father remembers. Rodolfo was a prominent newspaper publisher who owned the land behind the slice of Poneloya beach that my father picked as a camp spot. I've often wondered what would have happened if Rodolfo had called the cops on what were essentially foreign squatters. I have a feeling it was his wife who took the phone from his hand and said, "Let's hear their story first."

Yanina is a memory only I can recover, and I've returned to León to find her. Her cool hands and gentle words soothed me when my mother couldn't. She made salty soups and soft breads, and she squeezed guava juice from the fruit of trees in her garden for me to drink. I can't remember how tall she was or the color of her hair, only that she smelled of lavender and talcum powder. Her lap was never too tired for my sweaty, clingy body, and when she had to move from room to room she carried me on her sturdy hips.

"Mi mono mono," she called me—her cute little monkey. And when my mother and I recovered, she, like Yolanda in El Salvador, wrote her name in the front of my mother's journal. I am still clinging to the hope that I am not too late to thank her.

"What do you think are the chances she'd remember me?" I ask Gary.

"A camper with US license plates staggering up to her doorstep and depositing a mother and daughter with malaria in her lap?" Gary is sure that we made a lasting impression. "The question is whether she'll answer her doorbell if she sees you coming."

On our second day in León, Gary and I begin the search for Yanina and Rodolfo. The temperature is in the upper nineties, and I carry two bottles of water in my bag. It isn't enough to prevent the headache from returning.

"I think I'm having a malaria flashback," I tell Gary.

"It's a little early for gin and tonics" is his way of telling me to buck up.

Finding Ernesto in El Salvador has transformed my mother's journal into a treasure map. Connecting with actual human beings who crossed paths with my childhood feels like a resurrection—or at least confirmation that the slide show has roots in reality. I know time has replaced agony with adventure, that our collective, celebrated exploration of a continent is the unconscious camouflage of my family's grief. But however faded the truth has become, its faint outlines are still there. Names inscribed in handwriting other than my mother's offer more than third-party validation. They give me hope that the camper is also out there waiting for me.

But with the dentist, at least I had an address to go on. This time the journal simply lists the names Rodolfo and Yanina, plus all their kids and the underlined words León, Nicaragua. The owner of a local bookstore tells us that Rodolfo's paper, El CentroAmericano, has been out of print for years. Then, as if that isn't disheartening enough, "Pienso que él es muerto."

My head throbs with his casual surmise that Rodolfo is dead. If there is one person as invincible as my father, I have always assumed it is Rodolfo. The slide-show version of this man is a character I treasure. In Rodolfo my father found a fellow rebel, and he filled my head with man-crush tales of how tough Rodolfo was, how he could twist ordinary words into weapons. I studied journalism in college not to be like Bob Woodward but to be like Rodolfo. In the heirloom that is our family history he is heroic, a Sandinista rebel with a determined woman at his side. He can't be dead.

Almost as an afterthought, the bookstore owner tells me to check a sewing machine store a few blocks away. One of the women there might know where Yanina lives, assuming *she* is still alive. We duck back out into the searing, merciless sun. My hat feels like it is trying to choke my head as we make our way to the sewing machine shop. Life-sized, faded murals and protest graffiti dot our path like accusatory mile markers—the CIA as a giant, slithering snake; Ronald Reagan sitting on the head of a peasant woman in a field; Henry Kissinger wearing a clown's hat. Yanina's gracious sympathy for Americans might very well have been replaced with hostility and resentment.

We smell the rainstorm before we feel it, negative ions lifting and swirling the dust from the street under our feet. Just like yesterday's storm, it advances through León's streets in a frontal assault, and buildings only two blocks away are erased as we watch, edges and rooflines turned into a smear of chalky white. It keeps coming, and soon we can barely see each other through the downpour.

Someone shouts from a doorway, and I can make out only a Yankees cap and a waving arm. A sixteen-year-old boy named Pedro is apparently skipping school and invites us to take shelter in his living room. We step over a shinbone-high threshold obviously designed with the exact height of León's frequently flooded streets in mind. It is cool and dark inside, the walls above a high-water line painted bright turquoise and covered with baseball pennants.

Pedro's mother ducks into the house, sheltering a new haircut under a hasty hat of drenched newspaper, and instead of being annoyed to find two strangers dripping all over her living room floor, she invites us to stay for lunch. But when the rain stops, as suddenly as it began, we thank them both and head out for the sewing machine repair shop instead.

A dozen women are waiting in line for alterations when we finally find it, and after passing around my mother's journal there is general consensus that Rodolfo's wife still lives in León. Little girls adrift in strange countries latch on to comforting, maternal women with something close to desperation, and it may be too much to hope that the object of my adoration felt anything close to reciprocity. But still, a flutter of feeling lucky takes its place beside the squirming in my stomach that tells me I'm nervous, too.

"Ella es mi prima." A cousin is suspicious; she wants to know why two Americans are asking for Yanina. "¿Qué negocio tiene usted con ella?"

Twenty minutes later, we are standing outside a modest one-story home surrounded by a wrought-iron fence and flaming orange birds-of-paradise. The doorbell seems rudely loud and insistent, yet Yanina welcomes us into her living room as if she has been expecting us.

"Come inside, even hell would melt in León this time of day," she says. She is speaking deliberate, polite-hostess English, and I realize her cousin must have telephoned to tell her two sweaty Americans were on their way to her house. That is apparently all she knows. My heart sinks. She does not seem to recognize me; I look nothing like the little girl she nursed through the fevers of malaria thirty years ago.

Yanina is small, solid, and much older than the gentle angel I remember. Her dark hair is pulled back over a wide, square face, and a cotton print dress hangs off her broad shoulders at right angles. She is a grandmotherly warrior, kind and vigilant. Her home is fan-cool and shutter-dark, and every end table, countertop, and mantle is crowded with family photographs.

It is time to show her the prints I've made of my father's slides. There's one of me on a beach that could be anywhere—I am a purple sliver in sunset silhouette. Then there are blurry images of well-dressed children taking turns at a hanging piñata. It was her oldest daughter Monica's first communion party. Yanina squints and lifts the picture closer to her glasses. Then she pats it to her chest and squeezes her eyes closed.

"Teresita," she says when she opens them again, and I lean toward her for the kiss I know is coming.

She remembers me. Not the me who is the woman sitting in her living room fighting back unexpected tears of gratitude and barely dared hope, but the child I have always remained in her mind. On the wall hangs a photograph of a silver-haired, handsome man at a Roosevelt White House press conference, and Yanina addresses the image as though it could talk back.

"Rodolfo, look who came back to us."

We have missed greeting Rodolfo in person by seven years.

"She is strong and healthy now; it's a miracle."

Yanina has had no one to practice English with now that her children are grown and scattered across two continents. She is much more tolerant of my grammatical mistakes than her own so she switches to speaking mostly in Spanish. She still owns the Poneloya beach house, with its deep verandas, shady guava trees, sand dunes, and nesting sea turtles. Monica runs a travel agency now; Yanina's oldest son, Gustavo, lives in the United States. Yanina settles back in her chair as I translate for Gary. I need him to follow everything. These are nuances I will want to replay over and over, to fill the spaces between my father's slides.

"You wanted another brother so much that you asked me to give you one of my sons," she says, reaching over to pat my hand. "You didn't think I'd miss just one when I have so many."

Yanina excuses herself for a moment and leaves the room.

"She knows about your brother's death," Gary says, surprised. "Your mother must have finally talked about it."

Yanina returns to the living room with a bound set of *El Centro-Americano* from the early 1970s, and Gary and I flip through delicate, yellowing pages. Rodolfo was the godson of General Anastasio Somoza, but his beliefs were molded by the poets and laborers of León, and he wrote a column called *Mas o Menos*—more or less. He befriended an American family on the beach in Poneloya just five years before the Sandinista revolution.

My father's timing couldn't have been better. He drove our limping camper onto the beach in front of Rodolfo's home during a brief respite between his host's stints in jail. He may have been Somoza's godson, but that didn't protect him when he began criticizing Somoza's biological son in the pages of *El CentroAmericano*.

"Rodolfo did not always think of consequences," Yanina says. "A little like your father perhaps."

No wonder she showed such sympathy for my fevered, disconnected mother. She knew how hard it is to keep the horizon level for the sake of children. The Poneloya beach house was as much a safe haven for Yanina as it was for me. Holding a family together must have been second nature to her by the time ours collapsed at her front door.

I remember watching her strong arms reaching over me to tug on the chain that dangled from the ceiling fan above my hammock. It couldn't circle fast enough to bring relief. In my fevered state I flopped my head to the side to see the beach where Jenny and Monica were splashing in the waves.

Far behind them, I saw my father walk on water.

FEBRUARY 5TH–11TH, 1974

Lots of children to play. Rich. Were very well treated.

Dave rode surfboard.

There is something about Rodolfo's story that makes as little sense now as watching my father walk on water did to a feverish seven-year-old. Journalists unfriendly to the Somoza regime suffered worse punishments than jail time in the years that followed our departure from Nicaragua; it was the 1978 assassination of the publisher of Nicaragua's other major newspaper, *La Prensa*, that became a tipping point in the revolution. How did Rodolfo escape a similar fate?

"The new rulers assumed that any enemy of their enemy was a friend," Yanina explains. Rodolfo's history of jailings under Somoza's regime put him on the good side of the Sandinistas. "When the revolution came, the new government made Rodolfo ambassador to Colombia."

It is easier to picture Yanina nursing the wounded on the battleground than entertaining politicians in some faraway embassy. The woman sipping guava juice in her quiet living room a quarter of a century later tells us that she and Rodolfo grew disillusioned with the rigid controls of the Sandinistas.

"I had it up to here with politics and war," she says, drawing a thin finger across her wrinkled neck. "I read only poetry now, like most Nicaraguans."

The family ended up in exile, living in Miami. Far from her beloved homeland of arched verandas and guava groves, she watched American TV shows to improve her English.

"'Like sands through the hourglass, so are the *Days of Our Lives*,'" she says, eyes closed.

It was years before it was safe to return to Nicaragua, and even though *El CentroAmericano* was the oldest newspaper in the country at the time, it was forced to stop printing in 1979. Yanina's sister brings us fresh guava juice and marzipan cookies on a silver tray; we are nearing the end of the story.

"Él murió de un corazón quebrado." She says Rodolfo died of a broken heart, as though *El CentroAmericano* had been her husband's true love. I see a little of my mother's sadness in her eyes, those of a woman who packed up her entire family to follow her husband around the world. For both of them loyalty came with a high price.

The air between us is heavy, and I can't tell if it is sweat or tears that trickle down Yanina's glistening face. My parents never looked back when we left her care, never even wrote to her when they heard of the *La Prensa* publisher's assassination. Like the dentist's in El Salvador, hers is a story they have largely forgotten. But back then I was a needy weed clinging to the soil of Yanina's garden, and I wonder if my mother was as devastated as I was when we drove away.

"I don't think it really mattered to her," Yanina answers. The pink, syrupy guava juice in her glass is mingling with melting ice cubes, diluting. She presses the cool condensation to her cheek, and I can see that the effort to find soothing words is draining. "Nothing could bring your brother back."

We should be going. If we stay any longer this weary woman will feel as though she must take care of me again. Besides, she is leaving on a trip to Managua tomorrow. Gary takes a picture, and Yanina holds my hand long after the shutter clicks. What matters to her is that I found my way back. She is squeezing encouragement straight to my heart.

Another sudden downpour finds us behind the León market at six in the evening, where we take shelter in a bingo-hall-sized restaurant with dirt floors and crowded picnic tables.

"¿Un menú por favor?" Gary asks a woman carrying a plate of food.

She laughs and points to the sidewalk. Under a faded awning stand seventeen steaming cauldrons and a charcoal grill piled high with meat. For a total of three dollars, we fill our plates with avocado-and-egg guacamole, lemon-and-garlic butter beans, raw pumpkin coleslaw, stuffed cabbage rolls, and chicken that slides off the bone. For two dollars more, we buy an entire bottle of seven-year-old Nicaraguan rum called Flor de Caña.

Chapter Twenty

BUTTERFLIES

Northern Nicaragua defiantly straddles a hump of mountains that slopes to the seas on either side. It has always been a breeding ground for revolutionaries; leaving León we drive through villages that seem like backdrops of a war movie long ago abandoned. We pass cooperative coffee farms and dilapidated Sandinista relocation camps with billboards touting the country's impressive literacy rate.

We are trying to find a place called Miraflor. In the newest Nicaraguan guidebook it is billed as a nature reserve in the cool mountains with solar-powered bungalows. But when I stop to ask directions from farmworkers picking coffee beans, they have never heard of it. So it's up to me to decide which of the turnoffs vaguely leading north to take, interpreting the book's glowing descriptions by gut feel and crossed fingers. We lock the truck's hubs into four-wheel drive, and the F-350 picks its way over roads made more of boulders than of gravel.

Two kids, in ragged clothes and bare feet, stand like sentries in the dusty distance. When they see us approaching, they run out into the road and fill a pothole with shovelfuls of dirt and hold out their hands for tips as we pass. When the dust clears and we can see through the side-view mirrors, the kids have stopped counting coins and are retrieving the dirt. There will be an even deeper pothole whenever the next truck comes along.

In three hours we travel twelve miles. Even butterflies keep pace, bobbing alongside our open windows. At least they won't impale themselves in the truck's front grill, extracted by Gary in what has become a morbid twilight ritual. While I enter notes about each day's travels and epiphanies in my laptop, he collects the day's smashings and compares them to images in the one hardcover book he insisted on bringing: an oversized, illustrated text called *Butterflies of the World*. Across the camper's tiny kitchen table he begins to sketch, and before he puts his set of colored pencils back in its thin tin box, he makes notes of details like the temperature and elevation at each campsite. He is creating his own slide show, paying respects to those creatures who suffer for our progress.

We are making precious little of it today. The light is fading when we drive up to a group of villagers standing in the road and I hop out, hoping they will know the way to Miraflor. But even though they all speak Spanish the conversation is futile and one-sided.

"Isn't there a phone number listed in the guidebook?" Gary asks me when I return. He digs out the satellite phone. "If you get someone from the resort on the line then maybe they can talk to one of these locals and get us pointed in the right direction."

It is a good plan, but none of the men in the group will touch the phone. I try the only woman instead. She looks at me as though I have passed her a hand grenade. She stares at the phone in her palm as if deciding whether to fling it into the rocky field in front of us. Then she tentatively presses the keypad into her forehead. When nothing happens she turns it around the other way and presses it to her forehead again. I realize she has heard of phones but never used one. The men back away and she hands the phone to me without a word.

For only the second time on our trip, we have to camp on the side of the road. It is getting dark, and we begin a dialogue of rationalization.

"The last time we did this our steps got stolen," I remind Gary. We've been substituting a twenty-pound tree stump ever since the little-devils incident in Todos Santos, Guatemala.

"If you want to drive back in the dark we can try," he says. "But if I can't see to dodge the potholes, the water tank might crack all the way."

It would be crazy to continue; we can't risk losing the tank. Without the ability to store and chlorinate our own water we will be tethered to towns, restaurants, and hotels for the rest of the journey. We are surrounded by fragrant mountain orchids, but I feel on edge, conspicuous. The Avion is bigger than every hut we've passed. In a country with a population of five million people there are fewer than three hundred thousand cars, let alone one-ton trucks with four-wheel drive. We're glaringly wealthy North Americans in a place where the United States sabotaged a revolution.

"Babe, it's been twenty-five years. They may not have phones, but I'm sure someone's told them the war's over," Gary says.

Tonight his sketchbook entry reads, "80 degrees, 4,200 feet." Next to "Location" he writes only, "Somewhere?" We lower the miniblinds of the Avion's windows like it's an ostrich trying to stick its head in the sand. There are footsteps and whispers around the camper, but I am too drained to go outside and shoo onlookers away. When the night cloaks the camper in comforting anonymity, we climb into bed and I reach for Gary. No one will hear us. There are no streetlights or glowing televisions, and the star-splattered sky is cavernous and endless. It is so quiet I can hear Gary's quickening pulse, like the breeze fluttering through the stems of orchids.

And then, a single shot from a high-powered rifle splits the silence. There is nothing natural about that sound, no way for orchids

and dirt roads to absorb its mechanical, threatening crack. It is close
and intentional. We wait for another round but nothing comes; it is as
if the ghosts of revolutions simply want to warn us they are watching.
We are intruding in one of the most remote parts of the least popu-
lated country in all of Central America.

What seemed like a spontaneous detour twelve hours ago has
turned a corner into reckless danger. Not a soul in the world knows
where we are, including the two of us. Our bodies could decompose
under fluttering clouds of butterflies before our absence would even be
noticed, leaving my parents with nothing to bury next to my brother.

It takes me a full minute to process the fact that this is the second
time guns have fired over our heads. But this time I am consumed
more by remorse than the primal fear that gripped me by the guts in
Mexico. I am clinging to the man I love instead of digging through
a stack of paperbacks, searching for a weapon. My instincts have
changed from reactionary to resigned.

This time, I can't imagine gripping that cold steel weapon in my
hands. It would steal Nicaragua from me, and it is better simply to
spend the night awake.

Chapter Twenty-One

INNOCENCE

I am filled with Nicaragua's earnest verse, toughened by its lopsided struggles, frustrated by its secrets. We leave this country of warriors and poets never knowing if the bucolic-sounding respite of Miraflor even exists. It is only when we stop at a lodge just across the border in northern Costa Rica called Hacienda Inocentes that my shoulders relax and my jaw unclenches. It's a base camp, occupied mostly by visiting biologists, in the shadow of a volcano. Scientists gather around us to watch, as curious as if an Asian one-horned rhino had wandered into their midst, while we back up the camper to a trellis of night-blooming dragon-fruit flowers and a glistening blue swimming pool.

"Whatever they charge per night I'll pay double," Gary says.

I'm not certain I will ever want to leave. After Nicaragua's relentless tension and poverty resulting from decades of civil wars, Costa Rica seems almost obscenely tranquil. Instead of guidebook warnings to avoid camping, there is an embarrassment of options. More than 25 percent of Costa Rica's land mass is protected in national parks and preserves, a bigger commitment to conservation than that found in any other country on earth.

Gliding through cool, chlorinated water as the sun rises the next morning, I can't fathom why my parents are trying to build a tourist resort on an almost inaccessible, impoverished Nicaraguan island instead of in the primeval paradise that is its southern neighbor. In the course of one morning walk we are:

1. treated to the flutterings of giant blue butterflies called *Morpho peleides;*
2. followed by chattering orange spider monkeys through refreshingly cool jungle canopy; and
3. guided back to the hacienda pool by the calls of a pair of chestnut-mandibled toucans nesting in a guanacaste tree.

After a dinner served on a veranda with tropical hardwood floors and views of Mount Orosi in the setting sun, we sleep with the camper doors wide open. But this country has not always been as pure and blameless as the name of our first stopover implies. The United States–backed Contra rebels used a drug-smuggling airstrip near here to launch attacks against Sandinista forces in southern Nicaragua. Its discovery was one of the smoking guns in the Iran-Contra scandal during the Reagan years. But the Costa Rican government claimed no knowledge of the airstrip, somehow not noticing the rumble of planes in almost nightly takeoffs between volcanoes.

It would feel disloyal to the struggling country to our north not to try to find the airstrip. We stock up on fresh *panadería* rolls and Costa Rica's national beer, Imperial, and head deeper into the Guanacaste Península. My teeth grate at every police checkpoint, but instead of bribes we are asked only for verification of insurance and if we need help with directions.

We do, actually, because the airstrip we are searching for is not on official maps. The closest village is one I can't pronounce, Cuajiniquil, where the dirt road turns into a series of river crossings. The first one is shallow enough to cross with four-wheel drive, and it is easy to imagine supply convoys fording it under cover of darkness. A few miles farther and we come to evidence we are on the right path: an abandoned military police academy that was once a CIA training camp.

"You can't convince me no one knew what was going on here," Gary says. "They just looked the other way."

But in another few miles the dirt road washes out again, and this crossing is one that would certainly turn back curious villagers with no transportation options other than horseback or motorcycle. Gary wades out to test the depth and comes back wet to the waist. The truck would flood. If we are meant to find proof of our country's secret sabotage we will have to swim for it.

Gary holds his camera high above his head with one hand, like a war photographer in the Vietnam jungle. I am in charge of keeping the truck keys dry. The water is viscous with sediment but cool against the skin, and we scramble up the opposite bank with shoes squelching river goo and clothes plastered to our bodies. The canopy narrows into an arch overhead, and it is sauna steamy and sweat-lodge dark. That something sinister and secret played out here is not hard to fathom.

In another thousand meters we notice light filtering through the jungle to our left.

It is a clearing, overgrown but uniformly lower than the surrounding vegetation. I let Gary's body knock aside spiderwebs and clumps of willowy bamboo and follow him into the opening. The sun is so bright it takes a second for my eyes to adjust. We are at the edge of what was once a six-thousand-foot runway, easily capable of landing C-130s.

It feels uncomfortably complicit, two unaffected Americans standing out in the open of an ugly, forgotten war. It's as if the jungle is trying to cover up the evidence and render what happened here irrelevant in the grander scheme of natural splendor. From the air, only the runway's shape would give it away: a dead-straight scar slicing through the remote fringes of what is now a national park.

The outdoor showers at the Santa Rosa National Park campground are a perfect way to wash away the remnants of a day filled with muddy truth. By the time we arrive it is too dark to see the howler monkeys in the branches above us, but they are close enough that their hoots and grunts seem personal, even judgmental. It makes me nervous.

"Gary, is it true the males will piss on you if they think you're a threat?"

The monkeys hush, as if they're listening for his answer.

"Only if they don't have any shit handy to throw."

We wrap our sunburned, naked bodies in towels and dart back to the camper by flashlight.

FEBRUARY 14, 1974

What a trip. Had to ford two streams. Thought it might
be deserted beach—
Hah—a real tourist trap

My mother's journal is like a checklist challenging us to measure up. We've already crossed off river fording, but we haven't camped at a beach since Mexico, so we set out the next morning to find one. Within hours we are as disappointed as my mother was. I'm not sure what she meant by "tourist trap," but today the deserted beaches are off limits to tourists. They're part of giant resort developments that have turned the northern Costa Rican coast into a gated expat colony of rich Americans.

It is a bumpy day's drive south before we find a beach with public access. It is packed with surfers, and we park the camper next to the barbed-wire-topped wall of an overpriced hotel. After a few hours of watching the waves we return to find the Ford's passenger door pried open and my wallet stolen from the front seat where I had idiotically left it in plain sight. At least the Avion stood its ground. The screened window is slashed but the thieves didn't make it past the camper's old-school series of dead bolts. Still, it's the first break-in of the entire trip and a bleak welcome back to "civilization."

Even more disturbing is how quickly I revert to my type A, need-to-feel-in-control personality. All it takes is one call on the satellite phone to my aunt back in Oregon and my credit cards are deactivated, but I still insist on filing a police report for the stolen cash. It is Sunday and I should be grateful that a cop, in shorts and a soccer shirt, even opens the door to the un-air-conditioned, one-room Matalpo police station. But instead I'm irrationally irritated that he just adds our form to an overstuffed three-ring binder of thefts and break-ins. There isn't even funding for a computer, yet somehow I expect round-the-clock patrols and signs warning visitors of the danger. I demand an insurance form. We've been pulled over at every town in Costa Rica and asked to produce proof of the insurance we had to buy at the border, and I'm determined to get my money's worth. The cop hands over a photocopied form to fill out and tells me the nearest city with a fax machine is Liberia, halfway back to Nicaragua.

I can't let it go, and that night I'm both indignant and jittery. It seems like a lifetime ago that we slept with the door of the camper wide open just to smell the night-blooming dragon-fruit flowers of Hacienda Inocentes.

"What if they come back at night and try to finish the job?"

Gary groans but agrees to set the truck's alarm just in case. I have accounted for everything but the fact that two restless bodies lying directly over the cab create more movement than accomplished thieves. I roll over to get a sip of water and set off the alarm. It is earsplitting punishment for my paranoia, and I find it impossible to fall back asleep. Even the sound of tree branches scraping against the camper's roof unnerves me, and Gary climbs on top of the Avion in the middle of the night to break them off. Crawling back into bed, he doesn't have to say a word. I know I'm being unreasonable, but a few months on the road has not yet taught me to accept setbacks with equanimity.

The truck door's damage means that we will have to get repairs at the Ford dealership in the capital. On the drive to San José, we cross a bridge controlled by a troop of male howler monkeys. They balance along the cement railing on leathery buttocks, legs splayed wide enough to allow them to stroke their oversized testicles as we pass. Costa Rica's lushness seems a tad too lurid now, and I am relieved when we finally pull into a run-down, American-owned RV campground in a suburb called Belén. There's even a mall within walking distance, and I file the insurance claim that a more sanguine traveler would admit is ridiculous.

It has been a week since we've had Internet access, and opening e-mail is an unexpected attitude check. When we skim through news from Washington, DC, the exhibitionist monkeys of the Costa Rican countryside seem less vulgar by comparison. We are missing scandals, disasters, protests, and retaliations more consequential than anything that has happened to us on the road. But instead of my usual visceral reactions, I let myself feel the gratitude of distance. This trip is a chance to loosen the grip of outrage, and I will not rob myself again.

The parents of my best friend in high school have sent us the name and phone number of a foreign exchange student they once hosted from San José.

"We took in Arnoldo long after you girls went away to college. Look him up!" the e-mail urges.

I almost delete the message; I don't know Arnoldo or whether we will have anything in common other than brief teenage sojourns in Hillsboro, Oregon. But then I think of Ernesto and Yolanda and Rodolfo and Yanina and how much I would have missed if my parents hadn't wandered into their lives, however briefly. I cut and paste Arnoldo's address and send him an e-mail.

The next day, he picks us up at the Belén RV Park in a black SUV with tinted windows. Arnoldo has transformed from a shy high school exchange student to a Latin recording star with a hit CD. The liner notes are filled with smoldering, moody portraits, but in person he is teddy-bear cheerful and cheek-pinching cute.

He is married to the Costa Rican equivalent of a young Kelly Ripa. Mariamalia is seven months pregnant with twins and on maternity leave from her television show. She is craving Lebanese food and gracious enough to let two complete strangers tag along. They take us on a circuitous route through Escazú, their trendy, upscale neighborhood, the Beverly Hills of San José, only more historic. Exquisite colonial churches and leafy parks are connected by streets barely wide enough for their SUV.

"In Escazú they say all the women are witches." Mariamalia winks in the rearview mirror as we wait behind a horse-drawn cart filled with necklaces of dried onions. "My grandmother, my mother, even me—you never know."

Chapter Twenty-Two

BEWITCHED

There is a fine line between charmed and spellbound, and we drive along that line to a five-star restaurant tucked into the woods. We have been eating a steady street-food diet of beans and rice topped with pickled onions and hot peppers. But over white linen tablecloths and a view of the San José Valley, we dine on imported olives and rosemary hummus. In the cleanest fleece and cargo pants we own, Gary and I must look like uncouth American guests relaxing after a day on set with Mariamalia. For the first time on the trip, Gary doesn't have to rely on me to translate, and the meals we share with Arnoldo and Mariamalia over the next few days are food for his soul.

"So why is this country the only one in Latin America that manages to exist without a standing army?"

"It isn't that we're all super-pacifists in Costa Rica." Mariamalia is bantering with Gary, clearly proud of her country's priorities but not wanting to seem immodest. "It's that we don't really want anyone to notice how lucky we are."

Arnoldo finishes her thought. "We Ticos lead a charmed existence compared to our neighbors. We don't start revolutions, and the United States pretty much leaves us alone because we don't make waves."

Mariamalia nods between forkfuls of grape leaves. Arnoldo laughs. "I'm telling you, she never eats this much. I think we are going to have baby piglets."

She pretends to glare, and Arnoldo kisses a wisp of wavy brown hair from her forehead. Their affection is as touching as Ernesto describing Yolanda, and between the lines of dinner discussion I see the passion of Rodolfo and Yanina. More than anything they exude gratitude, and I realize our paths crossed just in time. I need some of it to rub off on me.

As soon as the babies are born, Mariamalia's smile will again light up the television screens of San José, and Arnoldo will start working on his next CD. But tonight, they are ours alone, and she is teaching us her favorite Costa Rican sayings.

"Okay, this one is what I used to say to my parents whenever I got in trouble for staying out too late," she says, acting it out with pouting lips and hands on hips. "'Nadie me quita lo bailado, lo comido, y lo viajado.' Or 'Nadie me quita bailado' for short."

I try it out, the round *o* sounds rolling around in my mouth like marbles. "So are you going to translate or make me figure it out for myself?"

This beautiful ambassador of a tender country says that it means "No one can ever take away what I have danced, eaten, and traveled." A blush rises from my throat all the way to my ears, and I hope she never finds out that she is talking to a woman who just a few days earlier filed a police report purely on belligerent principle. I have allowed petty annoyances and disappointments to detract from an incredible privilege. A year from now I won't even remember what my stolen wallet looked like, but Mariamalia's motto will stick with me for a lifetime.

What we thought would be a short stay turns into a weeklong wait for the replacement lock to fix the Ford's door, and we settle into a routine at the Belén RV Park. Every day in the rainy season starts with bright blue skies. Clouds build by lunch, and from one in the afternoon until one in the morning it pours. Mariamalia and Arnoldo do their best to distract us. He is opening a snack franchise called Get Nuts and a coffee shop, and he takes us to the upscale mall where he's hoping to beat Starbucks to the punch. Squealing girls carrying Gucci bags pose for selfies with Mariamalia and Arnoldo, and it's a head-spin to remember that a few days ago we drove through places still unpenetrated by cell phone signals.

Each time Arnoldo and Mariamalia drop us off at the campground, the ground is so saturated my boots leave heel-shaped puddles in the flattened grass. In five days our truck tires have sunk to their lug nuts in mud and I have returned to a mental state requiring sticky notes. I paper the camper's curved walls with pale yellow reminders of the kind of person I'm trying to outgrow. Check on the insurance claim just in case. Stock up on antibiotics. Look up the State Department website for travel warnings about Panama, the country we will enter next.

I stare at the blank strip of wood between the two cabinet doors above the sink, wondering if it's wide enough for another note. But Gary beats me to it. The note he wedges between the doors is decorated with a colored-pencil sketch of a tree with a little dialogue bubble coming from its branches: "Save me!"

He slaps another note on top of the pleading tree: "Stop writing these stupid lists and take off your clothes."

The patter of raindrops on the camper's metal roof reverberates like incessant knocking, but I'm laughing too hard to answer. Sloppy drips drizzle through the rubber seals around the ceiling fans, splashing off my naked shoulders. We flop onto our backs and take turns catching them with outstretched tongues.

The next morning Gary paints a gummy coat of aluminum waterproofing over the entire roof to stop the leaks, but he can do nothing to arrest the torment of the rainy season. We both catch colds, and I feel increasingly claustrophobic, confined to a small and stuffy space from which there is no escape. I can't imagine how my mother survived—cooped up in a camper with two small daughters pulling each other's hair and arguing about whose turn it was to turn the page in the *Little House on the Prairie* book. It must have driven her crazy, a condition I can relate to now that I have driven myself to that same place.

Despite my resolution to be more grateful and accepting, the notes I type into my computer each night begin to mimic the dreariness of my mother's journal. I should be committing my memories of Costa Rica's grandeur to the page: magnificent volcanoes, fish-full lakes, and operatic tropical birds. Instead I fixate on banal details—like the fact that there are only eleven inches between my nose and the Avion's rain-pummeled roof when I'm lying flat on my back in bed. If I roll over on my right side I squash Gary; if I roll over on my left side I have nine inches before my head will smack into an overhead kitchen cabinet. The walking space down the length of the camper is the width of an army cot, and we have to pass belly-to-belly for one person to climb into bed while the other brushes teeth in the kitchen sink. We play a hundred games of gin rummy because the sound of the rain on the roof makes it impossible to read.

One afternoon we kill time by dragging out the prints Gary made from my father's slides. The sun is shining in all of them. I am naked, soaping up in a Costa Rican stream. Shading my eyes with my hands on a deserted beach. Under a waterfall in a one-piece bathing suit. There's even one of my mother smiling into the camera with Jenny on her lap. I don't know which version to trust: my father's photographs or my mother's words.

There is the same disconnect in every country—exotic adventure on film, miserable pilgrimage on the page. I am beginning to realize they are equally unreliable as narrative. The very act of taking photographs contaminates reality, implying that a fleeting instant is somehow permanent and representative. But distilling an entire day into one or two incomplete sentences leaves out the pauses between exclamation points, the sustaining moments of tranquillity. What's missing from both my father's photos and my mother's words is the filter of time, the perspective of survival. The truth is what lingers, long after, in the chambers of the heart.

I can visualize the act of documenting the camper, if we ever find it, but not what Gary's camera or my words will really convey. I am not the first traveler to set out on a quest for place or origin, but finding the camper will be more than planting an I-lived-here flag in my history. It was built as the opposite of a permanent homestead, so can it ever anchor me? I am not sure I'll be ready to smile for a photo in front of a home I loved but that my brother never saw. I have no idea where finding it will fit along the continuum of grief to relief.

At last DHL delivers a replacement door lock for the F-350, and we hand a newly reissued credit card to the service desk at the San José Ford dealership. Our sojourn in the capital is over; we can embark again on our adventure. The camper I grew up in might still be out there, and Costa Rica has offered me fortitude for the search ahead. Yet somehow even a week in one spot has resurrected a little of the old me: the woman who constructs an order out of everything she can and relishes the little, predictable victories of schedules and checklists.

A part of me clings to the comfort of Mariamalia and Arnoldo's friendship. Like Shawn and Susie in Guatemala, they have become my Yanina and Rodolfo, my Yolanda and Ernesto. The difference is that I am no longer a child at the mercy of my parents' memories. I can create my own.

Mariamalia and Arnoldo send us back to the Pan-American Highway with a care package of candied nuts, Arnoldo's latest CD to play in the cab, and their address, printed neatly on a sticky note.

Chapter Twenty-Three

PANAMA

If there is a border I've been dreading most, it is Panama's. Not surprising, considering the welcome I got the first time. I was accustomed to my mother asking me to "go talk to the guards" and "help Daddy stay out of trouble." I just wasn't prepared to see him barefoot, tied to a chair, with his wrists strapped together by his own belt, refusing to pay another bribe. I started to cry and couldn't stop. Not when the man behind the desk pushed the hair out of my eyes and gave me candy. Not even when the guards gave back my daddy's shoes and untied his hands. Not even when he wiped my runny nose with his thumb and told me everything was all right. It wasn't. I could feel his heart pounding as he carried me back to the camper, and he smelled sour—just like he did when he picked me up from my sleepover on the night my brother died.

On to Panama, but not without a hassle.

This skinny, west-to-east-slanted country, split in half by a man-made ditch, will no doubt still be a hassle. The fact that Panama uses the dollar as currency or that its American expat population might someday equal that of Mexico or Costa Rica does not erase its status as the Central American country the United States has invaded most recently. All I want from Panama is a springboard between the first leg of our journey and the vast continent that I hope contains the old camper.

It turns out to be a relatively painless border crossing, once the requisite twenties are distributed among *tramitaros*. There isn't even a suggestion of searching the Avion; maybe my father's ordeal earned us some kind of karmic hassle pass. Whatever it is, I start to rewrite my mental script for Panama as soon as we peel off the Pan-American Highway onto a meandering road that loops through the Azuero Península.

To the left a thick cloak of jungle stretches to the ocean's shore, but if I look to the right we could be somewhere in Texas. Ours is not the only Ford; in fact, the shoulder is jammed with trucks attached to beat-up trailers. The occasion is a twice-weekly cattle auction, and we pick our way through Pepsi and sausage vendors to take seats in a covered metal grandstand.

All the men under thirty wear blue jeans and baseball caps with John Deere or New York Yankees logos, but everyone older wears straw hats with flipped-up brims and stylishly stitched cowboy boots. All of them juggle clipboards and pens, payroll pouches and handheld calculators. The enormous beasts jostle up a metal ramp into a holding pen, where two men hanging from scaffolding poke and prod them into an adjoining exhibition pen below the auctioneer. After driving through impoverished countries like El Salvador and Nicaragua, I think I'm hearing things when the auction begins. But the average bid seems to be between $350 and $450 a head.

I watch, horrified and mesmerized, as young boys dodge horns and hooves to attach paper auction numbers to the heaving sides of beef. Meanwhile, a crowd is gathering around our camper. A couple of Panamanian cowboys are pointing at the rows of stickers we've attached to the aluminum door: a flag for each country we've traveled through. We have just seen horns thrashing millimeters from their faces, but one of these tough guys asks us, "Isn't it dangerous to drive through Nicaragua?"

Panama isn't shaping up to be such a hassle after all. We drive away with the windows rolled down and doors unlocked. Gary leans back against the bench seat with one hand on the steering wheel and the other draped over my shoulders.

Under the weight of an impending downpour, the sky is glinting silver, pierced with biblical streams of sunlight. The southernmost ridge of mountains is backlit like the silhouette of a skinny horse's back: peaks and sways, curves and ribs. From a pull off at the top of the ridge, we look out over a herd of grazing cattle and a deserted scallop of pearly sand, palms, and mangroves.

There's a freedom and calmness to the quiet; I feel space settling in my soul and my blood flowing slower. The Azuero is so spread apart, so stretched thin, that jagged edges fall out of focus. Even the villages sprinkled throughout the peninsula seem to blend into the natural landscape instead of interrupting it. The houses are covered in crumbling red tiles the same color as the mud that made them, overlapped in graceful cascades. We stop in a tiny town called Parita to gas up, and while we're munching on stale potato chips the attendant asks if we're here to buy masks from Darido Lopez.

"Es famoso," he tosses out, as if a nonchalant tone will make up for bragging about the town's celebrity. He's even listed in one of the guidebooks. He works out of a lime-green house across the street. At first glance there is nothing to trumpet his fame, but when he comes to the door the bottom third of his white guayabera shirt is splattered with tongue red, fang ocher, cauldron black, and pus green. The inside of his house is as dark as the workshop of a madman ought to be. On a smattering of armless chairs and slipcovered sofas sit nine children—mixing, molding, and breathing life into outrageously freaky papier-mâché masks.

"I learned from my father and they learn from me."

I shudder to think of the bedtime stories told in this household. These quiet little kids are making masks with flaring nostrils, forked tongues, and razor-sharp fangs.

"In a few weeks there is a parade in a town called Chitré, and boys will terrorize their sisters and the meanest teachers," Darido laughs. "When they wear my masks their true identity is hidden and they are all dirty devils."

Darido's anticipatory delight reminds me of my grandfather in South Africa. He used to call my little sister and me "the devil's apprentices." When I tell Darido the story, the mask maker knows that I will, without a doubt, want a mask for myself. There is no gift shop in Darido's home; he makes each mask on commission.

"I always charge the same. It doesn't matter if you are a dirty devil or an ambassador. To me there is no difference."

We pay for two masks and promise to return to watch the Chitré parade and collect whatever monsters he creates. It is a luxury I'm still not accustomed to: the chance to double back and take my time. We have no deadlines or schedule to keep. This is a detour I didn't plan, a purchase I didn't budget, and I pinch the inside of my forearm to make sure it's still me.

Chapter Twenty-Four

BRIDGING THE GAP

Maps may show Panama's easternmost end butting up against South America like a normal border. But the bridge of connective jungle called the Darién Gap is impassable—fought over by competing indigenous groups, drug traffickers, jaguars, and crocodiles. The search for ocean passage around the Darién Gap took my parents about a month, an eternity even my slide-show memories can't reduce.

FEB 25TH, 1974

Found embassy. Closed 'til Wednesday

"Put that journal away," Gary teases. "A lot can change in thirty years."

He's grinning because the proof is in our guidebooks. Panama now has a bona fide RV park two hours west of Panama City called XS Memories, which is where we will stay while we search for a

155

modern-day Darién detour. It will be nothing like the first time. After 9/11, no passengers are allowed to travel on container ships, even to accompany their campers to another continent. We will have to send the Avion ahead of us by sea and catch up to it by air. But back in 1974 I didn't have to leave my home-on-wheels, as long as my father could find a ship big enough and cheap enough.

FEB 26TH, 1974

Drove around. Made some contacts. Found where people were waiting for ships—at Olympic stadium

I was more concerned with the half-blind kitten my sister and I found, wet and whimpering, behind the Panama City swimming stadium. We never knew exactly who or what poked out one of its yellow eyes, but my mother carefully scooped up the wounded kitten and brought him inside our camper.

"Girls, cover the table with the sheet from Mommy's bed," she told us. "I'm going to turn it into an operating table." I covered my eyes but I could hear the kitten squealing. I peeked through my fingers as my mother carefully scraped tendrils of pus from the empty eye socket and sewed it shut with her embroidery needle.

I am reminded of that crude operation when Gary and I pull into XS Memories. The American owners, Dennis and Sheila, have rescued dozens of wounded animals, and we park our camper among them, on a manicured lawn next to a freshly vacuumed outdoor swimming pool. There are sewer and electric hookups, and the sports bar at the heart of the complex is lined with championship pennants, rugby jerseys, and decades-old ticket stubs.

"We'll each have a bottle of whatever the local beer is," Gary says when we sit down at the bar that will become our base as we search for passage.

"You've clearly never had an Atlas before." Dennis laughs and hands us each two bottles. "Cheap stuff is so diluted you piss stronger than this."

Dennis is a muscular, moody man with a thinning ponytail under an endless variety of baseball caps. He met long and lanky Sheila in Las Vegas, where she ran a hotel and had something to do with raising and selling exotic snakes.

Now they are de facto zookeepers and camp counselors. Between the daily dramas of waitresses quitting and suppliers running out of ketchup, Sheila nurses animals to health and Dennis is organizing a through-the-locks kayak race across the Panama Canal. They are refurbishing an old ambulance for reliable transportation to the nearest hospital and trying to start a library for local kids. But instigating change takes enormous energy in the village of Santa Clara, even for unlikely guardian angels. The default setting of the expats who gather here is do nothing, collect a check, and drink too much. Dennis's dark tan doesn't hide the lines of frustration in his face. The weight of even a Virginia Slims cigarette slumps Sheila's tired arm over the bar, and I am reminded of my mother's face in all the photos from Panama.

It was near here that my father decided to drive us deep into the jungle, trying to camp for free while we waited for a way to South America. But even though the United States still controlled the canal, transient Americans were not allowed to camp in a military zone. So we went into hiding.

MARCH 8TH, 1974
Cop said it was against the treaty to camp here. Men!
Me and Jenny went to the authorities but it was a no
go. Went shopping and moved camp half mile from
locks—out of sight. Pleasant, tropical setting.

This is the other Panama I remember, days of hide-and-seek with my sister in the jungle and swinging from vines into rivers and lakes. Eventually, nineteen other travelers, in tents and campers, all trying to book passage from Colón to Colombia, joined us in our jungle hideout. Each day, to escape the attention of the zone police, we left our hidden compound and split up to go exploring.

MARCH 9TH, 1974

Went to Fort Lorenzo—the pirate Henry Morgan's
hideout. Climbed around rocks and walls and into dark
rooms. Hiked down cliff to a bay and went swimming.

Deal after deal fell through, and days turned into weeks. I was
glad. I learned to sneak up on giant blue morpho butterflies and hold
my breath while I plucked them from flowering vines. I tried to keep
them inside the camper as pets, but our half-blind kitten ripped off
their wings and squished their heads. My mother even showed us
how butterflies kiss each other, picking us up to her hip and batting
her eyelashes until they tickled ours. One afternoon the three of us
were walking back to camp from a swim in Gatun Lake when my
mother froze in place.

"Girls, don't move," she said in a low, I-mean-it voice. "See, over
there where the trees part? It's a mama panther and her babies."

I looked up and saw one solid black kitten in the mother's mouth
and another hiding between her legs. When I was born, my father
gave my mother a necklace charm: a solid gold cat with a kitten in its
mouth. On the day we saw the panthers, my mother and I looked at
each other in synchronized, unspoken astonishment. The charm had
come to life. The mother panther was slick and silent, and we held our
breath to better hear hers.

It was the exquisite fulcrum of instinct and curiosity, and we
were all six transfixed. The stealthy hunters broke the spell first and
padded off into the hills like shadows. At that moment, I decided
to name my half-blind, butterfly-killing kitten Pantera, the Spanish
word for panther.

Chapter Twenty-Five

RED MEAT

I have voluntarily gone without red meat for twenty years, smug in conscientious pseudo-vegetarianism. But in my nomadic childhood meat was a luxury. Gunfights over the roof of our camper were simply "Mexicans with guns," but each hamburger we ate was individually detailed in my mother's journal.

JANUARY 5TH, 1974—MEXICO CITY

Took subway to Western Union, got money—ate hamburgers (expensive) walked home

APRIL 9TH, 1974—CARACAS, VENEZUELA

Ate hamburguesas with papas fritas—yumm

On burger nights in my home-on-wheels, we took turns scraping the stuck-on crumbles from the cast iron skillet. I craved the fatty, rich flavor of meat, the way the smell smoked up the camper and settled into the cushions and carpet. That smell meant we were safe, for a while, not spending the night in a garage or on the side of the Pan-American Highway.

Tonight that smell is back, and it means something completely different: Sheila is grilling for the expats at XS Memories.

"We always do it for Oktoberfest," she explains. "But we could pretend it's for your birthday if you'd like."

I am about to turn thirty-seven, and the aroma of grilled meat is swirling all around me. I stare down at what will be my birthday dinner—Atlas beer and a mound of rice and beans—listening to my own inner lecture. Meat is the distance I have put between me and my childhood; my life is no longer a seesaw between feast and famine.

"I am in control," I whisper to myself. Okay, maybe it's more like a whimper.

I am so absorbed in my own memories that I almost don't see the tears in the corners of Gary's eyes. He is looking up at Sheila as if she might be an actual saint. Or his mother. They are the same, as far as bratwurst is concerned. His mother's cooking is the only part of his childhood he recites like a homily: Angie's tissue-thin apple-strudel pastry layers, her Depression-era penchant for margarine, the sausages that she soaked in beer and slathered with homemade sauerkraut.

He has admitted to no pangs of homesickness since we pulled out of his parents' Wisconsin driveway, but at Sheila's Oktoberfest he is overcome. He notices me staring, about to say something comfortingly mushy, and does what he always does to avoid being fussed over. He turns the attention to me. He spears a brat with his fork and slices it open lengthwise on my plate. Steam escapes from the split casing and rushes my resistance.

"Live a little," he prods. "You're not getting any younger."

Call it an emotional breakdown or breakthrough, but I begin my thirty-seventh year a carnivore again. That first bite of charred sausage casing is the next-best thing to hamburger crumbs on the bottom of a cast iron skillet. Gary leaps into the swimming pool fully clothed, a glimpse of the always-outdoors kid he once was. I plunge in after him, intoxicated with the smell of chlorine, salt air, and animal fat. The expats buy me weak Atlas beers all night, and I wander off to be serenaded by swaying palms, titi monkeys, and the starry Santa Clara sky. I'm not sure if Panama is changing me or resurrecting someone I once was.

I WAKE THE NEXT MORNING WITH A SPLITTING HANGOVER AND THE RE-alization that our drive has stalled. I check my laptop notes. We have spent twenty-three nights in the confines of a sports-bar campground. Worse yet, the agent of the freight line holding our $500 deposit tells us there isn't enough prepaid cargo to cover the ship's cost of passing through the Panama Canal. I might as well copy down my mother's journal entries and change the dates; nothing's changed except the prices.

MARCH 4TH
Boat fell through. Found another, better one—$50 deposit.

While we wait, the rainy season begins in Santa Clara, and daily torrential downpours take the place of sunny afternoons at the beach. If I stood in one place longer than the time it takes to drink an Atlas beer, I would look down and find mushrooms sprouting between my toes.

The rain pounds the camper walls closer together and compresses the air into barely breathable gel. Everything leaks. Even the drain plug in our Styrofoam cooler disintegrates, and melted ice soaks into the mezcal-stained carpet. Inside the Avion it smells like sweaty feet and rancid Wonder Bread.

The first actual spores we spot are in the bathroom, splotches of texture on the otherwise slick plastic shower walls. Then the mold spreads to the inside of the refrigerator, oozing from under rubber door seals. The screen over the casement windows turns mossy, and under our futon mattress we discover a thin, velvety carpet of light green sponge. We drag every last possession out onto the grass and give the camper's empty interior a sponge bath with bleach.

"And to think," Gary says as he snaps the fingers of his rubber gloves, "when you factor in crappy gas mileage and what we have to pay to camp every night, we could have ditched this giant germ jar and stayed in decent hotels."

I am not ready to admit that driving a camper as old as I am through a succession of Central American rainy seasons was a bad idea. Hotel hopping would have been even worse. I am not naturally nomadic and I feel safer sleeping in my own bed each night, even if it is moldy and perched precariously above four wheels. A part of me wishes for a pad of sticky notes to write down all the reasons this trip is still justified. Not that anything would stick on moldy walls.

"Well, at least we're saving money on meals" is all I manage.

"Sure," Gary says. "And how long ago was it cool enough to cook inside?"

I could look it up on my laptop. But then I'd sweat more, and it'd probably just prove him right. Sheila, with impeccable timing, pops over to feed our neighbors, the self-feather-plucking macaws. And to invite us to a party.

"It's Halloween," she says. "If you two are done fighting this losing battle, I could use some help hanging cobwebs in the bar."

A few hours later and XS Memories is decorated with crepe paper ghosts and ghoulish plastic pumpkins. Horror movies play on the big screen, and a cauldron of alcoholic potion steams on the stove. The expats and regulars arrive early to get first dibs at Sheila's costume box. This stretched-thin woman, with hardly the energy to lift her cigarette, knows how far from home we all secretly feel, and she has pirated away two suitcases filled with costumes.

"Get your mitts off," she snaps at Peter, the retired Canal Zone pilot, who divorced and remarried the same woman four times. She also swats away the hands of Connecticut Don, who moved to Panama after a heart attack six years ago.

"I'm saving my favorites for the new kids. Teresa, you're the hussy señorita, and Gary, you get to be her pimp."

I emerge from Sheila's living room layered in off-the-shoulder ruffles and squeezed into cleavage worthy of a brothel. Gary saunters out in a purple silk smoking jacket with black velvet cuffs, a plastic fedora, and Mardi Gras beads.

Canadian John is wearing a costume of his own: checkered polyester blazer, fake sideburns, and dark sunglasses. Women line up to drape over his wheelchair for selfies as he puffs on a cigar, does his best Sopranos imitation, and forgets about the military diving accident that occurred when he was twenty-two. His disability checks go further in Santa Clara than they would in Toronto, and he likes the politics better anyway.

"If you fall into a hole in a Panamanian sidewalk because someone stole the manhole cover, don't even think of suing," he begins, without a trace of irony.

Peter, Don, and Dennis finish the story in unison; they know it by heart. "The judge will just tell you to watch where you're going the next time."

My pimped-out husband shoots me a look that I know means "How in the hell did two people like us end up here?" But he clinks my Atlas bottle to his anyway, and in the collective laughter of the expats I hear the outlaw logic of my father.

Chapter Twenty-Six

PANTHERS

I t has been one hundred days since we left the United States, and I'm convinced it is only the holding pattern that is dampening our spirits, not Panama itself.

MARCH 10-15TH, 1974

Men trying to get us on boat. Skinny dipping at night.

Each night in slide-show Panama we floated naked under an onyx sky. The water was cool and soft, and skinny-dipping in the Panama Canal was like rolling in sheets of silk. I forgive a little of my parents' recklessness in return for the magic that sprung from it: jungle vines, pirate coves, and secret hideouts.

Gary and I decide to break camp, pay our staggering bar tab to Sheila and Dennis, and head for the canal. It has been under Panamanian control for three years; we know better than to try to camp in the jungle like my parents did. But I have to at least try to find our secret campground.

We drive through miles of arching jungle canopy: giant palms, bamboo stands, and rainforest hardwoods. Roots twist and branches tangle, rendering the cement canal locks all but invisible. The sun shafts down in haphazard patterns, dodging the patches of soft raindrops that melt through leaves and drizzle down without a splash. The vegetation is dense and disarmingly close; roots like bulging veins suck on the damp jungle floor.

I close my eyes and resurrect my father's camper here—parked between vines, fourteen thousand four hundred pounds of timber and metal pressing into the spongy, unsuspecting surface. Branches and palm fronds could never camouflage this monster in the Panamanian jungle, my sister's high chair dangling from the front grill like captured prey. It was too massive to be threatened, too mobile to be overtaken by hungry jungle vines. My father's gleaming aluminum creation proclaimed invincibility, and every night I slept with the security of a princess.

Driving through the jungle now is equally regal; I roll down the windows, blast the air-conditioning, and glide through my most vivid memories. I have the sense that we are only minutes late, that if we look down we'll see the tire tracks of the Jeep where my father peeled out and headed for South America. It is the closest I have felt in months to finding my childhood home; the trail is still warm and steamy.

But the Avion never makes it to the Gatun Locks, or to the clearing half a mile away where my family illegally camped in 1974. The national highway unceremoniously ends in the middle of a Colón slum. If Gary keeps driving forward we will be trapped in the chaos of a street market. Young, bare-chested men are hopping onto the bumpers and hoods of cars, hitching rides and demanding money to dismount.

I am thinking of the pledge we took at the start of this journey, the one where if either of us has a bad feeling about a situation, there will be no argument from the other. It had been a kind of traveler's prenup, a hedge against fights or inequalities we assumed would inevitably test our marriage. One hundred days ago I would have worried whether to speak up in the face of a situation only vaguely threatening as this one, the pledge untested by the truth of our lives together. But this drive has rendered words unnecessary. Gary's eyes meet mine in comforting solidarity.

"Not gonna happen," is all he says, and I get out to help him turn the Avion around without running anybody over.

On the way back to Panama City, we take a turnoff to the town of Gamboa. It stands near the edge of the passage known as the Gaillard Cut: the perfect place to watch ships pass and to shake off the disappointment of Colón. Gamboa could be a base town anywhere in 1970s rural America. There is a community pool, a Baptist church, and a two-pump gas station. There are two-story houses with porches; rocking chairs and swing sets from Sears; and soggy laundry hanging out front.

All that's missing are the inhabitants: men with starched uniforms and women with feathered hair. The streets are empty, and the air is so heavy I can't tell if it is raining or dissolving. There are no cars parked on the streets, no babies in buggies on the sidewalk. It is as though the people have disintegrated into the rising steam.

I'm glad; there is no one to disturb the sense that I have floated back through time. The ships we've come to watch are as oversized and out of place as the camper my father tried to camouflage in this jungle thirty years ago. Gary and I eat sandwiches from the back stoop of our camper like kids sneaking into a summer drive-in before anyone else arrives.

The picture is living color, surround-sound stunning, and the ships look close enough to touch. Each passing giant is tug-shoved through the jungle with distorted depth of field. I sit cross-legged on the ground, and a container ship slides by. The jungle disappears as the ship passes in front of me, its hull replacing the horizon. Rectangular metal freight containers in primary colors stack, like building blocks, all the way up to the cloud-streaked sky. I can picture John John, sitting in the living room of our single-wide trailer in the Oregon woods with Legos strewn around him. Deep in his belly, laughter would be bubbling up, ready to erupt when the blocks came tumbling down.

We sit for hours watching ships slowly squeeze through the jungle. I want to slip out of my sweaty clothes and swim through the silky water to the other side—where there are no lawns, no roads, no abandoned outposts of yesterday. The air is thick with memory, and I can almost hear the panthers watching.

Chapter Twenty-Seven

THE CROSSING

Somewhere along the two-day ocean passage from Panama to Colombia in 1974, my father snapped a shot of his family on deck. My mother is holding my little sister up to see over the railing. Jenny is gripping it with the strength of a ferocious toddler, her blond curls tangling in the sea breeze. I am squinting into the sun, horrified that my father is taking a picture of me, nearly naked.

"Princess, we have to throw your shirt overboard," my mother had explained. "It's covered in too much puke to wash out. You'll stink for days."

The girl in my passport photo has chubby cheeks dimpled with a confident grin. It had been only three months since we left Oregon. But on the boat passage from one continent to another, I looked like a walking skeleton.

"Jesus, were your parents so broke by then they couldn't feed you?" Gary asks. "Or is that just what a kid with malaria looks like?"

I want to hug this little girl, brush her tangled hair, and reassure her that everything turned out fine in the end. But when this photograph was taken the worst had just begun, and that haunts me as I contemplate crossing to Colombia once more.

Neither of my parents could have known that the speedboats passing our freighter in the Caribbean were transporting cocaine in large quantities. Drug-trafficking violence wouldn't peak for another six years, but it is full-blown anarchy today. To continue following my parents' exact route would mean plunging into drug wars and narco-terrorism. The dangers of Colombia are all Gary and I have been talking about lately.

"It's the most beautiful country in South America," my father encourages, over a satellite call to Nicaragua. We tell him that we are considering bypassing Colombia and Venezuela and shipping the camper to Ecuador instead.

"But you'll miss some of the prettiest countries if you take that route," he begins, then backs off as though offering a way of saving face. "Of course, we had two little girls; it was like having two extra passports to get us into places and out of situations."

The "situation" he's referring to is the one when he refused to pay another bribe, and all eleven vehicles on our freighter ship got locked up in a customs-impound yard in Cartagena, Colombia. For three days we were prisoners behind a razor-wire-topped wall, not allowed to leave even for food or water.

"But Pantera needs more cat food. Mommy says we're almost out," I remember telling my father. His response was far from comforting.

"We might all be eating cat food before this is over."

Just before the third dusk, one couple finally agreed to pay the bribe, and the aduanero on duty gave them a stamped exit pass and signed the logbook with their vehicle's license plate, make, model, and year: a 1963 red Volkswagen bus.

I have closed my eyes and listened to my father tell this story countless times, waiting for the moment when he rubs his hands together with impish glee and interrupts himself with snorts of laughter.

"So this couple drives away, parks their VW around the corner, and waits until the guards change shift. Then they waltz back into the compound, right past the night-duty watchman, and give us their pass."

In the space where my father was supposed to enter our vehicle's year, make, and model, he wrote "1963 red Volkswagen bus"— to match the information on the one legitimate pass. Then he drove around the corner, left the truck running, and sneaked back into the lot to give the pass to the next vehicle in line. Eleven 1963 red Volkswagen buses left the compound that night.

"The guard on duty was a young kid, maybe sixteen or seventeen years old, and he obviously couldn't read," my father explains. "I don't know what ever happened to that kid. He probably wound up in the salt mines or got beheaded when they found out the next morning."

By then we were a hundred miles away, after bribing an off-duty ferry to shuttle all eleven vehicles across the bay in the dead of night. The group split up and went in different directions. My father picked due north, and we drove day and night without stopping.

The stone in the shoe pestering our decision is that following my father's route through Colombia to Venezuela will place more than just me in danger. There is Alex to consider. I have no right to transfer the panic I felt at seven to my husband's son. This whole trip is about finding the camper, saying good-bye to John. There's no way in hell I want Alex to have to do the same for us. I think of my trusting, solid Wisconsin in-laws: Angie and Joe are too old to put through this. There is my own family, too. My grandmother is valiantly trying to master the Internet to keep up with our progress.

"Can't you fly home for Christmas?" Nellie Mae asks after one of our e-mail updates. "Just so I can wrap my arms around you for a moment." She has waved good-bye too many times.

Chapter Twenty-Eight

WHAT REALLY MATTERS

This is what circles back to me. It would be much cheaper to ship the Avion from Panama to Colombia, but there is a ferry leaving for Ecuador the next day. The freight will cost us $1,500—in cash—and the plane for us to get to South America another $1,000. But adding up the numbers somehow frees me. Our safety—our lives—is worth more than $2,500.

"We can give this money to a travel agent, or we can hand it over to some cocaine commando who carjacks us in the jungle," Gary says as I plunk down a credit card to buy our plane tickets out of Panama City. "Either way, we may never see the Avion again."

I am still thinking of my family's narrow escape through Colombia when Gary and I touch down at Bogotá International Airport en route to Ecuador. Our goal is to make it to the port of Manta to meet the camper arriving by sea. If we are physically present at the unloading, we'll clear customs at the same time as all the other cargo on the roll-on, roll-off freighter, presumably without being locked inside an impound yard for three days. If the beautiful Avion beats us to Ecuador and waits, conspicuously, on an empty dock, the chances of history repeating itself are higher.

I am rereading my mother's journal when the pilot announces that we are leaving Colombian airspace, about to cross the equator. We are flying over more than just a physical milestone. On the first trip we crossed the equator on what would have been the second anniversary of my brother's death, but there is not a word mentioned of it in the journal.

> APRIL 24TH, 1974
>
> Hot, tired and dirty. Found stream and took baths.
> Thunder and lightning storm. Dave had to move truck
> in middle of night as stream rose fast.

I am thinking of a grave, more than four thousand miles away, promising that John John's love and laughter would live forever. Somewhere on this massive, enigmatic continent is my chance to make good on that promise.

IT TOOK MY PARENTS THIRTY-FIVE DAYS TO REACH ECUADOR, MOSTLY ON dirt roads over the high mountain passes of the Northern Andes. It takes Gary and me about twenty-three hours. Still, it is the longest period of time we've been separated from the Avion since we drove it out of Gary's parents' driveway in Wisconsin. The plane's cabin feels claustrophobic. I am a turtle without my shell, cold and vulnerable. Gary can't just press the accelerator of the Ford F-350 and put distance between the present and the past.

We land in Quito and fly on to the coastal hub of Guayaquil to sign our bill of lading. The port where our home-on-wheels awaits, Manta, is farther up the coast. We taxi to a long-distance terminal for a four-hour bus ride through the steamy twilight. I am fidgety and nervous. We have to go through a metal detector, and the driver's helper collects cell phones from every passenger and locks them in a safe behind his seat. My unease grows. This collective phone confiscation seems foreboding, and once we are rolling along I ask the driver about it.

"Es así que un ladrón no puede llamar a su compadres," he explains. The drill goes something like this: a thief with a cell phone, riding the bus as a passenger, reaches out to partners waiting along the route. He gives them a heads-up when the bus is a few minutes away, and the partners stage an accident to make the driver stop. In jump his compadres. Out come the guns. Off go all the wallets of the passengers.

"Pero no se preocupe," the driver tells me. Not to worry, it doesn't happen every time.

The scenery is just as bleak. Where Panama was lush and green, coastal Ecuador is arid and brown. Piles of litter along the roads and under houses offer the only color visible through the fingerprint-smudged window of the bus. I plaster my forehead to the cool glass, searching for any signs of life and beauty straddling the highway.

Two-story houses made of mud or bamboo, or sometimes both, lean in toward the bus as though too weary to collapse. Through open windows I see women inside, peering at the faces flying past. We are inches, yet worlds, apart—the bus passengers wrapped in light sweaters against an artificial chill, the villagers barely enduring the heat. Grown men wear only briefs; naked children play in dry ditches.

I can't hear myself think; the passengers inside the bus are glued to a gruesome Hollywood action movie dubbed into earsplitting Spanish. We pick the hotel nearest the Manta bus station and collapse on a sagging, stained, and sheetless mattress. I would trade it in a heartbeat for the moldy futon inside the Avion.

I wake early after a fitful night's sleep and spend an hour organizing a manila folder with the papers required to collect our truck and camper. I'll need all the gumption I can muster. There is nothing more ridiculous than approaching the gates of a major commercial port in South America, on foot, and asking if you can go inside and retrieve your life.

"Estoy aquí para aceptar entrega de mi casa rodante." I announce my intention to claim the camper, holding out our bill of lading. We are sweating in front of a locked gate with no names to drop or bribes to offer. This is a place ruled by cranes and forklifts and men wearing badges and hardhats. I have no such legitimacy and have never felt more incompetent or irrelevant in my adult life. Seven-year-old me would burst into tears and pitch a fit to get my house back. But thirty-seven-year-old me waving my manila folder is as effective as chasing a Guatemalan earthquake with a broomstick.

For something like $300 I could hire a broker, and the Avion would be released in the customary fashion. Lots of stamps, photocopies for ten different files, here's a pen to sign on the dotted line, *no se aceptan tarjetas de credito*. But $300 is the equivalent of one week's budget, and I feel compelled to at least attempt to beat the system before capitulating.

I ask a man in a khaki uniform where I'd find the customs office. He points to a side building, and in its air-conditioned hallways we meet the aduanera: a large woman with silver hair that still holds the stiff tubular shape of plastic rollers. She is in the midst of celebrating her own going-away party.

"We're doomed," Gary says, but I can't back down.

I decide to capitalize on the general good cheer and join the line of people waiting to congratulate her. When it is my turn, I ceremoniously give her a copy of a magazine with a travel piece Gary and I did about Mexico.

"Estoy escribiendo un libro acerca de Ecuador." I shamelessly claim to be a guidebook writer. "¿Puede usted ayudarnos?" Can she recommend a way for me to retrieve our vehicle and continue on our journey?

"¿Tiene ustedes un carnet?" she asks as she thumbs through the article and compliments Gary on his photographs. I open my file, and as soon as she sees the navy blue ATA carnet cover she calls over a man in a tight brown business suit.

Then, in perfect English, she says, "Good luck, say wonderful things about Ecuador, and let this man take care of everything."

I feel invincible and vindicated. "No 1963 Volkswagen bus ruse for us," I brag to Gary as the aduanera's assistant takes our folder and walks us out into the hallway.

Out of earshot of the aduanera, the man in the tight brown suit tells us, "Vuelta sobre dos horas, con one hundred dólares en efectivo, y todos esperarán." We have two hours to gather a hundred dollars in cash, and our truck and camper will be waiting.

My pride plummets to the place in my stomach that knew it had been too easy. The official doesn't have to say a word; he is holding our passports, carnet, and the title to our truck in his hands. This is beyond any roadside shakedown, in a different league than common traffic-cop corruption. Our roles are suddenly reversed, and Gary puts his arm around my shoulders and steers me, seething, to the exit.

"But we vowed," I sputter, "never to cave to these bastards again."

"Look at it this way: you still saved us two hundred bucks," he tries to placate me. "We're ahead of the game, and nobody's chasing us with guns."

There is a dingy beach with rentable umbrellas next to the port of Manta, so we kill the requisite two hours fully dressed, downing beers and eating fresh ceviche among crowds of scantily clad sunbathers and souvenir vendors. When we return, with the bribe, our carnet is perfectly perforated, our passports are duly stamped, and a signed letter from the aduanera granting us passage through Ecuador is stapled to the front.

A customs agent accompanies us through the port's front gate. Parked on a flat, sizzling expanse of asphalt are one hundred identical, new GM compact cars and one 1968 shiny Avion camper. It is a giant among toys. The equatorial sun glints off its silver roof like the refraction from a diamond.

I understand in this moment that there is no way I should have expected to drive it away without redistributing some of the privilege and power it represents. A bribe to our eyes is simply delayed compensation to others. Gary checks the truck cab, bed, and camper for damage and finds nothing dented or missing except a pair of sunglasses he left on the dashboard back in Panama.

"Restores my faith," he says, and grateful relief lifts my spirits. We are on the same page again.

Gary and I drive out of the port of Manta, Ecuador, wedged among a convoy of cattle trucks. They are loaded down with tuna the size of great white sharks—black dorsal fins thrusting between the wooden slats of the trailers like daggers, inches from our windshield. *Don't let your guard down*, they are warning. Creatures far more magnificent than the two of us have been hooked and dragged into South America.

Chapter Twenty-Nine

ECUADOR

On a map's legend, we are driving through the slice of Ecuador where thin red lines signifying roads connecting the coastal wetlands to the Andes Mountains. What it does not indicate is how to get from sea level to six thousand feet in a reasonable amount of time.

The temperature plunges from thick nineties to the thinnest of sixties before we discover the secret to South American mountain driving: the Law of the Third Lane. It is invoked when an impatient vehicle attempts to pass a slow-moving vehicle on a solid white line. If the vehicle approaching from the opposite direction is smaller than the one attempting the pass, it obligingly moves over to the shoulder of its lane. The slow-moving vehicle being passed hugs the right side of its lane, thereby creating a narrow passage through the middle: the third lane. What we learn just as quickly is that the law is absolutely, unforgivingly Darwinian.

If the approaching vehicle is bigger than the vehicle attempting the pass, the driver of the latter nods his head and slips back into his place to wait for a more appropriate time. Occasionally an overloaded semitruck schools Gary in this unwritten law, but the combined mass of the Avion and the Ford F-350 is infrequently challenged, and our first day's drive in South America feels like a victory lap.

Until we get to the part where the highway disintegrates, just south of Quito. There is no advance warning to prepare for the shock of loose gravel and deep ruts after spongy-fresh asphalt. The settlement at the top of this particular peak in the Andes is a crossroad of construction and chaos. We arrive at dinnertime, and Indians with food carts are selling chunks of fried meat, marinated in exhaust fumes for no extra charge.

At one point there are nine lanes of vehicles, if you count the carts interspersed with traffic. Unlike a "normal" nine-lane highway—where presumably four lanes are grouped together in one direction, separated from five lanes grouped together in the opposite direction—this is a mix-and-match pattern. We are driving through a gravel loom with no idea whether we are the weft or the warp.

"The training wheels are off," Gary mutters. "We're in another continent now."

There is no going back; we literally can't turn around and drive home even if we wanted to. Everything will be different from this point forward: the languages, the food, and especially the climate. We are headed for an ancient Andean market town called Saquisilí that is so high in elevation that the sun blisters even the cheeks and noses of the locals. It sears Gary's uncovered head and my unshaded eyes, and I feel as if we are on another planet, one unprotected by an atmosphere.

We've been in countless Latin American street markets on this trip, but here there are no cell phones, televisions, or even portable radios entertaining the vendors or their customers. The most modern piece of technology for sale is a battery-operated toothbrush, and we only discover that because we squeeze into a circle of poncho-covered people watching a dental-hygiene demonstration. I am standing in a time warp, seven years old again and marveling in amazement.

The entire market is utterly efficient in a centuries-old sort of way. Nothing is worthless and everything is salvaged. It is organized in seven separate plazas—all the sewing notions here, all the sugars and spices there, all the hardware one block over. Between these plazas are curbside restaurants selling whole roasted guinea pigs, cattle-hoof-and-blood-sausage stews, and sweet steamed corn cakes.

I've never seen so many chickens for sale in one place; we could buy them alive or slaughtered, still feathered or plucked. Some are still screeching with fight while others are quietly resigned to their fate. Women stand in parallel lines holding out burlap feed bags filled with thrashing birds. Interested buyers make their way down the center, peeking into the bags and pulling out chickens by the neck to examine them more closely. Buyers and sellers alike wear felt porkpie hats with peacock feathers, neon-dyed wool shawls, and tiers of skirts over thick, sagging stockings. The whole interaction resembles a line dance with constantly changing partners and patterns.

Fat and furry guinea pigs, called *cuy*, squirm in straw baskets instead of bags. Customers pluck them out and pass them around by the backs of their necks—their little arms and legs stiffly extended like those of toy piggy banks. It is the same position in which they are ultimately impaled on a spit and rotated over open fires. They are displayed in front of the shops that sell them, crisp and golden, their mouths agape in silenced screams.

My conversion to carnivore is more tenuous with every squirming, screeching, or skewered animal I see. We stock up on fresh fruits and vegetables and head for what the guidebook calls the Quilotoa Circuit. The route isn't highlighted on my father's maps; the truck's brakes were so fragile by this point in Ecuador that he opted to stick to the Pan-American Highway.

I am ready for a dose of exploration, eager to chart a new course in this new continent. But determining just what constitutes the circuit and how to navigate around it requires language skills I do not possess. Getting directions in English is out of the question, but often so is Spanish, and I speak not a word of Quechua. I have to resort to basic sign language and pantomime to get from one village to the next.

When we reach a group of villagers huddled around a fork in the road, they never agree on which way is best. So a kind of dance ensues: toothless men with walking sticks flailing their free arms in every direction, turning and leaning and bending for emphasis; and me following their movements like a clumsy student at a ballroom-dance studio.

Gary laughs from the safety of the side-view mirror. "Mariamalia was right. I'll never forget your ridiculous dances."

The houses strewn between these mountains are dismal and defeated—stranded in dirt yards, dotted with litter and pecking chickens. Even though they are surrounded by felled forests, they are made of cement blocks and left unpainted, except for graphic political endorsements that banner-wrap their dimpled grey walls. The tin roofs have almost no slant, so as to minimize the gap between metal and cement at the peak, and the walls are less than six feet high. The people peering from them seldom wave or smile; old women wag their fingers when they see Gary's camera.

He is not tempted to shoot anyway; to document this poverty without some compelling reason would be like buying souvenirs in a ghetto.

"I would rather be a missionary than a tourist here," he mutters. "Even if it's only lies, I'd still have something to offer."

We camp along the side of the road, and Gary pries dead bugs from a new continent out of the truck's grill. We're at 10,099 feet, but the camper's thermometer isn't working, leaving blank spaces in his sketchbook records. The next morning there is a thin crust of ice on the carpet down the center of the Avion. The cobblestone roads of the Quilotoa

Circuit have aggravated the cracks in the aging water tank, and nearly half of the tank's contents soaked into the carpet during the night.

We are days from any sort of pavement, and the weight of the remaining water sloshing around in the damaged tank will hasten its ultimate demise. I drain our precious supply of water while Gary cuts a plastic milk jug into flat sections and uses contact cement to stick them over the crack like patches.

"I hope this holds," he says. "If not, we can't wash dishes or use the toilet or shower for the rest of the trip."

We both know it could be worse. By this point in Ecuador, the Jeep was deep into my mother's catalog of sixty-one catastrophic breakdowns.

> **MAY 7TH, 1974**
> Fixed brakes and radiator. Bugged all afternoon by
> kids. Drove on and stopped for bread. The truck
> wouldn't start. Battery dead. Night in shop. Terrible
> noises all night. Dave sick.

My gut is holding up and our Ford F-350 is blissfully reliable, but our thirty-five-year-old Avion is struggling to survive. If we ever do find my father's handmade camper in Bolivia, we may well need to salvage parts from its skeleton.

It seems like years ago that the Avion felt like an albatross, strung uselessly around our necks in Central America when overnighting in hotels would have been so much easier. Now our camper is the only vestige of familiarity in a bleak new world. It is a fortress of comfort and warmth compared to even the sturdiest of homes and hostels we pass. I would cover it in a million Band-Aids if that's what it took to hold it together. It goes wherever we go; abandoning it is unthinkable.

The nearest town where we might be able to replenish our supply of contact cement is called Chugchilán, and in its plaza a woman is

cooking meat-and-potato stew for workers coming in from the surrounding fields. She wants her daughters to meet the two sunburned
foreigners. Blanca Mariana is sixteen and Adriana is twelve, and
they speak just enough Spanish to giggle at mine. They have glowing
red cheeks and glossy black hair pulled so precisely over their ears
and behind their necks that their heads look like delicately painted
brown eggs.

Each girl is hunched over, carrying a burlap bag lumpy with potatoes. They keep the bags from dragging on the ground by strapping
them to their bodies with tangerine-colored shawls—like beauty-
queen sashes for hunchbacks. I can't tell how tall the girls are because
if they stand up straight the potatoes will tumble into the dirt.

I ask Adriana how far they carry the potatoes, and she can measure distance only by the hours. They leave for the fields while it is
still dark and they are returning only now, when the sun is setting. I
ask if Gary can take their picture and they agree.

"¿Puede mi padre verlo?" Adriana wants a copy of the photograph
to show her father. Gary is shooting black-and-white film; we'll have
to find a lab and process it when we reach the next major city.

"Claro." I tell her I'll mail her a print in a few weeks. Then I ask
where to send it. "¿Cuál es su dirección?"

The girls stare at me and offer up awkward smiles. They have
never sent nor received a letter; they have no idea what an address is.

For a moment I can't think of what to say, how to explain. But
then I realize I don't have to; they are teaching me. These girls don't
need an address to know where and who they are. They have a home.
They are home. I am the nomad searching for one from long ago.

Suddenly this quest doesn't seem so illogical. Everything that
rooted me disappeared when my little brother died. Tragedy compelled my parents to run away from home, but for me the camper
became home. And that home is abandoned somewhere in Bolivia
without an address or anything to document what it meant to me.

I will find a way to mail these girls their portraits, even if the envelope simply lists the names Adriana and Blanca Mariana and the town where their mother sells potato stew. And it may take hundreds of fork-in-the-road direction dances and the Law of the Third Lane to pass the obstacles in my path, but I will search for the camper until I find it.

Chapter Thirty

THE ANNIVERSARY

The road out of Chugchilán the next morning is punishing, requiring four-wheel drive and all the good luck charms I can fit on the rearview-mirror necklace. Evil-eye amulets and Navajo dream catchers replace the possibility of tow trucks or garages. The last time we drove along a road this grueling, the drive ended with shots fired into the emptiness.

Today we pass only one rusting passenger bus in the four hours it takes to drive just twenty miles. We inch along so slowly I can inspect every detail of the panoramic views from the comfort of the passenger seat. Footpaths lead to what look like huts thatched in long, unwashed blonde hair. Stretching to each one of these forlorn abodes is a thin black ribbon of electricity.

We climb to twelve thousand feet, and the hair huts and electricity ribbons vanish. Gary turns up the truck's heat to ease the cramping cold. If not for the jarring potholes, he would fall asleep at the wheel. I wipe the windows free of fog. At nearly thirteen thousand feet the llamas look filthy, the cows miserable, and the sheep too tired to move out of the road.

Thin thinking, we drive around them. The dirt on either side is no worse than the road itself. Intermittently, one side of the two-lane road is paved. So all buses drive on that side regardless of their direction or destination. Evidence of collision is strewn throughout the stubble of the surrounding fields: an axle skewered in the dirt here, a shattered windshield there.

Gary's hands are clenched around the steering wheel; he is struggling to stay focused. When we are so high that there are no more llamas to stare at, we marvel at the emptiness. I begin to fashion a new vocabulary for the Ecuadorian Andes made up of words like *impressive, striking, desolate,* and *melancholy.*

That's as close to beauty as I can truthfully come. I can't stretch out straight; my body curls and cramps from the cold. My head throbs, my lungs flutter, and my toes feel like tiny blue potatoes at the bottom of my muddy boots. Most of all I am craving a hot bath. Which is why my half-frozen finger is stabbing at a tiny dot on my father's map of Ecuador, trying to point out a town called Baños.

We begin a descent from one world into another, and the day's drive passes in a blur of incongruities. At eleven thousand feet, natives trudge on foot while their twice-as-tall pack llamas float past the camper at window height. At nine thousand feet, kids wearing blue jeans wash their soccer balls in the grey runoff of drainage pipes. At seven thousand, sidewalk butchers with bloodied cleavers separate hooves from legs of dangling hog carcasses.

At six thousand feet I start to see signposts for Baños, and for the first time since entering South America, we pay five dollars to park the camper inside the gates of a hotel compound. There is sleep deep enough to block out dreams, and then there is sleep so deep you aren't sure you've awakened the next morning. It isn't the altitude. Gary's journal notes six thousand feet and a balmy sixty-seven degrees. But the sky seems reluctant to let sunlight pierce through a hazy blanket.

Gary checks his watch. We've slept until nearly ten, and yet neither one of us feels relinquished by the clutches of night. While he inspects the camper's wounded water tank for more cracks, I open the screened windows. The air that rushes inside is sulfurous, somehow more alive than before. That's when we hear the first rumble.

The sound starts at our feet, as if the earth underneath the truck were moaning. It rises through the camper, resonant and omnipresent, like how I imagine a miles-long wave would sound to a creature of the deepest sea.

"Another earthquake?" Gary suggests. But nothing is rattling or rolling around, like it did in Guatemala, and the ground seems steady. So do my nerves.

"It must be the volcano."

Neither one of us has any idea how to pronounce the name we see above Baños on our crumpled map: Volcán Tungurahua. Leaning out from the camper's door we can't even see it. We have managed to pick a camp spot directly under the flanks of an active volcano. We are so close there is no horizon to measure its level, no tree line to gauge its height, no perspective from which to see where it starts and ends. What we need is some distance from this rumbling mountain. And caffeine.

"It's a little disingenuous to name this place Baños," Gary grumbles as we walk into what looks like a tourist town thirty years past its prime. "It should be called Volcaños or Eruptos—to give you a hint of what you're getting into."

Over mugs of tree-sap-thick coffee I consult a smattering of official brochures and guidebooks. Apparently the last time Tungurahua actually erupted was in 1918, but eighty years later two foreign mountain climbers got burned by exploding gases at the caldera. The whole town was evacuated, and it was months before the locals were allowed back in. By then, not even Lonely Planet could entice visitors.

It is still a bulging, unpredictable threat, and if it chooses to spew itself down the slopes, our tin-panel home-on-wheels will melt like a welder took a blowtorch to it. But the engineering marvel of thermal hot springs piped into communal swimming pools is too enticing to resist. The main pipe-fed pool looks like a submerged skateboarding rink, filled with squealing kids and old ladies dog paddling in circles to prevent the water from touching their flowery bathing caps. I shake my head to dismiss a wandering photographer offering steamy Polaroid portraits and find a quiet corner with underwater steps to lean against. I inhale the aroma rising from the mineral-rich water and examine toes that, after two days at much higher altitude, look more like prunes than potatoes. Gary finds it considerably less relaxing.

"That's not mine," he says, peeling a long strand of black hair from his forearm.

Washing it off in the communal, coed, thermal showers brings even more intimate encounters. A little girl, eyes squeezed shut against stinging shampoo, clings to my right thigh and wails, mistaking me for her mother. She could have been my little sister, thirty years ago.

What rushes back isn't homesickness—the Avion is home now—but something more like the memory of a life I borrowed once. In that life, today is Thanksgiving. Our friends and families are sitting down to turkey dinner and pumpkin pie, but here, three thousand miles due south, we are eating purple-potato curry and preparing for another night in the shadows of an active volcano.

This time, when the rumbling starts, I am too jumpy to stay flat on my back, listening to the eruptions from the confines of our bed.

"If it blows, it's not like the Avion can save us," I tell Gary.

"Agreed," he answers. "I'm not partial to tin tombs anyway."

We bundle up and drag our blanket outside, to spread atop the growling ground. Outside the Avion, unencumbered by man-made surfaces to absorb the sound, we are one with it. Each rumble rattles through my rib cage. A thousand jetliners queueing up to land could not approach the tone and depth of the seismic booms beneath our feet.

It is humbling to stretch our fragile bodies out on earth so restless and tensile. The ground quivers like a stretched-tight trampoline, reacting to unseen forces that could project us and every other living thing high into the night sky. It might be the blood racing through my veins, but I am literally quivering, too.

"Happy anniversary," Gary says, pulling me closer to him.

I stiffen, stunned and horrified. How could I have forgotten a date this important? I have written no verse, cooked no special meal, worn no sexy lingerie to mark the occasion. I haven't even properly bathed; my unbrushed hair still stinks of sulfur. I check my ring finger; a woman like this could only dream she's married.

But it's there, thin and snug against my skin. And so is the man who put it there. I can let go of my inner lectures, doubts, and insecurities. He doesn't need romantic reminders or rituals, just me.

"Pretty intense place to celebrate, right?" Gary says. "I could never have imagined this before marrying you."

I am listening to the comforting tick of his heartbeat when I hear the gasp of escaping gases. We both sit up to witness the black night above Tungurahua licked by tongues of fiery orange. I cling to Gary's hand, not out of fear but to the urgent need for contact, for grounding. If tonight is meant to change everything, I am ready.

Chapter Thirty-One

CATS AND DOGS

Ours is the only vehicle waiting to cross the dismal frontera between southern Ecuador and Peru. There is no obvious reason for the delay. It isn't near lunchtime. No migrants are being strip-searched. So I have a queasy feeling in my stomach when border officials with guns slung over their shoulders ask me, not Gary, to step inside a shabby customs building. I get out of the cab, unlock the box under Wipeout's seat, and take the satellite phone with me.

Gary looks confused; he's the driver, the male through whom all shakedowns normally pass. "It's not like you've got a get-out-of-jail-free number programmed in speed dial," he tells me. He wants to come with me, but one of us has to stay with the truck.

"I'll use it as a prop," I say. "Maybe they'll think I'm a reporter."

The customs building looks more like a hut the closer I get, and inside it is clammy and dark. There is only one electrical outlet in the wall. From it stretches one cord powering a portable heater and another leading to a beat-up Japanese boom box.

"Que significan las palabras 'gotta' y 'whoa, whoa'?" an Ecuadorian border guard in his early thirties wants to know.

"Y 'playing for keeps' tambien," the Peruvian aduanero chimes in. "De 'Wanted Dead or Alive.'"

It turns out they are not about to strap me to a chair and demand all my cash to enter their country. They are just Bon Jovi fans excited to come across an American who can help them translate the liner notes of a stack of pirated CDs. We drive away with windows rolled down, singing our good-byes to the border.

"I'm a cowboy," I belt out from the passenger side. The aduaneros twirl imaginary lassos over their heads, and on a steel horse we ride into our second South American country.

However bleak and dreary parts of Ecuador are, they are lovely compared to northwestern Peru. The soil is baked to a dull yellow, and whatever grass still clings to the surface looks sunburned to an ashen grey. The sky has no lift and so closely matches the charred grass that there is no discernible horizon. One hundred and fifty miles pass without a single tree.

Gary glances over at a photograph I am clutching on my lap. It shows my father's camper, pulled over to the side of the road, facing a landscape of desert sand dunes. There are no mile markers or signposts, no houses, shops, or even people as references.

"Are you sure your father even took that photo in Peru?" he asks.

Diesel fuel is more expensive than we've budgeted, we're running low on propane, and this photograph means nothing to him. It has come to mean everything to me, and I don't know how to begin to explain. The loneliness I see in it, for one thing. Until my father stopped to take this picture, we had been traveling in a convoy with other travelers headed for Lima. But somewhere in the desert of northwestern Peru, I made him turn our camper around, and I want to find that spot again.

We accidentally left the cat behind. So we had to go
back to get Pantera.

Gary is astonished. My father voluntarily backtracked to rescue a
cat. "You two girls must have howled like you were getting stuck with
forks."

I remember searching for brutal hours over an unforgiving road.
My mother's journal strips it down, like testimony of yet another
trial.

Hit some bumps, frame broke. Fixed frame

Our own camper is rattling and shifting above our heads, sliding too far right in the truck's bed to be stable. Gary pulls over and
we walk to the front to check. It looks like a two-headed monster,
the truck veering slightly right as if to hug the center line, the Avion
aiming at an angle to the left, straining to go its own way. It will take
both of us to ratchet it back into place. We've tried to prevent this
from happening by boosting the camper up on blocks of wood as if it
were a wobbly table with uneven legs. But it is as dubious a fix as my
father's welded wheel covers.

The Avion is chained from both sides to the frame of the truck.
Maneuvering the camper back to center involves a physicality never
demanded in Gary's former life. He has to grab one section of chain
with both hands while squatting horizontally against the side of the
truck, like he's rappelling down a short cliff. I have smaller hands and
less strength, so my job is to wedge scraps of wood between camper
and truck bed without leaving fingers behind. Our ability to work as
a team has never been more essential or miscommunication so potentially disastrous. In the Sechura Desert, one chain link at a time, we
coax the beast into balance.

"I can't even fathom how your father could repair the entire frame of the Jeep by himself," Gary says, beads of sweat dripping off his eyebrows.

My father's camper was far too heavy for crude leverage. It had to be jacked up and the truck driven out from under it just to assess damage. Even more amazing than the fact that my father somehow fixed the frame by himself in the middle of the desert is that he continued to search for the cat that caused the forty-fourth vehicular catastrophe of the trip.

It was my mother who spotted a black lump on the side of the road: tail flicking at flies. Pantera jumped into the laps of two overjoyed little girls, and before he drove off in an unsuccessful attempt to rejoin the convoy, my father took a picture of our camper parked on the side of the road.

It is the photo I am clutching in my hand. The wind has whipped the dunes into peaks and hollows like a stiff meringue. Over time the colors of the baked, pale sand dunes have faded into mauves and lavenders, but somehow the road is still as black as a ribbon of onyx across a snowy moon.

The odds of recognizing one lonely cross section of my memory are minuscule. The Sechura Desert is a vast plain devoid of any signs of life, except one. Miles from sporadic human settlements, plastic bags catch the cold air currents from the sea and ride until they strand themselves on tumbleweeds.

"Don't get your hopes up, Teresa," Gary says.

The wind is too fierce to roll down the windows. We are straining to see through a crust of sand slowly caking over the windshield.

"Oh, come on. How hard can it be to find a sand dune in the desert?"

I am trying to lower my expectations and laugh my way out of disappointment. But then, like a parachute landing on a target, a shredded plastic bag settles in the foreground, and I have something to focus on. Framing the bag are shapes that look intimately familiar.

"Quick, let me see that picture," Gary says, pulling over to the side of the road.

We turn on the windshield wipers to brush off the sand, and there they are—side by side. The crests of dunes before us match peak for peak those in the print I am gripping in my hands.

It is as if I never lived in South Africa, moved back to America, grew up, and married the man sitting beside me. I am staring at a landscape unchanged in thirty years. I am in the same exact place, overlapping my childhood like a sheet of tracing paper. A tissue-thin shiver pencils down my spine. If Pantera stood still long enough for me to find him again, the camper might be waiting too.

WE DRIVE UNTIL WE REACH AN ARCHAEOLOGICAL SITE JUST OFF THE Pan-American Highway and set up camp outside the gates of the Túcume ruins. Which is where we are serenaded by two of the ugliest stray dogs I have ever seen. Losing Wipeout has rendered me powerless to fight the emotional pull of any friendly dog, but these two make me physically recoil. They are grey, like everything else in their environment, and hairless save for clumps of orange, whisker-like fur jutting from their chins and ears. Their hides are cracked with open sores, and the female is in heat, leaving a trail of blood wherever she walks. An image of a forlorn cat, ooze draining from an empty eye socket, floats through my conscience. These equally repulsive dogs welcome us to Túcume as if they too have patiently waited in the desert for us to rescue them.

"I think we still have Wipeout's antibacterial cream in the camper," Gary says, accepting what must be done with his customary calm.

I cradle the female's festered head in my lap, and she doesn't even whimper as Gary squeezes the healing ointment into her open wounds. The male stops scratching his crusted ears and lets me clean them with a wet cloth and squirt medicine deep inside. The grateful dogs deposit themselves below our camper door to wait out the night.

The next morning they appoint themselves our escorts through the ruins. We are the only people here, and the hairless dogs lead us through a fence of low, scrubby trees and along a dry riverbed to what appears to be a huge termite mound. It is actually one of twenty-six pyramids of mud—carved out of the earth, supported with remnants of thick beams, and at one time plastered over with some sort of painted adobe. The Túcume site is still under excavation, and there are newly poured cement stairs that climb the hillside to a vista called El Purgatorio. Only from this vantage point is it possible to grasp the grandeur. Spread over acres and acres below are the buried foundations and eroded shapes that once sheltered a civilization: patterns of order that created a culture.

From a collection of guidebooks and signs, I piece together a timeline. The Lambayeque Indians occupied the site from AD 1000 to 1375, then the Chimú culture took over, and finally the Incas claimed it as their own. It was abandoned, like most of the great Incan strongholds, after the treacherous Spanish conqueror Francisco Pizarro deceived and captured the Incan emperor Atahualpa in 1532. To prevent reoccupation, the conquistadors spread the rumor that the site was haunted.

"Glad we didn't know that last night," Gary says. "It gets pretty dark out here."

But the clever suggestion of ghosts in tombs is why Túcume has remained relatively undisturbed for centuries. This morning, with only two hairless dogs at our sides, it is as if Gary and I have stolen upon the scene of a crime: the disappearance of an empire. Suddenly the chances that a single handmade camper has survived even thirty years in South America seem slimmer than they did a day ago.

Chapter Thirty-Two

THROUGH THE
LOOKING GLASS

We approach Lima from the north and end up lost—an hour
to the east of a city of almost nine million people. It is so
sprawling and stuffed full that I am certain we will never find a place
to safely park the camper. The most destitute of villages we saw in the
highlands of Ecuador and the deserts of northern Peru at least had
room to spread out; poverty came with some privacy. Lima feels con-
centrated and claustrophobic, clamping down conversation between
us. Even the hand that Gary gently rests on mine feels suffocating,
and I pull my hands to my lap. And then a pair of traffic cops spot us.

I brace for my body's usual reactions: guts cramping, palms sweating, temples pounding, guilt rising, spirit sinking. Soon I will be able
to hear my own blood pressure muffling out my rumbling stomach

and grumbling husband. This will be Guatemala, El Salvador, Nicaragua all over again; we are overdue. One cop waves us over while the other steps out into the road in front of us and holds up a fleshy hand. The scene is so familiar I can predict the choreography. When we pull over they move from center stage to the wings in an intimate, window-side duet. In perfect synchrony they bow from belted waists to be eye level with their audience: Gary. It is a performance I dread, a movie I want to switch off before it begins.

"Gracias, señor," comes the first line of dialogue. This cop can't be more than eighteen years old, but there is a hardness in his eyes. "Usted hizo una maniobra ilegal del carril."

Gary looks at me, rolling his eyes. He recognizes the illegal part; I figure out that we are being accused of changing lanes.

"Well, isn't this handy," Gary says as the second cop hands him a laminated card. "The fines for everything he could possibly dream up are right here, preprinted and everything."

Even more conveniently, the young cop goes on to explain that we can pay right now, on the spot. Our dubious infraction would only cost us twenty-six dollars, but it might as well be twenty-six hundred. In one deep breath I realize this is just an opening line. When the credits roll I will still be sitting side by side with the man I trust, and the lights will come back on. We are no longer rookie road-trippers, navigating a marriage untested by stress or danger. I can hear my own voice; it is not drowned by my fears. I take out a pencil and notepad and ask the cop to diagram exactly what he is accusing Gary of. He refuses and repeatedly demands the fine.

I try another tactic. "Mire, tu presidente dice que mordidas son ilegal en Peru." I am leaning over Gary, trying to convince an eighteen-year-old Lima police officer that bribes are actually more illegal than changing lanes. I need a visual aid, so I reach under my seat and pull out the satellite phone. I will call the US Embassy, I tell him, but the phone is having no effect that I can measure.

The word for bribe means "little bite," and I find myself making convulsive, snapping motions with my teeth as I repeat *"mordida"* over and over. I am vaguely conscious of Gary whispering something through my theatrics.

"Keep it together, babe," he says. "You're the only one who speaks the language."

I'm not following.

"You need to be the one they want to deal with. Instead of me."

We are two continents past stepping on each other's toes or second-guessing feelings. Even without rehearsal I anticipate the pivot: Gary will out-outrage the cops. In English, with a tone of voice that needs no translation. The color of his face keeps pace with the string of curses escaping from his mouth. Among more colorful names, he repeatedly calls the second cop a criminal, a word conveniently the same in Spanish.

Disbelief morphs into insult on the faces of the cops. Their collars seem too tight; the visors on their military-style helmets literally begin to steam. One takes the bait and starts swearing back, saying *"hijo de puta"* and worse. But I know Gary still has the upper hand, because both of them refuse to look this crazy American in the eye. Other vehicles pass by, slowing for a look at the scene we are creating. The first cop checks his watch. With every passing minute he is missing easier opportunities to collect *mordidas* from more compliant drivers.

"Look at him. He's afraid you're mental," I whisper to Gary.

"Good. Let him think I'm goddamn nuts," he answers back, shouting words the cops have no idea are meant for me.

"Tranquilo, tranquilo," the first cop says. But he is speaking in my direction, still avoiding a direct confrontation with the man on the verge of implosion beside me.

I shrug, palms up. He needs to believe I am both understanding and helpless. So that he can gallantly save the day by letting me go. It's working. I can feel the tears pooling in the corners of my eyes, ready to release at any point for more leverage. I point again to the satellite phone. See? I'm helpless but not completely without recourse.

The cops confer, lowering the voices they know I understand. Heads shake. Throats clear. Chins retract into tensely corded necks. They are trying on the costume of a stern warning layered over a thin undergarment of desperation.

"Por favor, señora. Controlese su esposo. No este en una rabia." He motions for Gary to roll up the window.

"So he thinks I'm some kind of rabid dog, eh?" Gary says. With pride.

"No, he wants to pass along some advice." I nod and shake my head at the cops, yes or no or maybe. This could go any way.

"What did he say?" Gary says. "I can't keep this up forever."

"Control your rage. I'm pretty sure he said control your rage."

Gary's mask drops, just for a second.

"Don't you dare laugh now. Just put the truck in gear and use your signals."

AN HOUR LATER WE ARE SQUEEZING INTO TOO-TIGHT ALLEYS AND DEAD ends, one of which deposits us at the gate of what looks like a huge green space or park on my map. It turns out to be a public recreational compound in one of Lima's infamous shantytowns.

I would be willing to pay any price just to stop and get my bearings, but the armed guard on duty charges us only the entrance fee listed to park for the night—literally pennies. It is midweek and the park is empty, so we drive through the parking lot and onto a shaded path between a swimming pool and public restroom. Every surface in the compound, from soccer fields to banana trees, is covered with fine grime the consistency of volcanic ash. What should be green is grey, and the absence of color is crushing. I look up to see where all the grit and dust are coming from. I would gasp, but inhaling too quickly would choke me. If there is a rabbit hole big enough for a one-ton truck we have fallen into it.

Our conspicuous rolling castle is surrounded by thousands of desperately poor people literally burrowed into towering piles of dirt. Their homes are chipped and staked into the sides of a disintegrating hill, connected by footpaths that look like the zigzagging trails of a toy ant farm. The soot in the air comes from cooking fires and burning garbage piles; there is no running water or electricity.

An hour ago I felt invincible, capable of talking my way out of any danger. But now, for the first time in South America, I think about the gun hidden under our books. It has been there since the earthquake in Guatemala, like a cancer in remission. I feel paranoid and contagious, a scary Alice in a gloomy Wonderland. I've read that almost half of Lima's population lives in places like this, officially called *asentamientos humanos*—human settlements. Gary does the math in his head.

"That'd be like if you took New York City and drew a line down, say, Madison Avenue. Everybody to the east of that line has to live in cardboard boxes and pee in the gutters."

The writer Sebastián Salazar Bondy nicknamed his native city "Lima the horrible," Herman Melville called it "the saddest city on earth," but I am determined to write my own description.

For the first time in months we have an appointment. We've been invited to lunch at the home of distant relatives of a friend back in DC. Cristina and Fernando live in a Lima suburb called Miraflores, a business and banking center with armed-guarded office complexes, functioning stoplights, and flowers in medians.

When Cristina greets our taxi she takes us on a stroll through the garden behind a high brick wall that separates her home from the bustling street. She has coaxed everything from fig trees to lemongrass from the soil. The aromatic scent of growth keeps the pungent traffic fumes at bay, and there is a calm to her garden that belies the tension outside the gates. This is a luckier Lima, but she and Fernando have not been immune to the struggles and violence of modern Peru. They live life fully but privately—always on guard. Which is why it is such a privilege to share a meal with this family and the two close friends they invite to hear our story.

Jorge is an art lover and businessman, and his wife Eleanora is a young and confident mediation lawyer. The four friends pepper us with questions of where we have been and what we think of all we've seen. But when Eleanora starts rattling off a list of wonderful places in Lima that we should visit, it is as if she is describing a completely different city than the one our camper is parked in. If she had never traveled outside Peru, I would discount some of Eleanora's enthusiasm as provincial hyperbole. But everyone in the room has lived in other places and seen other cultures—Fernando and Cristina lived in Maryland for years—and still they speak of their home country in loving largesse. Each person in the room has the means and the influence to leave, but they remain in their troubled homeland by choice.

"I just love living where there is so much to do and so much to feel," Eleanora explains. "The sky is so open and the sea is so vast."

There may not be an actual elephant in the room, but the one in my head is trumpeting, "How can you stand it here?" I can't stop thinking of the pollution and squatters surrounding our Avion. Traveling through the third world in a new truck and comfortable camper offers just a temporary taste of the tension and inequalities our gracious hosts live among permanently. I know that if I lived in the squatter settlements, I couldn't look down on a silver camper and two unburdened travelers without rage and resentment. If I lived in Miraflores, I would have to harden my soul to tune out the guilt. Yet Fernando and Jorge, Cristina and Eleanora rise above it. They hold on to their faith in the future and delight in sharing what they can.

We end the afternoon with a sampling of the national drink: pisco. Curiouser and curiouser, my first sip evaporates on my tongue like the Lima fog. Then it opens like a desert flower in the base of my brain, as piercing and complex as Peru.

"You must visit our cousin Claudio," Cristina insists when it is time to leave. "He makes his own pisco in the town of Pisco, and it's only a day's drive south of Lima."

THE MAD TEA
PARTY

A few hours down the coastline, the Lima fog lifts. There are tollbooths along the Pan-American Highway where it passes through swanky beach resorts, and we have to pay entrance fees—as if for permission to glimpse the glamorous.

Tucked into one cove is a villa that belongs on the cover of *Architectural Digest*—soaring white stucco walls and a cliff-perched turquoise swimming pool lean out over the Pacific. Around the next curve are empty reed mats skewered into the sand like cubes of straw. These huts are built by destitute residents of the nearby highlands in the hopes of staking a claim to land that might someday be valuable. There are billboards advertising pisco for sale but no signs of farming—until we pass the town of Pisco and take the turnoff to Claudio's distillery.

Here, rising from the desert like a mirage, are billowing fields of thigh-high asparagus and vine-wrapped trellises bearing thick-skinned, opalescent green grapes. We make our approach cautiously, as though around the corner we might disturb a giant rabbit with a pocket watch.

We pull into the sandy parking area of a one-story Spanish ranch house, but there is no one around, and all we hear is the breeze rustling through grapevines. The sun sets, flat and purple, and still there is no Claudio.

"Cristina wouldn't have forgotten to call him, would she?" I wonder aloud, too drained to even contemplate finding another spot to camp for the night. We are 184 days into this nomadic life, and it startles me to realize that squatting on a stranger's land no longer startles me. Or that I am not plotting how to find an Internet café to confirm, reschedule, control in any way whatever this night has in store. I'm beginning to understand that these are the chances that come before dips and twists in the plot of life. I am content to be the kite now instead of huffing and puffing like the wind. Finally, when the night's first stars are beginning to punch through the twilight, a pickup rumbles through the gates in a cloud of powdery, backlit dust.

"Dentists! Even their own mothers shudder at their offspring," Claudio proclaims as he reaches out to shake Gary's hand.

It turns out he was in Lima getting a tooth pulled when his cousins reached him on his cell phone. He drove back through the desert at ninety miles an hour to catch up to us at his ranch in Pisco. It is too dark for a tour of the distillery, and the anesthetic is still slurring Claudio's words. So the three of us sit around and drink pisco until the pain of the long drive and the dentist are merely memories.

The more pisco I drink, the better I understand Claudio's temporarily sloppy English and his dry sense of humor. When the temperature plunges in the desert night, we move the collection of half-empty pisco bottles from a stone outdoor patio to a tiled indoor sitting room. I can't help calling our host Don Claudio, and he does not object.

He is grizzled and callused yet elegant and amusing. It may be the pisco but I'm sure this man I've just met can waltz as skillfully as he drives a tractor. He tells us he is Italian and his ancestors were winemakers from Genoa. His grandfather came to Peru in 1900 and started making pisco, and the skill was handed down for three generations. Don Claudio now markets his pisco under the brand name Huarangal.

"Once upon a time there were forests of huarango trees growing along the Peruvian coast," Don Claudio explains. "But then the bad times came and they were all chopped down for firewood."

As much as the desert seems to define Don Claudio, I am startled to find out that he is actually a refugee. He and his wife, Isabel, raised their two daughters in Lima. They owned a restaurant for fifteen years, but in 1988 Shining Path guerrillas bombed the restaurant's street in Miraflores.

"The whole city was without power, and all you could hear was the roar of generators," Don Claudio remembers, his toothache suddenly throbbing again and in need of another dose of pisco. *Drink me,* I hear the bottle saying, and I feel shrunken and off balance, afraid to hear what happened next.

"So many people were getting killed that my daughters were afraid to go to school. So we packed it all up and moved to Pisco to grow grapes."

When the terrorism died down, his girls wanted to go back to school in Lima. Isabel lives with them in the capital during the week while Claudio runs the distillery.

"Could the Shining Path regain power again?" he rhetorically questions the room now slowly spinning around my head. "Never. They accomplished nothing and their voice was wasted. There is no longer an audience for communist or socialist ideas, and no leaders have risen to take the place of those in jail. It is over."

We toast to the end of the revolution, if not the struggle, and the next morning Don Claudio shows us his vision of Peru's future.

Grape juice and skins ferment in open-air, concrete tanks for three days. Then he seals the tanks, depriving the fomenting mix of oxygen for another twelve days. The pisco is pumped underground through plastic pipes and outside to a copper contraption that resembles a cross between a minaret and a giant tea kettle.

"It's called an *alambique;* it's Arabic in origin," the lab-coat clad Claudio explains. "It distills the liquid from eight thousand liters down to two thousand. For the first year it tastes like piss, and you can't sell it until it has aged for at least three years."

The sign of a great pisco, according to Claudio, is the tornado-like funnel of bubbles it makes when you cradle a bottle by its neck and twirl it in a slow circle. Don Claudio makes three varieties of Huarangal pisco, and over the course of our stay on his ranch we research each one. I can testify with no statistically significant margin of error that bottles of all three produce a perfect cascade of tiny bubbles when twirled and a pang of regret when emptied. I feel like a guest at a mad tea party, and if we stay any longer we might never return to normal size.

LINES IN
THE SAND

We are less than a day's drive to the mysterious lines of Nazca, but we arrive too late in the afternoon to sign up for one of the prop-plane sightseeing tours. It's a splurge worth indulging in because it is only from the air that the still unexplained, miles-long geometric lines and fantastical shapes emerge from the plains into which they are etched. We will have to wait until morning for the winds to calm and Don Claudio's pisco to clear.

Nazca is literally a landmark, the crust of the earth carved and lined by an ancient people whose motives are as fuzzy as my memories. On my first trip through Peru we drove on top of the Nazca lines and I never saw a thing. That's because when construction of the Pan-American Highway began in 1938, the asphalt was poured before the plains were aerially surveyed and the drawings officially "discovered." The route that was supposed to modernize a continent bisected and destroyed a part of its history.

The geography has not forgiven the transgression. It might be the lingerings of a pisco hangover, but ever since we left the wonderland of Don Claudio's ranch the desert has taken on a horrific harshness. So we probably shouldn't stop at a cemetery on the outskirts of Nazca that is renowned for the callousness of grave robbers. The sun has less than an hour left to hover over Chauchilla, and we lock the camper even though we are the only humans in sight.

"Make that the only humans still breathing," Gary says as he lifts his camera to document the most disturbing scene we have ever encountered.

We are standing at the base of what guidebooks claim is the world's largest sand dune, but it seems more like a giant pile of ash. Some four hundred pre-Hispanic tombs lie in its shadow, a dozen or so officially excavated and their contents preserved in far-off museums. The soil is so caked and blanched it looks too tight to stretch over what lies beneath.

In shallow depressions, femurs stick out of the sand where robbers disturbed ancient graves and then abandoned them. Tufts of hair and strips of burial cloth drift and bluster along zigzags of cracked earth. Bleached and broken skulls balance on the tops of boulders like sentries watching over their own graves.

I gulp, thinking of another, smaller grave a continent away. This drive down the Highway seems suddenly macabre, a dark quest lurching from one painful point in the past to another. If the original camper still exists, won't I be just as guilty as a grave robber, disturbing whatever peace finally settled with it?

The wind makes raspy, scraping sounds across the parched expanses; it is so wide open that there is nothing against which brittle bones can take shelter. They just bounce and jar along, at the mercy of taunting gusts. Gary is taking photographs just yards in front of me, but the wind is so strong I can't hear his voice, and I have to turn my face from the stinging kernels of sand.

That's when I see her: the skeleton of a woman squatting on her haunches. She has long, flaming-red hair. Present tense, as in a full head of hair still attached to an intact skull, fluttering in the swirls of wind that swoop down into what was supposed to be her final resting place. It is parted precisely down the middle, and I wonder whose gentle hands combed through it, preparing her for the afterlife. A grieving mother's? A beloved sister's? I can't imagine why they didn't close her mouth—her jawbone gapes open in a silent scream, and her eye sockets are stuffed with some sort of cotton.

She is faced east but will never see another sunrise. I run back to the camper and retrieve a bottle of Don Claudio's pisco to leave by her side. I know that it will probably be stolen by the same vandals who plundered her grave. But she should have some passing recognition; the pisco is a fellow traveler's token of comfort for whatever journey she is on.

WE MAKE A RESERVATION FOR THE FIRST PROP-PLANE TOUR OF THE morning, when the still-cool winds are supposed to be the calmest. My stomach lurches as we lift off into the empty sky, but almost immediately awe spreads like a soothing tonic through every clenched muscle. From the air, the plains of Nazca are a borderless sketchpad, and symbols emerge from the sand like rubbings on a faded gravestone. The lines look surprisingly fragile and delicate—more like erasings than drawings. Some figures, like the spiral-tailed monkey, have a whimsical quality. But the geometric shapes and random lines—created several hundred years after the animal figures were made—are more intriguing. Looking down on them from the perspective of a condor is irresistibly speculative, the possible answers as infinite as the questions they present.

"They were artists," Gary says through the mouthpiece of the headphones that connect us.

For him the Nazca lines don't need to represent anything; the fact that they exist and add beauty to the universe is enough. I am getting more accustomed to this absence of certainty. I am content with close, or maybe. It is dawning on me that the search is reward itself. But I can't shake the sense that there's a lesson in the lines below me.

Maybe, like the person I was at the start of this journey, the people who created Nazca were trying to impose some sort of order on the world around them. The lines could have been an ancient attempt at control, a stab at permanence. It didn't matter in the end. Time erased whatever seemed important at the time. Planning and plotting did not preserve their purpose. But instead of filling me with a sense of futility, the Nazca lines release me. The future will not judge my logic, whether I stuck to a map, plotted the right course, followed the rules, or kept to a schedule. There is only the present.

The plane touches down and I step onto soil that feels more solid than it did the day before. The wind is picking up when we drive away from Nazca's plundered graves and celebrated mysteries. We will follow my father's route up into the Peruvian highlands, through the looking glass of the girl I once was. I am ready. I have maps. I am prepared. But it will not matter. Whatever will happen next will do so without any regard for my plans or my purpose.

Chapter Thirty-Five

FLAMINGO DREAMS

I am holding thirty-year-old photographs of the ascent from Nazca into the Andes, comparing sand dunes. Every one we pass matches those in the photos. The road's curves bend in the same direction, and there are still landslides and boulders to dodge. The only difference is that the sheer drop-offs of Highway 26A are now lined with guardrails and the surface is smoothly paved. My ears are popping and Gary says he feels a little lightheaded. But the Ford F-350 purrs along at fifty miles an hour, as if the pistons and injector nozzles don't remember that they spent the past few weeks driving through a desert level with the sea.

The thinness of the air accentuates the clarity and intensifies the hues of the landscape we are zooming through. Lichens and mosses cling to the otherwise barren rock in shouts of triumphant green and plucky yellow. The sky beams with a piercing blue instead of listless grey.

"What's wrong?" Gary asks.

I touch my face; tears are streaking through the grit. Not a thing is wrong. I am crying because instead of the ugly grey llamas I remember, the wild vicuñas we pass are the color of butter and apricot jam.

We pull over to make sandwiches for lunch. My hands quiver as I slice the bread. I light a burner to make tea and stare, fixated on the flickering blue ring of flame struggling for oxygen. My ears don't register the sound of the kettle's whistle; it isn't until I feel Gary's hand on my shoulder that I snap out of it and pour the boiling water. Down the drain. I can't remember where we keep the plastic mugs. Gary brings out a roll of toilet paper instead of napkins, and I can't figure out which hand to hold it in.

"Maybe we should have a picnic outside," Gary says. "The cold air might feel good."

But when we walk away from the camper we forget about eating. It is all I can do to walk in a straight line, and Gary stumbles, as if the camera strapped around his neck were suddenly leaden.

"Look," he says. "There over."

He is pointing to a shallow lake a few hundred yards in the distance that quivers in the sun like a bead of cobalt in a pan of gold. Hovering above it, as though wading through a mirage, is a flock of neon-pink flamingoes.

"How did they get up here?" I ask.

Flamingoes go with zoos and neatly mowed front yards. I am too tall. My head hits the sky. I am swimming through my own tears. The flock looks up to examine us, utterly without fear. We are Adam and Eve, pale and wingless in a garden of wind.

We sit down on a boulder and check the altimeter built into Gary's watch. We have climbed from sea level to 14,261 feet. Since breakfast. Less than three thousand feet to go and we would be level with Mt. Everest's base camp. But instead of slowly acclimatizing, with oxygen tanks and Sherpas to guide us, we have made this ascent in a matter of hours. The realization sets off a minor panic somewhere in the back of my fuzzy brain. *I must be hallucinating. My nose will start to bleed. Gary might pass out at the wheel. We could get in a wreck.*

Nothing makes sense. I don't know who that big camper sitting on the white truck belongs to or why I'm sitting here watching flamingoes. *Where is my little sister?* I should look at my list. Somewhere I have a list that will say what to do. But it is so beautiful that I start giggling instead. I put our ham sandwiches on the dirt, next to each other.

"For a pillow," I tell Gary, and from our backs we watch silver clouds float over the top of the world.

Chapter Thirty-Six

THE ROAD

Except for the pink flamingoes, I am certain this is the same exact spot where we stopped thirty years ago. A memory of teaching my little sister how to play leapfrog floats through my foggy consciousness.

"I scrunched down into a tiny ball, like this." Telling the story to Gary, I feel as though it happened yesterday. I have to touch the earth to keep from falling into it, light-headed and off balance. "Then I told Jenny to run as fast as she could, straddle her legs, push off my back, and say, 'Ribbit,' like a frog."

I'm sure my father was underneath the truck, fixing something. My mother was probably trying to boil water for his coffee. Nobody was watching us until my sister's scream pierced through the thin air. Startled vicuñas ran away, bleating and tripping over the rocks. The curled surface of my back couldn't have been more than two feet from the ground. But after six months of sporadic nutrition, a two-foot fall was enough to snap a two-year-old's shoulder.

Normally Jenny bounced into the cab of the Jeep and flipped herself into the backseat in head-over-heels giggles. But now she couldn't reach for the door handle to pull herself up. Her lips were as purple as Tootsie-Pop stains, and all her words ran together.

"Owiemommyithurtssobaaaaaaaad," Jenny moaned.

MAY 30TH 1974
We think Jen broke her shoulder bone. Taped it and padded her seat. No doctor for day or so.

In 1974, the road cutting through the Andes from Nazca was a four-hundred-mile-long gravel rut, snaking through canyons of sideways-slipping slate.

MAY 31ST 1974
Put blanket on engine so wouldn't freeze during night. Everyone woozy. Jen very restless. I blacked out.

The fear of freezing was founded. The altimeter in my father's truck had already iced over, leaving the needle stuck at fifteen thousand feet. The next day we made it only ten miles before my mother took out her journal again. She committed the misery to paper, like a passenger on a plane about to crash.

JUNE 1ST
Road too terrible to describe. Still at 14,000 to 15,000 feet. Breathing hard. I think we've had it.

I think we've had it. My mother's spirit broke in those five short words. When you are seven and your mother shuts down, you stop fighting with your little sister. You remember how it felt when your brother disappeared, and his absence sits likes cold concrete in your stomach.

You pretend you are anywhere but in the mountains of Peru. You stop asking, "Are we there yet?" when the winding dirt road never ends.

Seven days later, when you finally reach the hospital in Cusco, you think the fluorescent light that shines through the X-ray box on the wall is the most beautiful picture in the whole world. There it is—your little sister's glowing collarbone in feathery white. Where it should be straight there is a vertical smudge of black. And then your mother leans in so close her nose almost touches the film and she starts to smile. There are threads of white knitting themselves across the gap; the bone is already healing itself.

> **JUNE 9TH, 1974**
> Beautiful. Ruins really something . . . met nice peo-
> ple—spoiled Jenny . . . went to bed tired but happy.

Eight days after the worst night of the entire journey, my mother held my sister's good hand and climbed the steep Incan terraces of Machu Picchu.

"Damn, this is hard work," my two-year-old sister muttered. Steps my mother could clear two at a time were thigh-high hurdles for Jenny. She stuck out her lower lip, blew the bangs away from her sweaty forehead, and grunted up each terrace.

"Damn, this is hard work," louder this time. My mother and my father laughed until tears streamed down their faces. Their tough, beautiful little girl had survived.

I am scouring my mother's journal, hoping she listed a place to camp anywhere on the road to Cusco. I can decipher her handwriting enough to identify one town, but the dates don't match up. For a moment I wonder if we are traveling on a completely new highway instead of retracing the original passage. Then I realize we have blazed past the scene of my sister's fall and covered, in less than one day, what my mother documented over the course of three.

I pack away the journal and continue on, sobered yet still exhilarated. Until this day it has seemed as though we are somehow continuing a road trip—one that was interrupted by thirty years. The parallels have amazed me: finding people mentioned fleetingly in my mother's journal, getting sick in the same places and hit with the same attempts at bribes.

Now the contrasts are coming into sharper focus. I am seeing things I couldn't as a child. The soil and the sky merge in dusty lilacs and olive yellows. Peaks in the distance are kitten's-ear pink, and the sudden canyons that slice from the grassy plains recede in glints of silver. It is not entirely wild and uncultivated. Mud clusters of farm huts and animal corrals interrupt wide swaths of emptiness.

We need to find a place to camp before we lose the light, but there are no more towns listed on the map. I have a strong sense of a safe place behind a mountain, but the memory is not a physical one, nothing I can describe aloud to Gary. The details floating back to me are sensory and peripheral. I am groping in the fading light, trying to remember. It had to have been a place where Jenny and I could crouch behind the wheels to pee and vomit without being seen by passing trucks or curious llamas. Up ahead, on the left, I see a crescent-shaped mound of earth, like a gently curving riverbank along a dry bed.

Gary maneuvers the Avion into its lee. The camper is blocked from sight. Tucked behind the mound, we are sheltered from intensifying wind. Gary goes through seven matches before one can hold its flicker long enough to light the wick of our propane heater. I hold my hands against the metal and I am filled with more than warmth.

I suddenly realize why it is that all my life I have been so compelled to control every detail and plot every possible outcome before I step out into the world. It is a reaction to what happened here. My little sister was broken and it was my fault. My father and mother couldn't fix her. They couldn't fix the road. They couldn't fix the truck. Every list I make, every decision I second-guess, and every precaution I take is one less chance of feeling like a helpless seven-year-old girl.

Blood is pounding in my ears and I want my mother to know the fairy-tale ending of the story she started so long ago. I dig out the satellite phone and call Corn Island, Nicaragua. Usually my father answers but this time I hear my mother's voice, timid and uncertain.

"Yes?" she asks, forgetting hello. She talks on the phone the same way she enters a room, hanging back, letting my father bluster ahead of her.

"Mom, it's me," I shout. Then I realize the connection is pure and close. We are so high there is nothing to block the satellite signal. I lower my voice. "I'm calling you from Peru."

The place where you thought we all might die.

"Did you say Machu Picchu?" she interrupts. "That's where your little sister learned to cuss, you know." I can hear her smiling; she wants to replay the slide-show version of the story.

"Damn, this is hard work," I dangle for her, something to hold on to. She giggles, so I say it again, just like Jenny did. Over and over. *Damn, this is hard work.* "I love you, Mom."

"I love you too, Princess. Daddy will be mad he missed you." I put away the phone. The connection is gone.

Chapter Thirty-Seven

MACHU PICCHU

O ur next night's campground is a gas station outside Cusco. It is noisy and filthy and smells like diesel fuel and grease traps, but the men's room has hot showers for truck drivers. We are the first to pull in for the night.

"Sea rápido; usted tiene treinta minutos." The attendant says I have a half hour before the bathroom will fill with drivers, all of them men.

He shows us how to fasten plastic bags around the faucets with rubber bands to avoid electrocuting ourselves by touching metal in an electric shower. Gary stands guard while I take the quickest, scariest shower of my life. I leave the water running for Gary as I bolt to the privacy of the camper.

As darkness falls, semitrucks fill in on all sides of the Avion. The backfiring exhaust systems and rattling diesel engines take hours to shudder to a stop. I can't sleep anyway; there isn't enough air to breathe, and the Cusco entry in my mother's journal is far from comforting.

> **JUNE 6TH, 1974**
> Got two good contacts to sell the truck. Sold our
> camping mats. Teri washed dishes.

It comes suddenly, this mention of selling the truck, the words like a mangy dog my mother rattled a stick at, hoping it would limp away on its own. Without the camping mats my father was forced to sell, there was nothing to cushion my sister's injured shoulder. In Cusco we started sharing my sleeping bag so that we could use Jenny's as extra padding underneath. There is nothing in my mother's journal of the outcome of the "deal" my father was working. We just moved on.

"Your dad would never settle for the first offer that came along," Gary says. "It's not in his DNA."

I am more compelled than ever to move on. The intensity of Peru is draining. In the nineteen days since we left Ecuador, we have camped in eighteen different spots. There is trouble brewing ahead, in Bolivia, the country where an expat finally bought my father's camper. We want to cross the border and search for it before the country explodes. Bolivia's disgraced president has fled to Miami, seeking refuge from the indigenous protestors who ran him out. Riots have killed more than seventy people, and more protests are threatened in the coming months.

If that weren't motivation enough, with each night in Peru it seems colder and harder to breathe than the last. The altitude makes my chest feel too tight for my lungs. Gary's jaw and shoulder blades ache in the mornings from the bitter cold. The futon that functions as our mattress collapses into a mean shelf that bruises my hips if I turn on my side to read in bed.

Other than the occasional stare at our silver camper, our presence in modern-day Peru is accepted without curiosity. Thirty years ago my wounded family was a spectacle. We stumbled, limped, and crawled from one good Samaritan to another, so routinely at the mercy of random rescuers that my mother stopped listing their last names or addresses in her journal. There is no context to the entries or explanation of how or why we met these strangers. But her tone turns reverential when one of them gives us the chance to bathe.

> JUNE 14TH, 1974
>
> Stayed in Hector's house all day, had a delightful visit
> and BATH. They have a 13-month boy. Dave visited
> the factory where he is the boss and he took us to din-
> ner. The maid did our washing. Pantera disappeared.

It is almost an afterthought, those final two terse words tossed into a description of more important things. Losing a loyal companion was nothing compared to all the losses we had already suffered, barely worthy of a mention. Our brutal, spirit-breaking journey through Peru began with my father's willingness to backtrack through the Sechura Desert to find Pantera. A month later he didn't look back, and my mother's journal never mentions the cat again.

"Listen to all she wrote next," I tell Gary. But I can barely get the words out.

> JUNE 15TH, 1974
>
> Dave fixed camper and we drove. Bumpy as usual, and
> cold.

Gary takes one hand off the wheel, closes the journal, and laces his fingers through mine. "We made her a gravestone," he says, and my unspoken guilt over leaving Wipeout behind is lifted and separated from the long-ago loss of a half-blind cat.

Gary and I leave Cusco and drive until we reach the last town on the road to Machu Picchu: Ollantaytambo. The only way to get from there to the base camp for the ruins is by train, so for the first night since crossing into South America we have to abandon the Avion.

"I don't like this," Gary says as he locks the dead bolt and sets the truck's alarm.

I am trying to fight my inner voice of doubt and distrust. We are in the same place where Pantera disappeared. Someone could hot-wire the truck in the middle of the night, and we would return from Machu Picchu literally homeless. Because all the vendors in Ollantaytambo's plaza are already gawking at our elaborate security precautions, I offer to hire one of them to guard the camper while we're gone.

"No necesita," says a woman bundled in shawls with coins sewn into their fringes. She just wants us to buy two of her llama-wool blankets when we get back.

We enter Machu Picchu hours before the waves of day-trippers from Cusco. The mist is slowly clearing from the mountains, patch by patch, revealing glimpses of stunning, verdant jungle. Jutting out above the ruins are snow-capped mountains like peaks graphed on an axis of earth by sky.

It is like opening a favorite picture book and watching it come to life. This one, for me, will always star my little sister as the heroine. Here she began the rebuilding of my mother's spirit with every step and arrested, for a while, my father's despair. Jenny was as strong as any son would have been, and her triumph still echoes between the stone slopes, bouncing back to me more vividly than my own recollections. When I was a child, Machu Picchu seemed miles wide with exhaustingly long, grassy fields, but now the aspect ratio is radically different. Everything is steep; terraces, altars, storehouses, and sundials are stacked almost on top of each other.

"No wonder your little sister cussed a blue streak," Gary says. "Even an adult could pull a hamstring on these steps."

When Jenny produced the first grandchild in our family, I asked her which was harder: giving birth or climbing the ruins at Machu Picchu.

"In the hospital at least they give you drugs," she said.

WE RETURN TO FIND IT IS 30.4 DEGREES INSIDE THE CAMPER. MIRACU-lously, the pipes didn't freeze overnight, and when we light the heater a wave of warmth and comfort fills the galley. Gary starts the long process of boiling water, and I search for a plastic bag of coca leaves. Forty minutes later we are sipping on the bitter, acidic tea that indigenous peoples use to dull hunger and open the lungs.

Our bones might not agree, but we both know how lucky we are. We can start up our diesel engine and leave whenever we want. The closest to truck trouble we ever encounter in Peru isn't with our own vehicle. It comes after a daylong hike to the top of the ruins of Písac in the Sacred Valley. As if out of a kid's fantasy, the clouds part and a vendor appears, peddling ice cream.

"How the hell did he get that cart up here?" I must be having another flamingo hallucination.

Gary points to a beat-up pickup truck with tie-down cables in the bed. I am too light-headed to make sense of it. The thought of trekking back down to the camper on foot is unbearable, so I walk over to the ice-cream man to negotiate a lift.

Franco speaks some Spanish and cheerfully says there is plenty of room. Gary will have to ride next to the ice-cream cart in the back, along with several poncho-wrapped men who materialize out of nowhere, but I am given the prime position in the front seat next to Franco. It is the perfect vantage point from which to notice 199,994 miles on the odometer, no glass in the front windshield, and no instrument panel of any sort in the dashboard. I have the distinct premonition that I am about to be punished for my laziness.

Tangled green, red, and blue wires thrust into the empty space like amputated bouquets. The steering wheel comes directly through the cab floor, the foot brake is missing its pedal, and the gearbox is almost rusted through. When the truck picks up speed there is a dusty blur beneath my feet, and I bring my knees to my chest because the seat seems sturdier than the floor. Franco doesn't seem to notice, and I realize he might easily have been one of the countless, unnamed strangers who stopped for my father while he thumbed a ride on the side of the Pan-American Highway. Franco's truck is held together just as ours was: by necessity.

He stops to collect more passengers as we descend into the town of Písac. Each time he stops, the pickup stalls. The passengers in the bed have to jump out and push-start it to life. At least Gary has something to do, a way to contribute. I am paralyzed with fear, wedged behind thrusting wires that spark when they touch.

The potholes aren't so much holes as collapsed gravel pits. To protect my spine I lift myself off the seat like I'm pedaling a bicycle over a curb. This is how bodies are flung from cliffs and piles of crumpled metal end up at the bottom of ravines. I close my eyes and promise myself I will never hitchhike in Peru again.

Yet Franco calmly steers through the remnants of landslides, and over the racket I manage to tell him that I visited Peru as a little girl.

"What do you think has changed the most in thirty years?" I shout through the rattling.

"When the terrorism stopped, the government rebuilt everything for tourists," he replies. "Thirty years ago this road was terrible."

IN THE ALTIPLANO THE AIR IS SO THIN AND THE SUN SO SLICING THAT the mountains are upthrust scars, eruptions of earth that block the winds from carrying rains inland and coating their slopes with gentle green. The people who survive here do so out of sheer force of will, their presence shouted out in shocking colors.

Chapter Thirty-Eight

CHRISTMAS
IN BOLIVIA

B y the time we leave Peru I have acquired the camping skills to cope with sub-forty-degree days and below-freezing nights. I can whip up a pumpkin and potato curry in one pot, frying onions in curry powder and turmeric and then pouring just enough water over the caramelized base to boil the vegetables.

I can take a shower in two, seven-second increments: the first as I hang out of the camper in my underwear and Gary pours a milk jug full of water over my head, and the second to rinse off the shampoo that I've recycled from my hair to my shivering body. Not that clean hair matters when it is shoved under a pointed wool cap twenty-four hours a day; in photos I am so bundled against the cold it is impossible even to recognize my gender.

Gary has decided that brushing his teeth with Coca-Cola is safer than water and that growing a beard is more sensible than trying to shave through goose bumps. I wake each morning next to a man who looks more and more like the one in my father's passport: grizzled, self-sufficient, and slightly deranged.

The altitude and harshness of Peru have hardened us both, and I am counting on this thicker skin to get us through Bolivia. Friends from home forward us dire State Department warnings of anti-American outbursts and frightening news reports. Protests over the government's plan to pipe natural gas through Chile to sell to the United States are becoming more violent. In thirty-three days of clashes between soldiers and demonstrators in the slums surrounding La Paz, at least seventy people died before multimillionaire President Gonzalo Sánchez de Lozada fled to Miami.

Opponents of the interim president have issued him a ninety-day ultimatum: prove yourself a worthy successor or the riots will begin anew. We do not want to be driving through Bolivia with Washington, DC, license plates when this window of grace slams shut. Gary and I must enter Bolivia, find my camper, and get the hell out by New Year's Eve. There is speculation that the US Embassy will close, severing a lifeline for travelers caught in the cross fire.

It would not be unprecedented. In the nearly two centuries since its independence from Spain, there have been almost two hundred coups d'état in this landlocked, downtrodden country, earning it a place in the *Guinness Book of World Records*.

It is also infamous in my family's history as the country where my father had to sit on a loaded gun so border inspectors wouldn't discover it. To lessen the chances of our own being uncovered, we decide to cross the least-traveled border, one that straddles a dismal frontier post called Yunguyo.

The town seems to exist only because of the border; the shops and market stalls along its one dusty road sell things like expired bottled water and stale, tongue-colored chewing gum. Just a few miles on the other side is the resort town of Copacabana, where trucks and buses, decorated by garlands of flowers and tinfoil streamers, line up to be blessed by the priests. If we make it through this border crossing, I will gladly join them.

"Esperate," says the guard with the entrada stamp. "¡Haga una contribución al policía!"

Bribes again, I begin to translate for Gary.

"Not a bribe," he says. "Just a contribution."

Grabbing a wad of dollar bills from the glove compartment, he hands them to the guard with a cheery "¡Feliz Navidad!" and we drive away, unsearched, into the country that was the last stop for my father's camper.

Gary's cheeriness just makes me feel worse. My husband may have been the first to suggest this retracing of my childhood odyssey, but I'm the one with firsthand knowledge of how reckless it really was. And now we have entered a country that is even more dangerous than it was in the 1970s.

I need something to distract me from such portentous thoughts, so I open the Christmas present we picked out before we left, ripping through faded Santa Claus wrapping paper. It is a stack of CDs— ranging from Bing Crosby's *White Christmas* to an Elvis yuletide compilation. I put in the first CD and begin to sing along.

"Deck the halls with boughs of holly, falalalalalalalala! 'Tis the season to be jolly. . . ."

I have perhaps the most unlovely voice in all the Americas, and I wait for Gary to take his hands off the wheel and stuff his fingers in his ears, begging me for mercy. But his jaw is slack, mouth unable to close. I follow his gaze and see children lined up alongside the road.

Some stand mutely with one hand out. Others go down on bended knee as we pass. Most pump their cupped hands up and down through the air in a gesture vaguely obscene in its desperation. There are hundreds of them, standing along the road like mile markers. Their cheeks are candy-cane red, chapped and blistered by the sun.

Hopeful grins stretch over broken, black, or missing teeth, and the wind whips matted hair around their faces like dirty straps of leather. Occasionally cars coming from the other direction slow down and passengers toss out bags that spill at the children's feet. Bread rolls and pastries tumble out, and the smallest children take turns shoving the goodies back in, saving them for later.

I push eject on the CD player; it's too hard to mix the merry and the misery. Even when we camped at the base of a Lima slum, we could watch the dirt paths leading into the hills and see that children had books and school uniforms. Now we are driving past malnourished toddlers begging for bread.

The paved road dead-ends at the foot of Lake Titicaca, in front of a row of flat wooden barges. Old tires are lashed to the sides of the boats with frayed rope, like floating bumper-rafts.

"Is it some sort of fish market?" I ask Gary.

He looks in the side-view mirror and sees cars and buses bunching up behind us. Horns are honking. Children are pumping empty fists, jumping on the sideboards.

"No. I'm guessing this is the Lake Titicaca ferry system."

We are facing a narrow pinch in the lake; across the water is the highway that cuts through the mountains to the capital, La Paz. The crew of the first boat in line has already lowered a sheet of plywood to serve as a boarding ramp. Gary puts the truck in first gear and gingerly inches aboard.

The camper lurches to the left as soon as the ramp is pulled in behind us; another boat is nudging into position and we are in his way. Under the weight of the Avion, the bow leans into the lake at a drunken angle and waves slap against the partially submerged sides.

Water splashes up through gaps in the decking. Whole planks are missing, and the sputtering, two-stroke outboard motor almost drowns the voice inside my head. *I should jump inside the camper, collect the cash and passports, and stuff them in my bra in case we have to swim to shore.* Not even my father tried to cross Lake Titicaca on one of these dilapidated ferries. Live animals are stacked in baskets, topped with spread-eagled men holding them in place like human cargo nets. There are no life jackets in sight; lit cigarettes dangle from the lips of men who can't seem to smell the diesel fumes around them.

"Look on the bright side," Gary says. "We might not have to sneak that gun of yours through any more border crossings if it sinks to the bottom of Lake Titicaca."

The barge men run to the bow. The engine has stopped, and they are poling us in to shore, dodging collisions with waiting ferries. To disembark, Gary has to drive the Avion over a small pyramid of planks. I jump off the front of the barge onto the pebbled shore, clutching Gary's camera. If I watch this through a tiny viewfinder, it won't seem so insane.

Chapter Thirty-Nine

THE HEIGHTS

There is smooth blacktop underneath us again, the best Christmas present we could ask for, and we head for La Paz at fifty miles an hour. Any slower and I would think of the gun again and whether we might finally need it to survive in this imploding country. If the contraption even still fires. It's been under molding paperbacks for months, untouched or cleaned all through the rainy season of every country in Latin America.

Guns fit right into the Bolivia of my father's slide show. I picture him not bothering to hide the pistol once he smuggled it past the border, letting it rest right between his legs and my mother's on the front bench seat. The camper was our covered wagon in a country he saw as the Wild West. There are even campfires and cowboys in this sepia-tinted recollection.

But the Bolivia I see through the windshield of the F-350 is apocalyptic. On the altiplano approaching the capital, we are driving through a war zone. Burned-out cars are left like carcasses on the side of the road, upside down and stripped of anything salvageable. Chunks of pedestrian overpasses as big as our truck block the side roads where they collapsed in the riots. I can't order the clammy fear coating my thoughts and sliding through my guts, telling me to retreat; this is a landscape where natural bleakness is topped by manmade destruction. Even the air whistling through the truck's vents is agitated and crackling with tension.

When the sun sets, the mountains will black out any hope of seeing where we're going or who is out there. And no matter how conflicted I am about the gun, what is clear is that we are driving through an explosive country. My principles might not stand up to standoffs in the dark. I don't want to admit it to Gary, but I am grateful that a seventy-two-year-old woman showed me how to shoot the weapon lying in wait under the floorboards of the Avion.

"You have to be ready to actually kill someone if you pull the trigger," I remember Nancy saying, back in Arizona. "Then you'll have to drive the hell out of there without looking back."

She's wrong about one thing. Another gunshot in the altiplano wouldn't even attract attention. Yet somehow people manage to go on living in the midst of all this violence. One-story huts made entirely of reed mats clump together around dirt alleys, the weight of their shared walls suspended by a hovering net of antennae and twisted wires. Each power pole is braided with coat hangers, sloping out to individual rooftops like strings of Christmas tree lights. This endless squatter's camp has spread across the entrance to La Paz like a thirsting vine.

JUNE 18TH, 1974
Made it to La Paz. Steering went out. Fixed once.
Went out again.

"How far from La Paz are we?" Gary asks.

My father's map is useless. We are threading our way through a slum universe that didn't exist thirty years ago. La Paz was a sudden sight when I was seven, dropping in front of us on the barren plain like a meteorite into a crater. Now, three-quarters of a million desperate people have staked a claim high above the capital. El Alto, this new city is called: The Heights.

I see a taxicab backed into an alley and tell Gary to pull over. I will knock on the door of the driver's home and offer to pay him whatever he wants to drive me to a safe spot to camp for the night. Gary will follow the taxi. It is a plan I would have dismissed as ridiculously risky six months ago, but it seems safer than two Americans trying to run the gauntlet of seething tension and poverty.

I climb into the cab of a man whose Christmas dinner I have interrupted, a stranger who has probably never answered the door and found an American woman asking for his services. The cynic in me says he could drive me in circles, running up the meter for a bigger fare. Or deliver the two of us to some political faction who could commandeer the truck and dump us where no one would ever look. Waves of spasms pass through my bowels, nerves wringing my intestines.

Stop it, I tell myself. *This man has three children. I saw them. His wife's homemade soup will be waiting for him when he returns.*

I lock the door, buckle my seat belt, and tell him to drive. The only way to fill the awkward silence is to launch into the story of our search for my father's camper. His jaw relaxes into a smile somewhere between confusion and amazement.

"¿De veras? ¿Hace treinta años?" His name is Eosebio, and thirty years seems like a lifetime to him.

He is Gary's age, and he tells me he has never left the confines of the city collapsing around him. He asks me to list every country we have driven through and what languages are spoken in each. He is driving over pavement, where it still exists, that is broken like the split-open seam of an earthquake. Intersections are flooded.

"Es normal," he tells me, shaking his head. "Desafortunada-mente." Corrupt politicians are to blame, in Eosebio's assessment, stealing all the tax revenue that should go to infrastructure.

We dodge sinkholes, craters, and raging currents of raw sewage. He stops every few hundred yards to check that Gary is still behind us. What I see in the rearview mirror drains the blood from my head, and I have to fight the sensation that I am about to pass out. Men are clambering onto the sideboards of the truck, banging on Gary's rolled-up windows.

They look less like gangsters or soldiers than hunters in a pack. The truck's side-view mirrors are convenient foot pegs, and one of them thrusts himself onto the hood. He's scrunched, gripping the windshield wipers like a swimmer on the starting blocks, inches from Gary's face. I am fumbling for the lock on the cab door, like somehow I could jump out and scare them off, when Eosebio's arm pushes me back against my seat.

In a split second, I know why. With his free hand he waves for Gary to follow and then guns the taxi up an on-ramp to a highway overpass. The hungry growl of the truck's diesel engine behind us is so loud I can feel it through the floorboards. One by one the men let go, peel off, and drop back to the ground. Eosebio gives Gary a thumbs-up in the rearview mirror, but when I unclench my fists it releases a wave of nausea.

"Hace solo un mes," he begins another story.

It's been only a month since a tour bus was held hostage for a week and four passengers wound up shot to death. Closer to Lake Titicaca, he assures me, not here in the capital city, but we should be very careful anyway. It isn't safe when so many people are suffer-ing. My stomach knows the truth I'm hearing; I don't need convinc-ing. We drop two thousand feet in elevation during a forty-minute descent, into a mountain basin filled with tinted-window SUVs and billboards advertising protein-rich hair conditioners and low-interest mortgages. It is suddenly overwhelming. Eosebio pulls the taxi to the side of the road so I can throw up in a ditch without getting out.

"¿Está usted embarazada?" He thinks I am pregnant. I shake my head, but Eosebio smiles knowingly, and there is no use in explaining how this is the price I pay for the gun I am smuggling through South America. He scribbles his cell phone number on the back of a card and hands it to me, in case I need anything during my stay.

Only more antibiotics and Dramamine, I think to myself. *And a hotel with good plumbing.*

The clouds lift and I can see jagged peaks of bare mountains ringing the city. The sun lights up the glass facades of modern skyscrapers just before it drops behind the peaks.

"¿Es milagroso, no?" To Eosebio, La Paz is a modern miracle, and at Christmas he delivers a woman he believes is pregnant to a fenced-in hotel compound in an elegant, tree-lined neighborhood known as Zona Sur. Eosebio convinces the owners to let us camp in their parking lot for four dollars a night, and even though he lives in a shantytown forty minutes up the side of a crater, my sweet shepherd will check in on me every day until I am well enough to leave La Paz.

Chapter Forty
LA PAZ

JUNE 20TH, 1974

Still working on truck . . . Aduana stopped by and asked
if we want to sell the truck. We said maybe yes. He came
back a half hour later with other men and offered to buy
it for $3,500. We'll attend to the paperwork tomorrow.

After seven months on the road and sixty major breakdowns,
there it is: a price on the life that had collapsed around us. By the time
we reached La Paz my father could no longer even steer the beast that
staggered under the top-heavy load of his homemade camper. With
$3,500 he could buy four one-way plane tickets from South America
to South Africa, an escape from his escape. My mother had passed
beyond disappointment and even relief. She was in my father's world,
mechanical: *We'll attend to the paperwork tomorrow.*

Only one thing stood between my family and the money that would free us. The broken steering column had to be cut off with a torch, refabricated in a machine shop, and somehow reattached to the front axle. Even in the poorest country on the continent, this repair would cost more money than we had left. But my father still had a few spare engine parts to trade for labor.

Traded ring and pinion for work done. Started to pack.

Parked in vacant lot

Eosebio has fetched us again, and I crane my neck from the front seat of his cab every time we pass a vacant lot. Each one could be the spot that was the beginning of the end for my childhood camper; it is as if time hasn't passed but traveled in circles. Like my stomach.

Eosebio is convinced that the sandwiches of La Paz's famous *cholas* will stop my vomiting. I'm leery of street food, but Gary is fascinated by these women. Their long black braids are tucked under stiff, narrow-brimmed hats straight out of a Laurel and Hardy skit.

I give in. Succulent roasted pork slices melt into a puffy cheese-bread bun. I would eat whatever Eosebio recommends for the rest of my life. He is showing me a different La Paz than the one I remember.

In that La Paz the air was grey and woolly with exhaust fumes, like a scratchy blanket. It was prettier at night, when I stood outside with my father, watching a mechanic loop a roll of scrap wire around his son's shoulders and make the sign of a cross. There was no electricity in the vacant lot, no way to reattach the repaired steering column. So the mechanic's son, not much older than me, climbed barefoot up a utility pole to an overhead power line. He scooted higher and higher, trailing wire behind him like Rapunzel's hair. His voice, tinny and far away, shouted, "¿Listo, Papa?"

When the mechanic was ready the son wrestled with the lines at the top, tapping directly into 440 volts of electricity. Blue sparks flew from every direction: the boy's hands, the coat hangers twisting around the pole, the welding torch his father held underneath our truck. Connected in arcs of current, the son stole from the lights of La Paz so his father could see.

> **JUNE 22ND, 1974**
> Aduana man came by to assure us that
> everything was okay, but then our battery
> wouldn't start.

It is never to the seller's advantage when a vehicle refuses to start. It was as if my father's unwillingness to stop a boy from risking electrocution circuited back on him in judgment: the end did not justify the means. The next morning dawned on a drained battery, and my father was out of spare parts to trade for labor.

> Boy were Dave and I sick during the night and
> all morning. Shits and vomiting—neighbors gave us
> some medicine.

The $3,500 sale fell through, but the neighbor my mother noted in her journal turned out to be the final guardian angel of my family's tormented trip. A Bolivian woman named Sonja was visiting her mother in La Paz when my parents puked through the night in a vacant lot next door. The mother happened to own property near Santa Cruz, on the other side of the country, and Sonja was married to an American man who needed a farm truck.

If my stomach ever settles, our plan is to leave La Paz and drive to Santa Cruz to see if the truck and camper are still on that farm. But I am still huddled over the toilet when there is a knock on the Avion's door. I peek through the windows and see Eosebio's taxi parked outside. He is pacing, one hand gripping the cell phone that is chained to his belt like a trucker's wallet.

"He must have bad news to give us," I tell Gary as I dress. "Maybe the political situation is heating up."

It has been a week since we arrived in La Paz, and I'm ready to leave. It's the rainy season in Bolivia, and the camper is closing in on me again. I duck inside the bathroom and splash water on my face before opening the door to greet Eosebio.

"Teresita," he begins. "Miras mejor que ayer."

I know my hair is still plastered to my forehead and I probably smell, but Eosebio tells me I look much better than I did yesterday. He is agitated, anxious to warn us of a problem. He remembers that I told him the farm where Sonja's husband offered to buy my father's camper was somewhere near Santa Cruz, days to the east of La Paz. Eosebio says to drive there now is impossible. According to other drivers in his union, a major bridge has washed away along the main highway to the eastern half of Bolivia.

"Debe ir en aeroplano," he says. He thinks we should leave our camper here at the hotel and fly to Santa Cruz.

"Not a good option," Gary says. Even if we never find my father's camper, we still have to drive south from Santa Cruz to continue on to Argentina and reach the end of the Pan-American Highway. "Ask him if there are any other cross-country routes."

Eosebio pulls out a map from the front of his cab. It shows only one route to Santa Cruz, and apparently the farthest east we could possibly drive along it is a city called Cochabamba. After that, major flooding has wiped out the bridge and closed the highway in both directions.

"Sonja's aunt lived in Cochabamba; my mother wrote about it in the journal," I tell Gary. We also have the name of a contemporary contact in Cochabamba, written on one of the lists I made before we left: a friend of a friend of my production manager back in the world I left behind.

"If we make it that far, maybe we can wait it out until they repair the bridge," Gary says. "How long could that take?"

Eosebio slowly shakes his head: I must be pregnant, Gary must be crazy. Still, he offers to lead us out of La Paz in the direction of Cochabamba so that we don't have to drive through El Alto again. For the last time, I sit beside a man who feels more like a fairy godfather than a taxi driver I met at random just a week ago. Gary follows, and our two-vehicle convoy threads its way through cobblestone streets and past concrete mansions built next to corrugated-metal shanties. *Chola* ladies in Laurel and Hardy hats shuffle past us in what should be gutters. Kids tug ropes around the necks of cows to move them out of the road. We climb for almost a full hour until we are level with the lip of the crater that cuts La Paz off from the rest of Bolivia.

Eosebio will have to drive another ninety minutes to return home, dodging burned-out buses and collapsed overpasses. But he seems reluctant to leave us. He fidgets with the map he insists on giving to Gary and digs through his glove compartment for a pressure gauge to make sure the truck's tires are ready for the trip ahead.

It is humbling, how much we have come to depend on strangers. Not on their sympathy but simply on their kindness. A woman who pukes a lot is not the same as a family forced to sell its possessions next to a broken-down truck. Yet I am collecting as many benefactors on my second journey as I did on my first. A handshake is all Gary can offer this man who has shown us the bravery and benevolence of Bolivia. But I can get away with hugging him.

"Buena suerte," Eosebio shouts when Gary starts the truck.

We'll need good luck. The last time I set out along this road, we made it only as far as the Jeep's sixty-first and final breakdown.

Chapter Forty-One

THE NEW YEAR

The entire country had only three hundred fifty miles of paved roads back in 1974, and it took Sonja and my family three days to travel from La Paz to Cochabamba, not counting my father's overnight hitchhike into a town called Oruro to replace a blown radiator. Gary and I make the desolate and bleakly beautiful journey in one smooth day. We are accustomed to the altitude; it doesn't cause bloody noses or shortness of breath anymore, just slowed movements and fuzzy thinking. We are so high that the clouds that used to float above me appear now to swirl below my feet. The horizon is a stack of layers I am swimming through.

The flat, high plains give way to the surly peaks and gorges of the Azanaques Mountains. The earth is the color of rust and black slate. There are veins of coal glistening along sunny ridges, and in the shadows clods of dark dirt look like purple bruises. The innards of the mountains have been sliced open and exposed to build this new

road to Cochabamba. We drive through a cross section of geology
and time. But for the modern road, we might have slipped into the
Middle Ages. The ponchoed people of the Azanaques live without
electricity, in mud huts with thatched roofs. Shared, low walls break
the bitter wind, and the water slopping over livestock troughs freezes
in dirty icicles.

Tucked into the hollow of one valley is a white stucco church. It
is resplendent with Spanish grace but off balance. We stop for Gary to
take a photograph, and I can't tell if it is leaning to the right or slowly
sinking out of sight. It is surrounded only by deserted adobe huts—as
though an entire community has abandoned faith. I wonder if this is
what finding the camper will be like: a physical record of my family's
pilgrimage withered and eroded by time.

I suddenly have second thoughts about looking up an American-
Bolivian couple when we reach the town of Cochabamba. We have
a physical address, but Don and Margit are two levels of connection
removed from anyone we actually know, and it seems a presumptuous
imposition. Is a friend of a friend of a friend ever really welcome? But
in almost two weeks in Bolivia we have spoken only to Eosebio and
each other. Since Margit is married to an American expat she probably speaks English, like Sonja did. I dial her number from a telephone
booth, and when she answers I am seven again, swooped into the
arms of another strong, decisive woman.

"Stay right there," Margit tells me. "It's too hard to explain how
to get to our house, so Don will come find your camper. I'm sure
you'll be easy to spot."

Don and Margit live in a rural bedroom community of Cochabamba called Tiquipaya. Their home is nestled between a woman
with two cows, named Marta and Rosita Amoracita, and another
family with six pigs and twelve children. Don and Margit have a huge
television tower in their backyard, around which scratch and peck
half a dozen ducks, hens, and roosters. Their garden smells of citro-
nella, cilantro, and lemon basil. They grow alfalfa for the birds and

enough vegetables to feed a village. A minuscule Jack Russell terrier growls from the safety of an insulated windowpane, and a nervous German shepherd darts between our legs and chases chickens. Above the graceful arabesque of their Spanish stone gate loom the snow-covered peaks of the Tunari National Park—none of which can compete with the force of nature that is Margit.

She is a tiny woman with flaming red hair and a personality that would dwarf anyone's but that of her equally charismatic husband. It is difficult to be glamorous in Bolivia, but Margit has the beauty and flair of Ethel Merman. Don is a silver-haired teacher from Los Angeles who now has Bolivian grandchildren and godchildren and speaks of the United States as a foreign country. When I ask him what he and Margit will do if the riots resume, he says he won't consider leaving.

"I've seen LA burn twice, once in the Watts riots and once after Rodney King," he answers. "It's not so different here."

I worry that our new Ford truck and silver camper, beacons of American consumer power, will somehow undermine the delicate and deliberate integration Don and Margit have achieved, but they won't hear of us staying anywhere but here, with them.

"Tomorrow is New Year's Eve," Margit exclaims as if it is a holiday declared in our honor. "And you and Gary must meet my aunt; everyone calls her Tia Eva."

JUNE 28TH, 1974
We stayed with Sonja's aunt and visited. Ate
hamburgers.

On both journeys, Cochabamba is an oasis. Gary and I plan on staying only one night, but Margit tells us rescuers are still looking for survivors swept away by swollen rapids when the bridge Eosebio warned us about collapsed.

"So the road is still closed?" Gary asks. We are sipping wine in front of a warm fire, and I am secretly hoping for a delay.

"You mean both roads: the new and the old highway," Don corrects.

It turns out there are two parallel routes that straddle a mountain range to the east of Cochabamba and normally reconnect near Santa Cruz. Floods and mudslides have made both passages impassable. Under the circumstances it would be both rude and foolish to refuse Don and Margit's invitation. So we give them a tour of the Avion and settle in for our first night in Tiquipaya.

"You will love Tia Eva," Don says as we climb into his pickup the following evening, New Year's Eve. "She's probably the most famous German in Bolivia, if you don't count Klaus Barbie."

Margit swats at Don's arm. "Tia Eva was sent to Bolivia to marry a family friend when she was eighteen," Margit explains. "After she left Germany both of her parents were sent to Auschwitz. Bolivians saved her life, so she has dedicated her life to helping Bolivians."

It is a startling story, one that puts a temporary highway closure in proper perspective. We take the back roads to Tia Eva's house, those less likely to be blocked by police checkpoints or protestors, and arrive at a one-story sawmill that once produced the wooden beams lining the shafts of silver mines in Potosí.

The floors are poured of smooth concrete, and the ceilings are so low that Gary and Don have to duck through door casings. The heavy mud walls are filled with photographs: Tia Eva in a nurse's uniform, handing out food supplies, accepting awards, and shaking hands with dignitaries. She has outlived her Bolivian husband but is still surrounded by extended family, much of which is converging in her long and narrow dining room tonight or phoning her from countries continents away.

Tia Eva is sitting in a corner near the head of the table, and we join the line to greet her with hugs, kisses, and New Year's wishes. I can barely see her over the sea of heads because she is even tinier than Margit. Her face is as round and layered as a pink camellia, and even bundled in bulky sweaters and scarves she is delicate and elegant. Her mahogany hair is curly and bobbed, and her eyebrows regally arched and refined. Her eyes water when she laughs, so it looks like she is crying when Don and Margit explain how Gary and I landed on their doorstep.

"To survive in Bolivia you must learn to laugh at what life throws your way," she says and waves us to a seat.

Long before midnight—Tia Eva makes no apologies for not waiting up—the crowd draws to a hush and Margit stands with a glass of champagne in hand. In a clear and ringing voice, she reads from a list of blessings to be thankful for and effortlessly slips in a mention that her new friends Teresa and Gary arrived in time for the celebration. She is often interrupted with good-natured heckling and murmured agreements, but not a single guest makes a move to drink from the glasses they hold in their hands.

Until Tia Eva rises from her chair at the head of the table. Only when the matriarch declares the definitive "Próspero Año" do glasses begin to clink.

"I grew up in that house," Margit tells us on the long drive home. "My mother left when I was little, and Tia Eva raised me since I was four years old. Let me tell you, that woman was so-o-o strict! The boys were terrified to ask me to a dance."

It may be the champagne, but it all makes sense to me now: Bolivia saved Tia Eva, Tia Eva saved Margit, and now Margit is saving us.

Chapter Forty-Two

WITCHES AND
SPELLS

The dawning of the new year brings no such clarity to the issue of when, or whether, the roads between Cochabamba and Santa Cruz will ever be back in service. Gary and Don scour maps of Bolivia to see if there are any routes that detour around the collapsed bridge, or any frontage roads that we could use to bypass mudslides. But between the two parallel routes are undeveloped national parks crisscrossed only by rivers. To the north of the northern highway, all the splinter roads dead-end in the Amazon. And to the south of the southern highway, the paved roads all lead to the capital, Sucre, and the mining city of Potosí. It is as if tectonic plates have shifted and Santa Cruz is now another continent.

By our third day parked in Don and Margit's driveway, our predicament is major Tiquipaya news, and friends and neighbors drop by with information and speculation.

"Six months," says the neighbor with the cow named Rosita Amoracita. "It will take six months to rebuild the bridge and reopen the highway."

"Give it a year," says the wife of an American university professor. "Remember, we just had a coup and the natives are restless."

In Tiquipaya, there are no television news networks or radio stations with traffic helicopters, so no one knows exactly where the roads have washed away or how much ground clearance is needed to ford the flooded rivers. If we wait long enough, our parade of visitors advises, the rains will stop and the roads will reopen.

DON GOES BACK TO TEACHING CLASSES AFTER THE NEW YEAR'S BREAK, and Margit calls a cab to take us to the long-distance bus terminal in Cochabamba.

"We should talk to the people who really know the roads: bus drivers," she explains. Within minutes of arriving at the terminal, she persuades a ticket taker to make us a photocopy of each bus line's schedule and route. Most have crossed out the entire fortnight of departures to Santa Cruz with thick felt pens. Margit is not deterred. In her one-inch pumps, pleated skirt, and buttoned-up floral cardigan, she flags down bus drivers and climbs aboard double-decker buses asking questions.

An hour later she has cobbled together an alternate route to Santa Cruz, over dirt roads and through towns not even listed on our map. But the same rains that turned two major highways into mudslides also fell on these more remote locations. None of the drivers can tell Margit how long this primitive route might take to drive, if it can be driven at all.

"I really don't think it's safe," she tells us reluctantly. "I haven't even heard of some of these towns and I grew up here. But you can decide later. Right now, let's go home to have a meal together."

Normally, taxi drivers deliver passengers no farther than the town square in Tiquipaya; beyond that point its roads are tire-swallowing mud bogs that regularly ruin suspensions. But Margit knows the driver's mother and answers his shy questions about how to apply for a home loan at a bank. Without being asked, he drives through troughs of mud and right up to her front gate. Margit presses a generous tip into his hand, and the driver not only boosts her over a mud puddle when he opens the door but carries her packages inside as well.

"On the news in America you see only the anger and protests in Bolivia," she tells me as she waves good-bye to the driver. "But all Bolivians want—all anyone wants—is a little gentleness."

I think of the begging toddlers of Lake Titicaca, the burned-out buses of El Alto, and the fear I felt asking a stranger to drive me through the streets of La Paz. And standing before me is the lesson I've been stranded here to learn. Margit comes from a family that harbors more than lucky travelers; people like her are the bone marrow of Bolivia. We are witness to the kindness and bravery that hold countries together.

Chapter Forty-Three

PACHAMAMA

The discussion over when and how to leave Cochabamba continues over wine and roasted chicken. Margit wants us to stay a little longer, to see if the rains will stop.

"Mi casa es su casa," Don says.

"We are having a wonderful time," Gary says. "The thing is if we hang out here too long we're pushing our luck on the political end."

Don looks unconvinced, so I jump in. "The truck can ford a stream or two, but we can't barrel through riots and roadblocks."

"Teresita," Margit says, extending her arms in a gesture of both question and embrace. "Why risk your own safety, and Gary's safety, just to find an old camper? It's probably chopped up for firewood. Your father moved on and forgot about it. Why can't you?"

I am tempted to run into her outstretched arms, let this gentle woman protect me from disappointment. But she is waiting for an answer.

"I had a brother I barely remember who should have been beside me in that camper."

The Jack Russell terrier is whimpering and pawing at Margit. This woman, who can fend off haggling street vendors, is wiping away a tear.

"In Bolivia, we have a saying that wisdom comes through the soles of our feet," she says. "This is because the earth is Pachamama, the one to whom we all return."

Now I am the one fighting back tears, and Don leans over to pinch my cheek.

"So if you want Mother Earth to clear these mudslides and help you find that camper," he says, "you always need to spill a little of whatever you're about to drink on the ground. She likes the strong stuff."

Margit's eyes widen and she claps her hands. "Don, you have given me a wonderful idea," she says. "Tomorrow I will take them to the witches market and we will buy an offering to Pachamama."

The witches market is hidden in a city-within-a-city called La Cancha. This outdoor trading post, notorious for pickpockets and counterfeit goods, sprawls over fifteen city blocks. Margit, luckily for us, is well practiced at spotting forgeries and has a sixth sense about people following too closely or watching too carefully.

"See that bottle of Lysol?" she points out. "It is just water with yellow food dye. And those radios from Sony? Pick them up, what do you feel? They are as empty inside as the brain of a Santa Cruz beauty queen."

We are shopping in La Cancha's witches market just before the first Friday of the new year. Margit laughs as she guides us through a tarp-covered maze of bundles and boxes, and it's hard to keep up through the market's cluttered canals. She flutters and dodges, twirls and dips, advances and retreats with such unpredictability that pickpockets eventually find someone else to trail. She never ignores the pleas of earnest merchants and finds a tactful recourse for every sales pitch. When we reach her favorite vendor, her arms gesture back and forth in the universal language of introduction as if she were conducting an orchestra.

"You must be wondering if she is really a witch," Margit whispers in my ear.

"Do you believe she is?" I ask.

"She says so, and who am I to doubt her?"

I have never seen so many powders, roots, and tiny vials of liquid. Peering down each aisle is like examining a chemistry set through a kaleidoscope. Apparently everyone in Cochabamba believes in witches at least some of the time, because they alone can prepare the monthly offering to Mother Earth.

"It's called a *q'owa*," Margit explains. "You pronounce it like co-aaaaah. I'm going to ask her to make two: one for us and one for you and Gary."

The basic ingredients of a *q'owa* include piles of dried flowers, herbs, and incense glued to a stiff sheet of construction paper and sprinkled with myrrh in a vaguely biblical offering. If the believer wants Pachamama to grant good luck with livestock, the witches mold tiny figures of llamas or sheep out of sugar and food coloring and attach them to the *q'owa*. Car trouble is addressed by sugar molds of vehicles. Homes are protected by tiny sugar dollhouses.

"Mis amigos necesitan la protección de Pachamama para su. . . . " Margit is trying to explain that we are taking a dangerous trip in a camper, but the witch looks confused.

"Casa rodante," I interject. I stick my finger in a pile of sugar and draw a house with wheels.

The witch smiles and lifts an armadillo off a stack of boxes in the back. She hangs it on a hook from a string tied behind its tiny ears and underneath its belly. I am still staring at the swinging armadillo, wondering if it's alive, when she peels the lid off a Tupperware container and holds up a pink sugar mold of a truck.

"Looks like a Ford F-350 to me," Gary says.

Then, underneath the pile of sugar trucks, the witch pulls out a green, boxlike canopy that looks remarkably like a camper.

"I can't believe it," Margit exclaims, congratulating the smiling witch.

"Um, do I want to know what the animal innards are for?" The witch is scraping the lining of a twisted pile of intestines over our *q'owa*.

"Grease from guts makes enough smoke to fill each room of the house with blessings."

Gary raises a bushy eyebrow.

"Don't give me that look," Margit laughs. "We are going to burn the other *q'owa* inside your camper."

The final, and perhaps most important, ingredient of the *q'owa* is the dried, aborted fetus of a llama or a condor. I am staring at baby llama skeletons tied to a rope in the back of the stall like emaciated toys hanging by their necks on a laundry line. Their tiny leg bones are bent at the joints, and their jutting chins tuck down in fetal position. Margit points to one dried fetus for herself and a second for us—as though it is no different than selecting produce.

Each llama is delicately wrapped in cotton balls and added to the *q'owa*, which is rolled in several sheets of newspaper like a fish-and-chips cone. I have no idea how much such sorcery costs; Margit presses a wad of bolivianos into the witch's palm before we can object. On the bus ride back to Tiquipaya, almost every passenger's shopping bag is topped with a carefully wrapped *q'owa* sticking out between plastic handles.

When we get home Don is back from the day's classes and already firing up the charcoal grill on his deck. "I get the coals really hot and then scoop some out with this shovel and put the *q'owa* on top to catch fire," he explains, as though he has been burning llama fetuses all his life.

For added effect, he runs into his closet and brings out a bizarrely pointed stocking cap.

"This is my favorite *chulo;* it's quite dashing, don't you think?"

He stands in front of us in a pointy red hat with pompom ear-flaps, holding a shovel with burning coals and what looks like a flaming grade-school science project. We follow the man in the dancing dunce cap around the house like he's the Pied Piper of Tiquipaya, draining an entire bottle of wine as Don inundates the four corners of his home with acrid *q'owa* smoke. Margit adds the finishing touch to the First Friday ritual: a sprinkle of rubbing alcohol wherever Don wanders.

"So Pachamama is never thirsty," she reminds us.

The *q'owa* burns out just as Don comes gasping from the last room of the house. Now it is time to burn ours.

"You leave tomorrow; may this bring much luck to your travels," Don pronounces with the seriousness of a shaman. The green sugar camper bursts into flames, and we run around the back of the house and through the chicken coops to reach the Avion in the driveway.

"Hurry," Don shouts. "We have just enough time to bless each tire. Then we must take it inside the camper before it smokes out."

He kneels in front of each tire, moving counterclockwise, and in the cold air the *q'owa* burns quickly. Gary holds the shovel of glowing embers while Don leaps into the Avion and then passes it up to him. Ashes of an unborn llama waft through the air, floating to rest on top of llama wool blankets. I help Margit up the back steps, but her entire bottle of rubbing alcohol spills over the seat cushions in the commotion. Our camper smells like smoke and rotgut, but faced with the prospect of mudslides between Cochabamba and Santa Cruz, Pachamama's protection is worth the stench.

Chapter Forty-Four

THE DECISION

Bolivian tour books stop just short of boasting about the country's terrible roads; they've become something of an attraction. Footprint's *Bolivia Handbook* lists "things to do" in highlighted sections, one of which is "Brave the helter-skelter ride down the world's most dangerous roads." Tour companies in the surreal and desolate salt flats compete with each other by the degree of assistance they provide to broken-down drivers. "We won't leave you stranded," one advertisement claims. The fact that you will break down is a given. Getting to Bolivia's remote regions requires Land Rovers in the dry season and private helicopters the rest of the year.

But Gary and I are not attempting to drive our disintegrating camper to extreme destinations; we are just trying to get to Bolivia's largest city: Santa Cruz. According to the map highlighted by the bus drivers Margit interrogated in Cochabamba, we will be traveling over pleasant-sounding "secondary roads" and "carriage routes." We have no idea whether we can buy diesel along the way, but the entire drive looks to be less than three hundred miles, and if we get decent mileage we should be able to drive that far on one tank.

The secondary road that bypasses the mudslides starts out as a single lane of faded yellow cobblestone. It feels like we are driving on a sidewalk or up someone's private driveway. The road stops when it reaches remote villages and picks up on the other side, so we have to backtrack, zigzag, drive over fields and through streams to wiggle around these road-squatting settlements. Gradually I wrap my head around what should have been obvious: secondary roads are used more by pack animals than vehicles.

In the flat stretches between villages, it is slow going but stunning. We could be rowing through an ocean: waves replaced by a patchwork of overlapping hills, seagulls by Andean condors, crested glimpses of shoreline by the purple haze of distant mountains. Eventually there are no more villages to circumnavigate.

That's when the cobblestone secondary road becomes a cobblestone carriage route—which in plucky Bolivian map-speak apparently means lumpy wagon tracks. The air smells of peat and evaporating rain, and the vistas are so clear that the horizon slices the sky like a razor's edge. In a place so pale and thin, it is irrelevant to look at the map, pretentious to imagine any sense of control. On paper we are a mere fifty-five miles south of the Pan-American Highway, but there is no way to connect the dots.

The carriage route to the next town on our detour, Aiquile, is a slick trough of mud one minute and a dusty washboard the next. When a Ford F-350 begins to toboggan sideways and slide up one wall of a giant ditch, the camper it is carrying leans precariously in the other direction. We can hear dishes flying from the cupboards and our eight-gallon drum of drinking water rolling down the center aisle. There are no other vehicles on the road. No one would find us if we landed upside down in a field.

"Why are we the only ones out here?" Gary asks me.

There is no good answer. If the Pan-American Highway is impassable, as the bus drivers say, there should be a convoy of trucks and buses sharing our route. I am not comforted by the solitude; this wretched route may be an exercise in the unnecessary. There is so much dust pouring through the cracks and crevices of the cab that I have to squirt water from a bottle directly into Gary's mouth as he drives; he can't afford to take his hands off the wheel for even a second.

We are bone rattled and parched by the time the skies crack open with thunder and pelt the carriage route with rain. It is as if the dust-packed air were tinder for bolts of lightning, and there are only four rubber tires between us and instant electrocution. Each time the rain stops, our windshield wipers clear a view more terrifying than the last: rivers in place of gentle streams, sinkholes where there was once solid cobblestone, gorges where guardrails and gravel shoulders should be.

A rocky outcrop ahead hovers like an oasis, the space below its overhanging ledge providing protection from some sort of waterfall. Until we realize we have to drive through it. The road doubles back on itself in a hairpin turn directly under a torrent of water cascading over the ledge. It is as if two giant fingers pinched the sky to the road and flicked the edge of the earth three hundred feet down on the other side just for spite.

We get out and stand behind the camper, gaping at the prospect of turning back. Going forward requires the logic of a lunatic. The force of falling water could spin out the back wheels and sweep us to the bottom of the ravine. Even if we were to miraculously survive, and somehow surface near some kind of phone, any call I would make would sound like one of those Nigerian scams. *My home fell over a cliff in South America and I've lost everything. Please send money so I can eat.*

I close my eyes and flash through my own slide show of the last seven months. Me squeezing the trigger at an Arizona gun range, angry men waving machetes in the Ocosingo jungle, Gary chasing earthquakes with a broom, shovelfuls of dirt filling Wipeout's grave, and the smoke of burning llama fetuses wafting through the camper.

All these images will fade, just like the memory of my little brother. This journey will have been for nothing, and I will spend the rest of my life wondering if we could have made it. I am relieved, in a cowardly way, when the skies open up again and the road behind us begins to dissolve. A rock and a hard place would be a nice choice to have, but the ground is literally washing out around us. There is no benefit in hesitation; I have been delivered from an agonizing decision. Cut off from alternatives, I am forced to acknowledge the vanity of control. There is only survival.

I will have to serve as Gary's eyes, checking the condition of the road that is slowly crumbling under the weight of the truck and camper. He will inch us through by feel, relying on me to say if we are too close to the rock face. I crack open the door. It might be the waterfall pummeling my eardrums but it sounds like Gary is telling me to jump out if the road gives way.

The door is heavy, and even with my forearm pressed onto the window ledge I can barely hold it off the latch. Mud spins off the front wheel and hits me in the eye. I'm blinded and try to wipe my eyes, but when I remove my left hand from the dashboard, the weight of the door lurches my body to the right.

Gary grabs for me.

"What are you doing?" he screams. "We're almost through."

This time it is the image of John John that flashes behind my squeezed-tight eyes. He is struggling with a heavy door, looking down, panicking. I can't help him. But I force myself to inhale through my nose. The truck is starting to fishtail, tires scrambling for traction. Keep breathing. Hold on. Stay calm.

Then, suddenly, the roaring noise is behind me. We have pulled clear of the ledge; a flooded river is no longer crashing onto the camper's roof. The relief is a suction force pulling me forward, first my lungs, then my heart, then my brain. I open my eyes; the windshield

Chapter Forty-Five

THE MAP

Finding my father's camper has never seemed so unlikely, but we are past the point where giving up or going back is possible. I have often wondered why it took sixty-one breakdowns before my father sold the camper—why breakdown number thirteen or forty-seven did not bring him to his knees. The same numbness I feel here, in the Bolivian outback, must have rendered counting calamities moot. Rational alternatives evaporate in isolation; logic is inversely proportional to desperation.

> **JUNE 29TH, 1974**
> Drove all day. Prettier scenery—mountainous but
> not so high. Finally arrived in Santa Cruz and took
> showers.

At this point in the first trip, my mother could see an end to the misery, but Gary and I have no idea where we are or when it will be over. There isn't even a place to pull over and declare a campsite; Gary just steers the wheels off the ruts of the road and drives through low shrubs and stubby cactus until the ground underneath us feels somewhat level.

Stars emerge from the murky twilight in cold, sparkling splendor. Strange noises gurgle from unseen animals all around the Avion, but I am too tired to be jumpy. We finish Margit's leftovers and fall asleep somewhere near the center of a country in the center of a continent that feels like the farthest place from anywhere.

DAY TWO ON THE CARRIAGE ROUTE TO SANTA CRUZ FEELS LIKE YEAR two. The road continues to deteriorate, and we inch forward at less than ten miles an hour. When we finally reconnect with the Pan-American Highway, it is so quiet I can hear all four tires humming against the surface as we work up speed.

"Shift," I remind Gary. He has spent two days driving in first gear.

It takes several minutes before I remember to swallow and breathe through my nose again. The landscape celebrates our arrival with welcoming, outstretched cacti, then transitions into verdant valleys and gentle woodlands. We roll down the windows and let the scent of ferns and pine needles waft away the dust suspended in the air.

There is a kilometer marker on the road just ahead; we are at least close enough to Santa Cruz to warrant measurement. I am expecting a burst of energy, a wave of confidence to carry me forward like a victory lap. The mudslides are behind us; grocery stores, clean water, and gas stations are within reach. We have come as far as my parents did; I have proved at least that this is possible after thirty years. We could press on for another hour and make it to the outskirts of Santa Cruz, but something pulls me back.

I am not quite ready to arrive; my thoughts have not caught up to my longitude and latitude. It will take time for the last two days to drain from my aching muscles. I need to sob for almost turning back, weep for the frightened little brother who flashed before my eyes when I thought we would be washed away. I am shaken by the ferocity of panic, the suddenness of survival. I feel beaten down, unable to get back up and take more punches. Gary pulls me closer to him and we drive another five miles with my head resting on his shoulder.

We pull up to the gate of a private picnic ground just as the manager is locking it up for the night. He hears the weariness in my voice and agrees to let us in. We have not quite reached Santa Cruz, and this park consists of nothing but wooden benches, tables, and a cold outdoor shower. But the air is warm and the ground is level, and we still have another meal's worth of Margit's kindness in the cooler.

"Now what?" we ask each other after scrubbing off the grime of Bolivia's outback. I dig out an e-mail from my father that I printed using Margit's computer back in Cochabamba. It is too hot to close the camper door; we pore over the e-mail through swarms of tiny mosquitoes drawn to the light above our kitchen table.

Sorry didn't answer your questions sooner, but we seem to have forgotten where we sold that camper. I think they're divorced now but as best I can remember, Jim's wife would be between 55 and 60 now, and the kids' names were James and Mary Sonja. There was a third but I can't remember the name. Sonja also had a brother a few years younger who was good friends with Jim but I can't remember his name either.

The last time I saw the camper it was on a farm south, southeast of Santa Cruz and I think it was on the road to Puerto Izozog. Then continue south to Puerto Abapo then cut off S.E. on the road to Aymiri and Charagua and Boyuibe.

The farm was somewhere slightly east of the road to Boyuibe, maybe between Aymiri and Boyuibe. It was a cotton farm and quite big. I also remember passing a military outpost camp on the way there and crossing a big railroad track from West to East. The track itself ran North and South.

Hope this helps you—Love Dad.

Gary and I have been so preoccupied with finding a route from Cochabamba to Santa Cruz that we haven't cross-referenced my father's recollected directions against an actual map until now. Bolivia is a country the size of California and Texas combined. It is bordered by Peru and Chile to its west, Brazil to its east, and Paraguay and Argentina to its south. My stomach sinks as I scour the map.

The closest town to where my father remembers leaving the camper, Boyuibe, is actually two hundred twenty-five miles south of Santa Cruz. It is also so far to the east that it is only fifty miles from Paraguay. The route to the border is listed as "often impassable" during the rainy season. I find the north-south railroad line my father remembers, but it parallels the entire route. He could have crossed it at a million different unmarked points. Nowhere on the map is there a town named Aymiri.

The scope of our miscalculation and the degree of my father's imprecision are staggering. We don't even swat at the mosquitoes draining our arms of blood. We have driven almost sixteen thousand miles in search of something that may no longer exist. We are contemplating the impossible and rationalizing the irrational. I am forced to admit that all I really know is that my father thinks he left the camper on a cotton farm somewhere east of a town I can't find on an impassable road to an entirely different country than the one we're actually in. Gary says nothing but pops open a can of beer. Then he walks to the door of the camper and starts pouring it all out.

"What the hell are you doing?" It's hot and there is only one other beer in the cooler.

"Mess we're in," he says. "Seems to me Pachamama's going to want more than just a sip."

Chapter Forty-Six

LOST

The next day we drive south, down Highway Nine, in the general direction of Paraguay and the last spot described in my father's e-mail. Hopefully somewhere along the two hundred twenty-five miles to Boyuibe we will stumble on landmarks he mentioned: a town called Aymiri or a military outpost. As Gary drives, I scour through my mother's journal for details my father might have brushed aside.

"Does it say what your folks eventually got for the camper?"

"No, but I'm assuming more than $3,500 since that's what my father apparently turned down in La Paz."

This is how I avoid acknowledging the obvious, that this search is thirty years past probable. I have no reliable records, so I fill in the gaps with speculation. I am digging through the words my mother left behind like an archaeologist working only with the evidence of discard.

Suddenly Gary slams on the brakes and we skid to a stop in front of massive steel pilings poking up from a flooded riverbed. There is a lone bulldozer on the other side of the river, bucket stretched out like a neck craning to see who might be coming. To our right is the old bridge—amputated between unconnected sections of road.

"Are we supposed to walk on water?" Gary asks aloud. We are still staring, in disbelief, when a semitruck rolls up behind us and the driver begins honking his horn.

"You got a better idea, buddy?" Gary yells out his window.

He does, actually. Without coming to a complete stop, the trucker downshifts and angles his sixteen-wheeler down the embankment to our right. It is a well-worn detour passing literally an arm's length in front of the screen porches of a line of riverfront shacks and running about a quarter mile to a railroad trestle.

"No Bolivian way," I say, reducing this entire country to a surrogate swear word. "That truck is going to cross the river on train tracks."

"So are we."

He begins to follow the truck, mud-coated gravel spitting up at our windshield. I'm just about to invoke our pledge—at least to think this through for a minute—when a semitruck approaches from the other direction. There is no room for us both to pass side by side, and this time the Avion is the smaller vehicle. The Law of the Third Lane demands that we back up, through the mud, climbing the embankment in reverse to let the smirking truck driver through. That's when we hear a deep thud. Gary gets out of the cab to inspect the damage.

"It's just a signpost," he yells. "Probably says keep the hell out."

About twelve vehicles are backed up behind us. The semitruck driver trying to climb the bank honks his air horn one too many times.

My husband is a man whose steady, delicate hands can adjust the f-stop on a lens without his even lifting his eyes from the viewfinder. He can hold a video camera still for hours, controlling the pace of his own breathing. I've watched him film gory surgeries without even clenching the muscles in his neck. But out of the truck's side-view mirror I witness his composure finally snap.

That signpost the Avion hit? Gary yanks it out of the ground like it is a matchstick. He flings it down the hill with a bloodcurdling yell. All around him men are getting out of their vehicles, trying to reason with him.

"Tranquilo," one of them says.

"Get out of the goddamn way or I'll throw every last one of you over the side too!" Gary yells as he climbs back inside the cab.

No translation is needed; his is the universal language of a man pushed too far.

Chapter Forty-Seven

BOYUIBE

I walk backward between oil-stained planks of the railroad trestle, directing Gary a little to the left and back to the right. Through missing boards under my feet I can see the muddy, flood-swelled river swirling and breaking over the tops of exposed boulders. The sound is terrifying; with each rotation of the truck's wheels the bridge moans. The Rio Grande Guapay, thirty feet below this creaking trestle, slurps and snorts like a caged monster.

I did not sign up for some extreme, Bolivian version of a demolition derby, but I will not let this testy country beat me now. Gary has already started to lose his mind; I can't afford to lose my nerve. Plank by plank we nudge toward the other side, as gingerly as a one-ton truck and vintage camper can manage. Then we lock the hubs into four-wheel drive to plow through the muddy ditch that stretches infinitely into the distance.

"You'd think your father would have warned us about this pathetic excuse for a road," Gary says.

I remind him this is the same country the famed bank robbers Butch Cassidy and the Sundance Kid used as their final hideout. Che Guevara tried to launch a worker's revolution in southern Bolivia in the late 1960s, only to be assassinated here. The Nazi exile Klaus Barbie became a naturalized Bolivian citizen and a close confidant of the brutal dictator who seized power in 1980. Roads are an afterthought in a country like this.

"So what's in Camiri?" Gary asks.

I look up; he is pointing to a rusted signpost that says Camiri, eighty miles. "A place to eat, maybe camp?"

According to my guidebook, Camiri holds only the dubious distinction of serving as headquarters for the US-trained Bolivian death squad that hunted down Che Guevara.

"Well, that explains this lovely welcome mat of a road," Gary says. "They don't want any other American to ever find this place."

I read the last paragraph of my father's e-mail out loud. The town he calls Aymiri sounds almost the same as Camiri. In an instant I realize that my father probably just dropped the consonant. If he actually meant Camiri, then the road that leads to the camper could be anywhere off to our left.

I am so lost in thought that I don't see the approaching semitruck bearing down on us, too far in our lane. In half a second it shears off our side-view mirror. The mirror's metal bracket smashes into Gary's door, and bits of shattered glass scatter across the windshield like a collapsing wave. It happens too fast to scream.

"I guess that's payback for the signpost," is all Gary says when it is over. His outrage is exhausted.

The last outpost my father remembers consists of two blocks of mud houses and a dirt road that crosses a north-south railroad line. The road is the color of a gumbo's roux, and along it the stripped branches of skinny trees are lashed together into uneven fences, marking property lines. Windows have no glass, and the beams that support the sagging roofs of storefronts serve double duty as hitching posts for horses. Scrawny donkeys nuzzle clumps of littered grass.

I carry with me a photograph of the old camper and another of my bearded father standing waist high in a field of cotton, even though I know it's hopeless. The men of Boyuibe are drinking beer on the railroad tracks. Gary is with me, so they are obliged to at least acknowledge my questions.

"Muy linda," they agree. Everyone I ask says that the camper is beautiful, but they have never seen it. No one has heard of an American named Jim and his Bolivian wife, Sonja, or even of a cotton farm in the vicinity.

"Posible atrás en Santa Cruz," slurs one man, watching his sons kick a soccer ball along the tracks. "Hay fincas allí. Y gente rica." There are still farms in Santa Cruz, he thinks, and rich people. Ask them your stupid questions.

I'm angry with my father for not remembering where he sold the camper. But Gary reminds me that finding it was our idea, not his.

JULY 18TH, 1974
Finally we leave.

My mother was finished with everything, including complete sentences, by this point in her journal. Reading it I am torn between wanting to push on toward Paraguay and a fear of actually finding the camper, abandoned in this wasteland like a carcass. Somewhere out here my father relinquished his getaway vehicle. What a bitter place to surrender.

Gary and I return to the Avion as uncertain of the future as my parents must have been thirty years before. Our camper is bruised and battered and so am I. There are no more addresses of travel angels tucked into my mother's journal. Even my father doubts that the camper could have lasted thirty years in this hardscrabble country.

It would be easier to let grass grow over the dirt I have disturbed. I could let it go and write a new ending to the story. It would go like this: two wiser souls follow the Pan-American Highway to the end of the road—Tierra del Fuego—and never look back.

But it is Gary who refuses to give up. I have shut down, just like my mother, but he is breathing life into my fluttering hopes.

"Look, we haven't exhausted all possibilities; we just haven't thought them through."

We are thousands of miles from the two people who stood on a beach in Mexico and said yes to a life together. We have spent every waking and sleeping moment of our marriage within arm's reach of each other. We've shared the same forty-two moldy paperbacks and read each other's personal e-mails from home. After two hundred fifteen days in the cab of the same truck we can recite the words to each other's favorite songs, stupid jokes, embarrassing childhood stories, and indignant rants. Yet there are still possibilities.

"We're never going to stumble on the camper on our own; that's obvious," says this man I will never be able to completely predict. "We need a plan."

This is another possibility I never imagined: Gary admitting we need a plan. If he takes out a sticky pad next and starts writing a list, I will have to check the photo on his Washington, DC, driver's license against the man in front of me in Bolivia.

"Let's backtrack to Santa Cruz and poke around town for a few days. Some clue may turn up yet. For all we know, Sonja and her kids still live in Santa Cruz. One of them might know what happened to the camper."

This time it is my turn to pour a lukewarm beer into Pacha-mama's thirsty dirt. Then I take off my shoes and stand in the soggy spot, willing the wisdom of Mother Earth to rise through the soles of my feet.

Chapter Forty-Eight

ANOTHER BOY

Santa Cruz is a city of 1.5 million people and overflowing roads jammed with SUVs and four-wheel-drive pickups. Drivers pass on the right, block intersections, and park on top of sidewalks. There are car dealerships and fast-food restaurants, but I see very few hotels; Santa Cruz is less a destination than a destiny. So it feels like the first stroke of luck in a week when we spot a public swimming pool and recreation complex on the side of the Pan-American Highway a few miles west of Santa Cruz.

"Look, a *balneario*," we both shout out at once.

Two Olympic-size swimming pools take up the front of the property, and dotted along a wide and sandy driveway are twenty camping spots nestled under mango trees. Each tree is strung with electric power outlets and extension cords. Across an irrigated lawn are men's and women's locker rooms with sparkling-clean toilets and private, hot showers. Behind the campground stretch acres of rolling farmland and grazing horses. It is not the first time we have pulled into a swimming-pool day park and asked if we could pay to spend the night. But at this one, curiously called Fabio Andres, we are greeted by a handsome man in his early thirties wearing pressed slacks and a short-sleeved button-down shirt.

"Hello, my name is Richard," he welcomes us in practiced English. "I see from your plates you're from DC; I have been a few years in Maryland for my studies."

He brings over cold beers after we park and level the Avion, and I expect a valiant attempt at remembering verb tenses and Redskins scores. Usually these introductory conversations get pulled out to sea after "What's your name?" and "Do you have any kids?" But Richard swims against the rip currents with grace. His eyes are warm but direct, like he can sense we share more than vocabulary. I ask him how he got into the Bolivian balneario business. The Fabio Andres complex is named in memory of a beloved nephew, he explains, a child killed in an accident.

For an instant my head is underwater, tugged down by an undercurrent of John John before I can close my mouth. Gary puts his arm around my shoulder and I surface, spitting out the first words I can think of.

"Is that his picture?" I ask, looking at a billboard near the front gate.

"Yes," Richard says, with gentle finality. "The way we will always remember him."

A dozen questions are splashing inside my head, but Richard is smiling and offering me a lawn chair.

"So what brings you folks to Santa Cruz?" he asks.

"We are trying to find a woman who might know where we can find an old camper. Kind of like this one, only bigger, that my father sold somewhere in Bolivia thirty years ago," I answer.

My sentences sound circuitous and illogical, but I am too tired to organize them. Why bother? After this past week's futility I am expecting only polite smiles and awkward silences. Instead, Richard calls for his mother, Carmen, to join us under the mango trees. Then he waves forward a group of workers raking leaves a few rows behind us. Gather around, he is telling them. You are among friends, he is telling us.

"Teresa, Gary, let me introduce you to the balneario's groundskeeper, Celso, and his eight daughters."

Richard is both interviewer and translator for our growing audience. I realize with relief that I will not have to pantomime the story, draw pictures in the dirt, or proffer photographs from the past. I can ease back into my chair and let the strain and disappointment of the last week drain from my body. Gary squeezes my hand and backtracks through our story, from the blank stares in Boyuibe just a day ago to a three-year-old boy killed in an accident in 1972.

Richard says only, "What was his name?" not "How awful" or "I'm so sorry." He has been there himself, and the unlikely parallel settles on my shoulders. We are meant to be here, under these mango trees. After driving for almost nine months, incredibly, we have found a family who has traveled the same road.

"When I take my mother home tonight, we will look through old phone books," Richard tells us as darkness closes in. "She has saved them since I was a boy."

Carmen feigns vindication, hands on her hips, for being the pack rat everyone teases.

"Don't worry, we will find this Sonja and your father's camper," Richard says. "We should go now and let you get some rest."

Carmen kisses both my cheeks, and Richard gives Gary his home and cell phone numbers and says good night. There is no one to watch us take off our clothes and slip into the deep end of the swimming pool, moonlight glancing off the swish and splash of cool water. We are alone in the still, fragrant sweetness of a Santa Cruz summer night. Perfect for the conversation I have been avoiding for ten countries. I dip under the surface, tilt my head back, and let the water pull the hair away from my face as I come back up for air.

"I want out of it," I start.

Gary splashes me. "Go ahead. Nobody's stopping you."

He thinks I mean the pool when I actually mean my own skin. I want to be the person Richard and his mother assume I am, someone who is searching for her past but not chaining herself to it.

"Why did you let me do it?"

It isn't pool water sliding down my cheeks. He glides through the water to wipe away tears.

"Babe, it's okay. If we don't find it we don't find it," he says. "Not all experiments prove their hypothesis, but you always learn something anyway."

This is as close to philosophy as I have ever heard my practical, no-drama husband utter. But he still doesn't understand why I am crying.

"No, I mean why did you let me buy the gun?"

He thought this trip would allow me to say good-bye, but I have dragged everything wrong and paranoid and angry and dangerous with me. This continual, willful resurrection of every frightening memory of my childhood belittles its joys and erases the good of the Samaritans who stepped in to lift my seven-year-old spirits. Not to mention the kindnesses of Shawn and Susie, Mariamalia and Arnoldo, Ernesto and Yanina, Eosebio, Margit and Don, and now Richard and his mother.

"You learned something anyway, didn't you?"

Now it's me not following.

"Your hypothesis was wrong. So what? We're here, together, and even if we never find the camper you can still say good-bye."

That's just it. I can't. Not while I've got that gun. And I have no idea what to do about it.

"I can't hit reset and have it disappear. Or walk up to a cop and say, *Here, take this. I'm sorry, can we just pretend this never happened?*"

I want him to say I should have thought of that, or it's what I deserve. But he won't let me pick this fight.

"You'll think of something," he says. "I trusted that all along. You were wrong, but you had your reasons and it wasn't worth the time it would have taken to argue with you about it."

It is a tactic I should have recognized. It's one we used in every shoot when clients wanted something I knew wouldn't work. I would nod and listen to the client while Gary would film what he intended anyway. His job was to make it look beautiful, and mine was to make the client think it was their idea all along.

"It's not like the gun was going to sit out in the open on the dashboard," he continues. "Why do you think Dad and I picked a hiding place that takes a map and a metal detector to find? I knew you were too terrified to ever use the stupid thing."

He could have been thrown in jail or worse. His fate and my complicity in it has stabbed at my conscience every time we drove past cops or passed through borders. But all the times I was certain that he was seething in silence, choking on suppressed *I told you so*'s, he just was nodding, listening, and doing what needed to be done.

I wrap my naked, shriveled body around his. Anyone could walk up and see, but I am too relieved to care. I've already been exposed, and I could float forever in forgiveness.

Chapter Forty-Nine

THE PHONE CALL

I wake the next morning knowing how my parents must have felt when strangers dusted off their hopes. We wave to Celso and his daughters like they're new neighbors. I shave my legs in a hot shower for the first time in weeks and then drape them across the camper's table, crossed at the ankles so Gary notices. He is just about to abandon the scrambling of morning eggs when Richard knocks on our door.

"Teresa, Gary, I have some phone numbers for you," he calls out, and I slide my smooth legs off the table and jump to the door. In a phone book saved for decades, Richard has found two promising listings: one for Sonja and one for James, most likely the little boy who rode with us from La Paz to Santa Cruz in 1974.

"Let me see that," Gary says, reaching for the phone book like it's one of my father's slides he has to hold up to the light to see. "After all the hassles we've been through, it's suddenly this easy?"

Unspoken gratitude spills from my gaping mouth. I can't believe this is happening. We have just arrived in a city roughly the size of Phoenix, Arizona. What are the chances of finding a campground owned by an English-speaking man whose mother keeps phone books dating back to the time when Sonja still used the last name written inside my mother's journal? The setbacks of the past few weeks seem suddenly fortuitous. Without the mudslides in Cochabamba, we would have arrived in Santa Cruz during the peak holiday season. Richard's balneario would have been filled to capacity; we might never have met Carmen.

"If those don't work, we can try another long shot," Richard says. "I order the balneario's beer from this distributor named Ann Juliet. Long blond hair and blue eyes. Kind of girl you don't forget in Santa Cruz. Anyway, I checked our receipts, and she has the same last name as Sonja and James."

"Could she be the third kid in your father's e-mail?" Gary asks. I know he is trying to keep a check on his enthusiasm, but every muscle in his body is coiled tight, ready to spring from the camper and run a victory lap.

I don't even have to look at the e-mail. The minute Richard says Ann Juliet, the memory of a gurgling baby girl reaches up for the name like it's a shiny bubble floating by. Richard hands me his cell phone; the numbers are already programmed in. I have no idea what I will say if Sonja answers or if she will even remember me.

"What if she doesn't want to talk to me?" I hesitate. "She might think we want the camper back, or that we'll hang around for weeks on end." It took her twenty-six days to be rid of us the first time, according to the dismal entries in my mother's journal.

"Just call," Richard says, smiling.

Is he encouraging me for the sake of a little boy he never met, whose death was a loss like the one his own family has found a way to survive? Or is he caught up in the simple thrill of solving a mystery? I haven't told him that my mother never wrote or spoke to Sonja again. She has every reason in the world to slam the phone down, but all my doubts dissolve when I hear her voice.

"Teresita, I can't believe it is really you!" she begins. I can hear that she is fighting back tears. Her voice is thin, weathered by the years. But then again, this has to be a shock. I have called her without warning. She has had no time to collect herself or decide what to make of this intrusion.

"Are you still reading so many books? All these years and I never know what happens to you. How is your mother?"

If she feels ambushed she covers it with questions. Gary is hugging me from behind, trying to overhear Sonja's voice. Richard waves a hand in front of my face to get my attention, then points to the cell phone and makes stabbing gestures with his index finger.

"You can put it on speaker." He is like a puppy bringing a ball he hopes I'll toss. "But only if you want."

I hold the phone out in the space between the three of us and hit the speaker button. I tell Sonja that my parents are healthy, still married, and living in Nicaragua. Richard pulls a pen from his pocket and scribbles down directions as we make arrangements to meet the next morning at nine.

"Adios, Teresita," Sonja says.

I am suddenly scared to break the connection and lose her. "Don't say good-bye. Just hasta luego, until tomorrow."

"Okay, hasta luego, mija," she says, laughing. "Hasta luego."

For the first time in months we have not just one appointment but two. Richard's mother has invited us to a traditional Bolivian meal to meet the rest of her family and to share the story of Sonja and the search for the old camper. Gary and I spend the rest of the day in the tingle of anticipation. I am grateful for the distraction of a family meal. I dig a dress out of the camper's dusty closet, hoping it will somehow convey a measure of appreciation and respect.

"You're going to wear that?" Gary asks. "It looks like prune skin."

"Have a little faith," I answer, hanging the wrinkled dress outside. "This humidity will breathe some life back into it."

Richard loans us two bicycles, and we pedal through bumpy mango orchards and spongy pastures. Richard's mother, Carmen, is bending over an outdoor brick oven pulling paddles of golden rolls from its depths. She is wearing a long feathery skirt that hovers in the draft of the escaping heat, and her silver hair is smoothed off her forehead with a blue scarf. If there is anything to the last-frontier appeal of Bolivia, Carmen embodies it.

The yucca in her canapés is pulled from the ground by her own hands. The cheese in her empanadas comes from the neighbor's goat milk. The rice-flour rolls she draws from the oven are made from the recipes of her Spanish grandmother. Bolivia seems pioneering and idealistic as we sit down to this feast; for a few hours I will set aside the nagging doubt that it still harbors the camper that was my childhood.

"In Spain they call this dish paella," Richard says. "But without the sea, Bolivians changed it to *majadito*."

Carmen ladles dried beef and fried eggs on top of mounds of slow-cooked saffron rice. If even the celebrated national dish of Spain can be molded into the shape and form of Bolivia, surely I can adapt. Sonja will say whatever she needs to say, and I will go from there. The camper either exists or it doesn't; it is out of my control.

For dessert the entire family accompanies us on a walk through Carmen's "secret" garden: a plot of fruit trees tucked behind the campground, enclosed by a living fence of vines. We sample oranges, limes, and mandarins straight off the branch—so juicy and tart that we finish each succulent offering with a nibble of its peel to cleanse the palate. Richard and Carmen take particular delight in introducing us to the most bizarre of Bolivian fruits: achachairú, translucent, pulpy seeds that look like eyeballs covered in spiky leather, and ambaiba, clusters of drooping, fuzzy, fingerlike pods. Carmen laughs as Gary and I get sticky; tangerine juice dribbles down our chins as though we were children, and the oily essence of guayaba leaves stains on our fingers. When she finally closes her garden gate behind us, we are coated in the complex flavors of Bolivia.

Chapter Fifty

SONJA

I t was my mother's journal that jogged the dentist's memory in El Salvador; photographs of the camper placed us in context for the editor's wife in Nicaragua. But on Sonja's face the recognition is instant and total. Gary and I, standing on her doorstep, transport her.

"You look just like Beverly and David!" she blurts out before even introducing herself, her hand covering a gasp.

Seeing Sonja is a little like returning to elementary school as an adult. She is shorter than me, and I feel like this will overwhelm her. There is no way I can ask about the camper yet; there are fluttering hands to settle, nervous giggles to escape. I can't reconcile the woman brushing bangs away from my eyes to get a good look at my face with the Sonja who hitched a ride with us from La Paz to Santa Cruz. She wears blue suede boots and her English is hesitant. Despite the heat, she wears a light cardigan to cover up the looseness of her outstretched arms. Her blue eyes are heavy with mascara that smudges into surrounding creases. She seems like a kindly grandmother, not a woman who engineered my family's salvation.

"Your mother was such a sad person," Sonja begins. "You have to tell me, Teresita, did she ever have another son?"

In all my adult life I have neglected to ask my mother if she wanted more children. I suddenly feel shallow and inconsiderate, but I never pondered whether the love of two daughters was enough to make up for the loss of a son. When Sonja met my mother, only two years had passed since John had been killed. Every day in Santa Cruz my mother watched her daughters playing with someone else's son.

"Her heart was heavy with missing John John," Sonja says. "She wanted so deeply to give your father another son."

I can't stop myself from dissecting the words that Sonja chooses. "John John," she calls my little brother. This Bolivian woman in blue suede boots speaks the private language of my family. My mother's heart was "heavy," and she wanted to "give" my father another son. Maybe I am reading too much into the words of a woman who probably hasn't spoken English for years. But perhaps her words reveal a heavy truth—that my mother blamed herself for my brother's death.

"We shared many tears together," Sonja says, softly.

I think of my mother now, isolated on an island off the coast of Nicaragua, and I am sorry she let Sonja slip away. The connection must have been too painful to maintain. This friendship was like an itching scab from a time she wanted to forget. When Sonja puts her arm through mine, I know she understands.

"Here is where your father parked the camper," she points out as we stroll through a walled-in front yard. It looks too crowded; a gardener is packing topsoil around newly planted fruit trees.

"That camper was so big, but David, he could make it go anywhere he wanted. He could make anyone go where he wanted. He had a very strong, macho personality."

I laugh and tell her he still does. "Mom settles for occasionally steering him in directions she wants."

I am camouflaging the truth. Now that my sister and I are grown and gone, my mother has no daughters to use as leverage. My father still drifts from country to country, chasing dreams and attacking windmills, and my mother follows without question. Sonja chose a different course.

"I finally divorced Jim," she says, flatly. "I would not let him take away my mother's land."

I'm not following. My father has always described Jim in glowing, almost envious terms. Jim was Butch to my father's Sundance; even as a kid I thought of them as a pair of adventurous pioneers. But Sonja tells me that the two of them, her ex-husband and my father, wanted her to sell her family land and use the money to build a steel factory. It is an uncomfortable pause in the slide-show history I remember of my time in Bolivia. Instead of another romantic, sepia-tinted image projecting on the wall inside my head, it is as if my father's whirling carousel is sticking on a blank slot.

This steel factory was not a plan developed with the input of wives or discussed in front of children. The men simply expected to get their way and for the women and children to learn to like it. There was money to be made, frontiers to conquer. I struggle to imagine what growing up in Bolivia would have been like, and all that comes into focus is that I would never have met my grandparents in South Africa. The silent pause in the slide show is filled with the soft, re-gretless voice of a woman who stood up to men in a time and a place where most women did not.

"The children could have claimed US citizenship and moved there, because of their father," Sonja says. "But our roots are here, in Bolivia."

I have an urge to bend down and touch the smooth, grey concrete floor of Sonja's house. I can picture my Monopoly game spread out here—piles of pastel money tucked under the board and dice sliding across the slippery floor. I can hear my sister turning one-armed cartwheels while waiting for her turn.

I hear heavy footsteps and look up as Ann Juliet waddles into the living room. The baby girl who used to suck on strands of my hair is seven months pregnant and as blond and beautiful as Richard described her. We stare at each other, archaeological specimens, laughing to cover the absence of an instant bond. Our shared history is proven but not present; it is an awkward intimacy.

"So, Teresa and Gary, do you want me to take you to the camper?" Sonja asks, jolting me back to the reason I am standing in this house again. "The roads are too much for Ann Juliet to come with us in her condition, but I don't have to work tomorrow."

The room seems suddenly loud; the drone of the window air-conditioner drowns out the shouts of protestors marching across the living room TV. My ears pop when I swallow, and I am conscious of my feet scuffling over the concrete floor. I can't seem to put one in front of the other. I need to repeat Sonja's words aloud, as though I were in a spelling bee, to make sure I understand them in context. Sonja doesn't have to work tomorrow; that means she is offering to spend her day off with us. To take us to the camper.

Sounds streak past me, and my peripheral vision closes in. Suddenly I am back at the beginning, confronting a giant creature bolted and welded together in the laboratory of my desperate father.

"Sit down, Teresa," Gary says. "You look like you're about to faint."

I sink into the sofa and stare at Sonja, letting the cushions reach around my hips like a seat belt. *Buckle up, relax, enjoy the flight*, I tell myself. *This is what you've come so far to learn.* The camper my father built still exists, and Sonja, unlike my father, knows exactly where it is.

"So it's close enough to drive to?" Gary asks, handing me a glass of water from Ann Juliet.

"Of course," Sonja says, her intonation rising for confirmation. "Isn't that why you came to Santa Cruz?"

She laughs when I tell of our blunderings through the Bolivian outback and the e-mail that drove us to the brink of Paraguay.

"That may be where your father saw it last," she explains. "We had some property near Boyuibe a long time ago. But we needed to use the truck on a farm not too far from here, near Puerto Izozog. We took the camper off the back of the truck and left it there; it has been waiting in one spot for the past thirty years. If you have four-wheel drive, I think it would only take a few hours to reach."

I feel dizzy, like I am seven years old again, blindfolded and flailing at a piñata. Sonja's hands are steady on my shoulders; my heartbeat slows, and the past stops spinning around my head. We have driven 16,397 miles, across two continents, and the camper is waiting not fifty miles from this living room. After thirty years, I will see it tomorrow.

Ann Juliet phones for a cab to take us back to the balneario, and I watch modern Santa Cruz slide by my window in a stream of diesel exhaust and sagging telephone lines. I am grateful that Gary and I have our own space, beside Carmen's secret garden, to contemplate and savor the flavors of anticipation.

"Are you ready for this?" Gary asks, hours later. We are sprawled atop the Avion's bed, ceiling fan swirling inches above our sweaty, spent bodies. "It might not be the fairy tale, castle-on-wheels that you remember."

"I don't expect it to be," I tell him. "The slide show is over."

Chapter Fifty-One

THE CAMPER

We have been driving ever since we picked up Sonja two hours ago, but we still seem to be on the outskirts of Santa Cruz. It is pouring rain, and in the grungy industrial districts the dirt streets overflow with rainwater. The truck is thick with tension, and not just from the dangerous driving conditions. I am sitting between Gary and Sonja feeling like I should hold her hand or something. So much was blurted out when we first met, but we are still essentially strangers, suddenly thrust together, thigh to thigh.

Sonja is disoriented; road signs are obscured by steam, and there are cars stranded in intersections. She is embarrassed when she mistakes a turn and we have to double back. I am staring at naked children paddling plastic oil drums like boats from house to house.

"Don't worry, it is just a flash flood," Sonja says. "This happens all the time in the rainy season. The politicians in La Paz say they will

fix the streets, and they forget as soon as the sun comes back out. In
Santa Cruz, if you want something fixed it is better to do it yourself."

My father's camper has waited thirty years; I can't justify rushing.
We decide to park the Avion and wait for the waters to recede at a
roadside diner at the edge of a petroleum refinery. Dozens of customers are crammed around mud-splattered plastic patio tables. Refinery
workers in denim coveralls and neon hardhats hunch over bowls of
soup and plates of fried chicken in thirty-minute lunch-break inter-
vals. The owner seats us under the sturdiest portion of thatched roof,
farthest from his cinder-block wall of naked pinup calendars and *Play-
boy* centerfold posters. We have an unobstructed view of the flooded
dirt road and an oil well less than two hundred yards away. The grey
sky is torch lit by a roaring orange flame that burns off natural gas.

"This is all new, this oil discovery," Sonja explains. "Ten years ago
it was only farms—like ours—but the government owns all the rights
to the oil and gas under our fields."

The revolving door of Bolivian presidents has sold these rights
to multinational corporations, at prices that prompt deadly riots far
away in El Alto and La Paz. None of which seems to upset Sonja; she
says the violence never makes its way this far east. I am opening my
mouth, about to ask about the impending coup and the window of
time left before the next flare-up, when Gary interrupts me.

"So what crops do you grow these days?" he asks.

I smile. This is Gary wisely steering us into the easier conversations of hostess and visitors, saving strength for the floodgates he
knows will open when I see the camper. A horse and buggy pull into
the parking lot right behind the Avion. Holding the reins is a blond,
blue-eyed man wearing farm overalls and a straw hat. Behind him, in
the trundle seat, sits a silent woman in a prairie dress and three little
girls with bonnets covering their blond heads.

"Mennonites, from Paraguay," Sonja whispers before we ask.
"They are persecuted everywhere, but here they are just left alone."

The man hands the reins to his solemn wife, walks over to stare at our camper, and then climbs back in his buggy without saying a word. The family rides off with the refinery flame burning in the background and the girls' pink ribbons streaming behind them in the breeze.

"Did my family seem as strange as that to you when we first arrived in La Paz?" I ask Sonja.

"Maybe a little more strange, because your father's camper looked like it came from the future, not the past," she laughs.

When the rain stops and we can see through the steam rising from the mud, we set off again for the farm and the futuristic camper of my past. The road makes sucking, slurping noises as we slip and skid along it.

"On the left, those fields used to belong to my grandfather," Sonja points through the open window. "Up there, around the bend, all of that was my mother's."

It dawns on me that Sonja is describing the disappearance of a dynasty. Her great-great-grandfather settled the area and cultivated some ten thousand hectares of land. Over the years, the family holdings have been sold and expropriated by the government until they are down to less than two thousand hectares. No wonder she refused to relinquish control of what remained to my father and her ex-husband.

"Did all this happen because of Che Guevara and his revolution?" Gary asks.

"El Che didn't have anything to do with it," she answers with a dismissive laugh. "In Bolivia the land reform started in 1953. We were giving land to the poor long before that troublemaker came around."

She seems ambivalent, even charitable, about the redistribution of 80 percent of her family's land.

"Now it is more equal," she says. "It is only fair."

Sonja nods to the men on horseback who tip their hats when they recognize the woman riding past. Their faces are as weathered as the raw curtains of hide serving as homemade chaps. Their sweating horses are protected from the scratchy brush by heavy shields of leather.

At last Sonja recognizes one section of the tree-limb fence we have been paralleling, in first gear, for a full hour. She hops out of the cab, into ankle-deep mud, and nonchalantly slogs through overgrown brush to unlatch a wire loop from a post.

"It's to keep the cows away from the soybeans," she says as she hops back in. "They love them."

We pass through three separate barriers of wire fence, each secured with naked tree limbs stabbed into the soil. Each field we drive through seems to drag our camper a little deeper into the mud and a little farther from what we have come so far to find. Even four-wheel drive isn't enough; we have to wedge pieces of wood and rocks in front of the back tires to rip away from the muddy suction.

We are agonizingly close. Finding the old camper has gone from a remote possibility to a potentially dangerous exploit in the face of a looming coup. We have nearly beaten our own camper to death in the process. *This isn't a quest*, I have to keep telling myself. *There is nothing to prove.*

At one point I might have been able to accept that the camper would stay a part of my past, lost forever in the Bolivian outback. I might even have preferred that to discovering that it was picked over for scrap or chopped up for kindling. But in the last few days, under the shade of mango trees, I have allowed myself to picture a cinematic ending to this journey. It is a glorious wide shot, Gary tracking the camera over a landscape of grit and determination. In the distance, the camper will crest above the horizon. A rising swell of music ushers in the closing credits; soon the screen will fade to black.

Reality is considerably less dramatic. Sonja's farm is a quilt of damp soybean fields sliding under thorny trees to butt against a swollen, muddy river. Surely nothing as vulnerable as a handmade camper could be protected here. The sun beats down relentlessly, and the air is thick with mosquitoes and blackflies. The ground greedily pulls at our feet, as if to devour, not deliver us to the camper. My legs have forgotten how to flex at the knees, my ankles how to articulate and release my toes.

"I don't know if I'm ready for this," I confess.

But Sonja misinterprets my reservations.

"Oh, don't worry. We have the spray."

She coats me in repellent to ward off swarms of mosquitoes. Scruffy children materialize like ants from an unseen mound, opening another wire gate and leading us through a cattle corral. My eyes struggle to adjust to the glare.

"It's over there," Sonja says. "Just a little more to walk."

I am breathing like a little kid, in spurts and gasps. It's as if I can't exhale properly; the heavy air of expectation is sucking me backward. This soggy field feels somehow like a fairground, our journey to get here a rickety carnival ride. I can't walk so I am being tugged, rung by rung, up a steep track, and I am scared to peek.

Through squinting eyelids I can make out an unmistakable silhouette. Under a lean-to shelter made of raw tree trunks and a thatched palm roof, sharing the outermost wall of a brick farmhouse, squats the camper.

It is both too close and too far away. The emotional roller coaster I have been riding for almost a year suddenly peels off its tracks. I am suspended somewhere in the air above the twisted, tangled route that led here.

"Look, babe, there it is," Gary shouts. "Still in one piece!"

Not me, I want to say. I am split in two, wanting to believe this and not sure I can. But in the horizontal, stripped-lean landscape of a Bolivian soybean farm, my father's creation stands tall. We approach from the front. The white aluminum skin is still stretched taut over a massive wooden frame. It looks injured and awkward propped up on sawed-off tree stumps instead of straddling the mighty Jeep. But even indisposed, it is impressive. The rectangular window of my parents' sleeping berth is a huge, unblinking eye staring down at the search party fanned out below.

I always imagined that if my childhood home were actually still on earth, not burned for firewood or dismembered for its parts, in the moment I discovered it time would stand still. But it's rushing past, like a time-lapse movie, in every direction. I am the only object rooted, motionless. The sun zips westward through the staggered sky. Clouds race by, forming one shape after another, all from the corner of my frozen-forward eyes. Sounds barrel past me, too: John John laughs, my mother sings "Frère Jacques," and Wipeout pants in my ears. But they are all just the bees, scoring this moment with a sound track of relentless buzzing.

The back door of the camper hangs a little crooked. The hinges are rusty, and the brass doorknob is tied open with a string to let a fog of insecticide disperse. The smell is acrid and burns my eyes, but it masks the mildewed scent of neglect, so I gratefully inhale the poison. Even with the door wide open, the dark wood paneling sucks away the light as if to hide the signs of aging.

I know how the camper feels; I'm not quite ready to share the guts of this reunion either. The camper feels hollow, or is it me? My skin, hair, and clothes are just membranes stretched over the outline of my body. Inside the lines is empty space. I should celebrate, but if I smile I might dissolve. This weary shell was once my armor.

The carpet has worn through to the plywood floor, warped into a heavy sag. The camper seems to buckle under its own mass, fittings and fixtures too bulky for its bones. My parent's empty sleeping berth is king-sized. But the mattress is long gone, and without it the space is a dark, receding cavern lined with shed snakeskins, insect carcasses, and dust.

The side bench seat where my sister and I slept is no wider than a cedar hope chest. For a moment I can't visualize how even two tiny children could fit. Sonja watches my reactions, laughs, and grabs a hidden handle, pulling out a nesting drawer within the drawer that doubled as our bed. How ingenious my father was, and how small and fragile his daughters must have looked as he tucked them in each night.

"I'm going back to the truck to get the satellite phone," I tell Gary.

"They're never going to believe where you're calling from," he says. He's already taking photographs, busy documenting our discovery. "I'd love to see the look on your father's face."

But it isn't my father whose voice I am craving. I need to thank my mother for what she did here. As I am dialing the number to the Corn Island Dive Resort, a place as isolated as this soybean field, I realize my father never got over Bolivia. Nicaragua is just a substitute frontier.

"Joe's Bar and Grill." He has no idea who is calling.

"It's me, Dad. Gary and I found the camper."

I am expecting a string of questions. Where? How? There is nothing but the low hum and crackle of the satellite connection.

"Dad, have I lost you?" I am turning in circles, ninety degrees at a time, and fiddling with the antenna.

"No, I'm here," he says, and I hear him sucking on his lips and swallowing. He is crying. "After all this time, I just can't . . . " believe, accept, understand, all of the above.

"I know, Dad, me too."

He sucks the tears back through his nose, snorting everything inside. He is overwhelmed, and when my father begins to lose control, he claws his way to the mechanics, pulls himself up on the back of detail.

"How's the truck holding up?" he asks.

"It's gone, Dad. Sonja says it was sold for parts. Years ago."

There is a long silence, then a deep inhalation through his nose before he asks, "So the whole rig is up on jacks?"

I picture my sun-withered father teetering on the verge of disappointment, and I race to shore him up.

"No, more permanent than that. It's blocked up against a farmhouse. Sonja even built a thatch roof over the whole thing."

"Well, that's a little overkill," he says, collecting himself. "It never did leak. I made sure of that."

Here comes the father I know, shaking it off, looking around to see if anyone saw him slip.

"So it looks as good as new, eh?"

The carousel is in my hands now; I project images for him to lean on.

"Damn, even I didn't know I was that good."

He is behind the wheel again, me in the backseat doing everything I can to please him.

"Hey, did you happen to notice if the gun is still in the hidey hole?"

My stomach drops. He wants me to check, sweet talk the guards, get him out of jail.

"Dad, are you saying you don't know what happened to it?" I ask. "What if a kid found it, or a criminal?"

I walk back to the camper as I talk, looking for Gary. He's not going to believe this.

"I might have given it to Jim with the rig, or sold it," my father muses. "Christ, I can't remember."

This is something he and Jim probably kept from Sonja. My mother documented every other possession we were forced to sell, but there is no mention in her journal of the gun.

"Have Gary feel along the edge of the refrigerator for the corner molding," my father begins to instruct. "Follow that around next to the bed, and you'll hit the seam."

This he remembers exactly, like a blueprint. I am losing the signal, so Gary crawls up into the bed compartment alone to search for my father's hidden gun. He must be thinking he has married into lunacy, with a wife who insists on buying a pistol and a father-in-law who forgets where he left one.

I look over at the Avion and wonder what will happen to it one day. We've talked about selling it in Brazil or Argentina and flying back to the United States. But not with a gun hidden under its floorboards. If I could travel back in time, I would argue with the person I was when I bought it, convince her she wouldn't always over-think things. But I made a bad decision, and I can't run away from it and abdicate my responsibility to some stranger who discovers the gun in the future. If Gary finds the gun my father abandoned along with the camper I grew up in, the sins of the father will be added to the daughter's.

"Okay, Dad, Gary's coming out of the camper now."

Damn, he is holding something. How will I explain this to Sonja?

"And behind false door number one," Gary says as he steps out into the light, "an empty hornet's nest. That's it. Relax, babe, nothing to worry about."

"Well, I'll be damned," my father says when I tell him it is no-where to be found. "Guess we'll never know what happened."

I can hear him downshifting into second gear, first gear, coming to a stop. This is all the information he needs, enough to distract him from deeper thoughts and implications.

"Well, your mother's sitting here chomping at the bit, so I'll let you go," he says. "I love you."

My mother wants me to repeat everything I told my father; she has heard only one side of the conversation and knows he won't bother to fill her in.

"You know how your dad is," she says. "Thinks he'll remember but he won't."

"Okay, Mom, but I really need to say something first," I tell her. "I know Dad wanted to go into business with Jim and live here. I am so proud of you."

"Proud of me?" she asks.

"After everything that happened, it must have been incredibly hard to stand up to Dad and get us out of here," I say. "You can't imagine how lonely the camper looks. Thank you, Mom. Thank you so much."

I am expecting any response from my mother other than a giggle, but that is what fills the awkward pause. It is her little-girl voice I am hearing over the phone, the one she uses for asking favors and saying pretty please. She doesn't know how to accept gratitude.

"I'm glad you found the camper, but it's your dad who deserves the credit," my mother says. This is the role she is accustomed to: loyal follower. The line crackles, and the silence between us surges and retreats in my ear. I realize I cannot expect excitement or even curiosity from my mother. I have found the physical remains of the pain she wants most to forget. She says she'd better go; the guard dog is barking at something.

"Your dad's yelling. He has a conniption fit if the locals try to walk across our beach. Thinks they're out to rob us," she says, bowing out of the conversation. "Say hi to Sonja for me. Bye-bye, Princess. Don't let the bedbugs bite."

This is a bedtime story for my mother, one with a happy ending. She has tucked me in, and I sleepwalk back to my father's camper. Sonja is inside; if she overheard the phone call or anything about the gun, she clearly doesn't want to talk about it.

"Come look in the bathroom, Teresita," she says. I follow, numbly. "We took out the toilet so there is more room for the shower."

She shows me that my mother's oven still works, fueled by two oversized propane tanks like barrels braced against the camper's side. I mutely nod, brain elsewhere.

"I should go check that the caretaker's kids closed the last gate all the way," Sonja says, patting my hand. "Take your time."

Time is what I can't take, or keep. The evidence of its passing is all around me. Above the sink I pick at a peeling plastic label my father stuck to the backsplash. I am surrounded by instructions.

"Turn off when traveling," the strip above the water pump reads. And, "This is hot!"—intended, no doubt, for my seven-year-old benefit. I laugh out loud.

"What's so funny?" Gary asks.

"Dad must have dragged that label gun all the way to South Africa and back to Oregon," I answer. "I remember him sticking these things to every potentially dangerous appliance, I swear, until I left home for college."

"Huh, sound like anyone we know?" Gary says, innocently rubbing his chin.

It is too sweaty and humid for my lips to create any suction against his, but I kiss him anyway. There aren't enough sticky notes in the world to list the emotions draining from the pores of my skin, my head, my heart.

The cabinet doors still open but with creaks of reluctance. I peer into every empty cupboard where once we crammed the trappings of our transitory life. I run my hand along their inner surfaces, hoping to feel the scrap of a drawing, or a Barbie doll shoe. I expected finding the camper to tell me something about myself—that standing inside it would reconnect me with the little girl who talked her father out of jail and believed in gypsies who could see the future.

But there are no souvenirs of the child I was; I find instead a record of the childhood my mother vetoed. In the back of the closet where my parents hung their clothes is a rolled-up tube. I smooth out two sets of blueprints on the camper's countertop. They are for the steel factory my father planned on opening with Sonja's husband, and for a house I presume was meant for us.

"It looks more like a jail than a home," Gary says. "It's just a square box of cement and rebar."

I see my father's tidy handwriting in notes along the margins—numbers and instructions as unemotional as the writing in my mother's journal. The distance between my parents was never greater than when he drew up these plans; they were living in separate worlds. When Sonja walks back inside the camper, I lift my hands from the blueprints and the edges roll up like a guilty secret.

Sonja thinks the camper is beautiful, or at least she thinks that is what I want to hear. In truth it is a little sad and dingy, but triumphant. It has managed to survive, just like my family. All around me are physical links to my mother, father, and sister: the mirror where she brushed her hair, the secret compartment where he hid the gun, and the tiny bed where Jenny snuggled next to me. Yet more vividly than my parents, or my sister, John is beside me in the dark, enveloping heat.

I feel not the physical presence of my brother, like a ghost, but the absence of him. It is a gravitational pull, his missingness, a tug on my soul. I will never really know my brother, what he would have looked like or who he might have become. He was taken long ago, and I thought I needed to find this camper to say good-bye to him. But it is his absence that I have to leave behind.

I want to take some memento, something tangible to hold in my hands and prove he was real. But what is left of him is me. The proof is in the journey that taught me I don't have to understand or fix everything. I can go on now. I know that John John is beside me. He always has been. He is there in the questions and the doubts, the spaces between life's certainties. There is only the whisper of the hours passing, the smell of earth, and pale yellow butterflies fluttering between the walls. And that is enough.

Afterword

THE RESTING
PLACE

My parents dreamed of driving to the end of the Pan-American
Highway in 1974, so Gary and I finish the trip—with John
beside us. Argentina is the gentle denouement after finding the
camper, a chance to hold each other and exhale. It is what I imagine
the American West was like in generations past: open country, rug-
ged and unspoiled. Everyone camps in Argentina. From young lovers
to families, they pile into beat-up old Fords and pitch tents alongside
mountain roads, next to glacial streams, and in free municipal campgrounds in every town. Instead of roasting hot dogs and sipping coffee, Argentineans grill great slabs of meat around red-hot coals and
pass the mate gourd.

Gary and I are no longer quite the oddities we were in the rest of
the continent: our skin tones blend, and even our 1968 camper is less

conspicuous. We are left in peace to enjoy Argentina and let it soak into our hearts. We can camp without any fear of overstaying our welcome. We leave our lawn chairs, muddy hiking boots, and drying laundry outside our camper just like everyone else. We walk away from unlocked doors to bathe in crystal-clear, trout-filled streams.

Argentina is our reward and renewal, a richer compensation than any imagined sufferings along our journey. The left and right sides of my brain are in complete balance; I plan only so far ahead as to arrive safely. Each day I am more comfortable letting go and relying on my internal compass. In Patagonia, on the long drives that the guidebooks shudder to mention for the monotony, we find beauty and peacefulness unparalleled. If I could fill my life with paintings of the way the land arches to meet the convergence of clouds in a Patagonian steppe, I would never need windows.

The sun doesn't shine here; it spreads and settles and seeps into your soul like a lingering kiss. The colors are a state of unfolding grace: soothing mustards, lifting lavenders, and calming greys against a sky the blue of childhood. There is nothing here to distract from the sky because no worry or concern could possibly compete. It is the sky both of awakening and of remembering seasons past—gentle seasons, the softness of daydreams, the cadence of a melody hummed. It is sky the blue of eyes closed, fingers crossed, and happily ever after. There is only one thing left to do.

When we have driven as far south as it is possible to drive, to the Tierra del Fuego National Park, we take the gun from its hiding place under the camper floor and uncork a bottle of Argentinean champagne. As the vestiges of light drip down behind the peaks, I fling the gun into the Beagle Channel and watch it sink out of sight.

I am free and new again, and everything is as fresh as history revealed and the future imagined. I had no idea the end of a journey could be so gentle and sweet-smelling. The sky and the land relinquish their rigid boundaries and melt into liquid and cloudy horizons. The colors whisper and blend into soothing halftones. The breeze stirs the scent of clover, salt water, mussels, and rain into something like a sigh. It is a place where even dreams can rest.

ACKNOWLEDGMENTS

Travel and writing are utterly communal ventures for me. Driving to the end of the road and back again required the love, support, and trust of so many people that the list is hard to begin. But family first, because without Gary's and mine this book would be an uncompleted journey. To my mother and father, thank you for my tough little sister, for your faith in roads that others never attempt, and for sharing your memories, photos, and dubious sense of direction. To my aunt, thanks for saving letters and replacing stolen credit cards along the way. To Gary's brothers, sisters-in-law, mother, and still-missed father, thanks for never saying aloud what you undoubtedly thought. And Alex, thanks for being the gut check and reason to return that you probably never knew you were.

On both my first drive down the Pan-American Highway and the second, I collected a new family of fellow travelers and uncommonly kind strangers. Thank you Lawrence, Big Alex, Christy, Nancy, Theo, Marc, Shawn, Susie, Ernesto, Yolanda, Yanina, Rodolfo, Mariamalia, Arnoldo, Hooper, Betsy, Sheila, Dennis, Margit, Tia Eva, Don, Sonja, Richard, Magali, Yamil, Audrey, Mike, and finally my agent, Adriann, and equally brilliant editor, Stephanie.

ABOUT THE AUTHOR

Writer/producer Teresa Bruce comes from a background in public television. *God's Gonna Trouble the Water*, a one-hour documentary on the Gullah music and culture of South Carolina and Georgia, aired nationally on PBS during Black History Month and won the CINE Golden Eagle Award. Her first book, *The Other Mother: A Rememoir*, won the Independent Book Publishers Association Gold Medal for best memoir of 2014, and her screenplays have won top honors at the Beaufort and Oaxaca, Mexico, International Film Festivals.